Shoes and the Georgian Man

Shoes and the Georgian Man

Matthew McCormack

BLOOMSBURY VISUAL ARTS
LONDON • NEW YORK • OXFORD • NEW DELHI • SYDNEY

BLOOMSBURY VISUAL ARTS
Bloomsbury Publishing Plc
50 Bedford Square, London, WC1B 3DP, UK
1385 Broadway, New York, NY 10018, USA
29 Earlsfort Terrace, Dublin 2, Ireland

BLOOMSBURY, BLOOMSBURY VISUAL ARTS and the Diana logo are trademarks of Bloomsbury Publishing Plc

First published in Great Britain 2025

Copyright © Matthew McCormack, 2025

Matthew McCormack has asserted his right under the Copyright, Designs and Patents Act, 1988, to be identified as Author of this work.

For legal purposes the Acknowledgements on p. xi constitute an extension of this copyright page.

Cover design by Adriana Brioso
Cover image: *Portrait of John, Lord Mountstuart, later 4th Earl and 1st Marquess of Bute*
by Jean-Étienne Liotard (1763)

All rights reserved. No part of this publication may be reproduced or transmitted in any form or by any means, electronic or mechanical, including photocopying, recording, or any information storage or retrieval system, without prior permission in writing from the publishers.

Bloomsbury Publishing Plc does not have any control over, or responsibility for, any third-party websites referred to or in this book. All internet addresses given in this book were correct at the time of going to press. The author and publisher regret any inconvenience caused if addresses have changed or sites have ceased to exist, but can accept no responsibility for any such changes.

A catalogue record for this book is available from the British Library.

A catalog record for this book is available from the Library of Congress.

ISBN: HB: 978-1-3503-5867-6
PB: 978-1-3503-5866-9
ePDF: 978-1-3503-5868-3
eBook: 978-1-3503-5869-0

Typeset by RefineCatch Limited, Bungay, Suffolk
Printed and bound in India

To find out more about our authors and books visit www.bloomsbury.com
and sign up for our newsletters.

Joey's book

Contents

List of illustrations viii
Acknowledgements xi

Introduction 1

1 Georgian men and their shoes 13

2 Shoes and the body 35

3 Shoes and politics 55

4 Boots and masculinity 73

5 Gout shoes and disability 95

6 Dancing feet 119

7 The soldier's shoe 139

Conclusion: Wearing Georgian shoes 161

Select bibliography 183
Index 191

Illustrations

0.1	Man's straight black leather shoe, 1760s	2
0.2	Shoes owned by William Cowper, late eighteenth century.	4
1.1	Man's black leather shoe with silver buckle, 1790s.	15
1.2	Sole of straight shoe, 1760s.	16
1.3	Anon., *Cobler's Hall* (*c.* 1793).	18
1.4	John Dempsey, *Black Charley, Shoemaker at Norwich* (1823).	20
1.5	Mourning buckle, 1795.	24
1.6	Artois buckle, late eighteenth century.	25
1.7	Man's silk brocade shoe, *c.* 1730.	26
1.8	Men's shoes with red heels, 1740–79.	27
1.9	William Hogarth, *The Strode Family* (1738).	28
1.10	Women's slippers, 1805–15.	30
1.11	Théobald Chartran, *Edwyn Burnaby, MP*, *Vanity Fair*, 10 March 1883.	31
2.1	Anon., *The Corn Doctor* (1793).	37
2.2	Wellington boots, 1800–25.	38
2.3	The bones of the foot (1830), after William Cheselden (1733).	40
2.4	Slip-on man's shoe, 1700.	41
2.5	W. H. Lizars, *Leg and foot: dissection, with blood vessels and nerves . . .* (1822).	44
2.6	Man's shoe, 1828.	46
2.7	Children's pumps, *c.* 1830.	48
2.8	Lewis Durlacher, plate 4 from *A Concise Treatise on Corns, Bunions and the Disorders of Nails* (London, 1845).	50
3.1	*The Elected Cobler*, from M. Darly, *Macaronies, Characters, Caricatures, etc.* (London, 1772).	57
3.2	William Hogarth, *O the Roast Beef of Old England* (1748).	61
3.3	*Welladay, is this my son Tom* (1774).	62
3.4	James Gillray, *Independence* (1799).	64

3.5	James Gillray, *Un petit Souper a la Parisienne: or, A Family of Sans-Culotts refreshing after the fatigues of the day* (1792).	65
3.6	Clogs, early nineteenth century.	66
3.7	Man's cut-down leather boot, early nineteenth century.	67
4.1	Joshua Reynolds, portrait of Sir Banastre Tarleton (1782).	77
4.2	Postilion's boots with splatterdashes, 1790s.	78
4.3	Man's leather jackboot, *c.* 1720.	82
4.4	Man's black-and-beige leather top-boot, 1810–20.	85
4.5	Richard Dighton, sketch of George Bryan 'Beau' Brummell (1804).	87
4.6	Dress Wellingtons, *c.* 1840.	88
4.7	William Heath, *A Wellington Boot, or the Head of the Army* (October 1827).	89
5.1	James Gillray, *The Gout* (1799).	96
5.2	Pair of gout shoes, nineteenth century.	98
5.3	Thomas Rowlandson, *The Tithe Pig* (1799).	101
5.4	Anon., *The Gouty Husband and his Young Wife* (1760s).	102
5.5	Charles Grignion I, after Thomas Rowlandson, *Men Dancing in a Coffee House, an Illustration from Tobias Smollett's The Expedition of Humphry Clinker* (1793).	104
5.6	Isaac Cruikshank, *The Treasury Spectre, or the Head of the Nation in a Queer Situation* (1798).	107
5.7	Two pairs of slippers owned by George IV, 1820s.	109
5.8	Gout shoe, eighteenth century.	109
5.9	Gout shoe (slit), eighteenth century.	110
5.10	Henry Bunbury, *Geoffrey Gambado, Esq.* (1786).	111
6.1	George Cruikshank, *City Ball at the Mansion House* (1 November 1824).	120
6.2	Kellom Tomlinson, *Passacaille* from *The Art of Dancing* (London, 1735).	123
6.3	Joshua Reynolds, John Stuart, 3rd Earl of Bute (1758).	126
6.4	Man's black leather buckle latchet shoe, 1820s.	130
6.5	Man's black, woven textile pump, 1840s.	132
6.6	Man's brown leather shoe, 1830s.	134
6.7	Man's black leather tie shoe, *c.* 1830.	135
7.1	Replica of a military shoe buckle from the late eighteenth century.	141
7.2	Sir William Young, sketch of a Grenadier Private, Royal Buckinghamshire Militia (King's Own) (1793).	143
7.3	Charles Hamilton Smith, *Soldiers of the 1st Regiment of Foot Guards in Marching Order, 1812* (1812–15).	144

7.4	Franz Joseph Manskirch, *Anecdote of the bravery of the Scotch piper of the 71st Highland Regiment, at the Battle of Vimiero* (1819).	145
7.5	Pair of army boots, 1850s.	147
7.6	Thomas Rowlandson, *Measuring Substitutes for the Army of Reserve* (1815).	153
7.7	Rating's shoe, 1750s.	155
7.8	Rating's shoe, 1750s.	156
7.9	Daniel Orme, *John [Jack] Crawford*.	157
8.1	Andy Burke in his workshop.	165
8.2	Clicking the soles.	167
8.3	Uppers of rough-out leather.	168
8.4	Completed shoes without buckles.	169
8.5	Fixing the buckles.	169
8.6	Applying black ball.	170
8.7	James Gillray, *Very slippy weather* (10 February 1808).	173
8.8	Uppers showing the shape of the foot after ten days' wear.	175
8.9	Uppers showing the shape of the foot after forty days' wear.	175
8.10	Outline of the foot visible on the sole after forty days' wear.	176
8.11	Wear to the heel after forty days.	177

Acknowledgements

This book was made in Northampton, as shoes have been for centuries. Having lived in the town and worked at the University of Northampton for twenty years, it feels inevitable that I should write a book about shoes. Shoes are everywhere in Northampton: the factories and former factories, the physical fabric of the streets that housed the shoemakers (often named after manufacturers or parts of the shoemaking process), statues in the town centre, murals in the Guildhall, the football team known as 'the Cobblers' and their fans 'the Shoe Army'. The university itself is a centre for the study of leather, fashion, podiatry and many other shoe-related subjects, which means that I am almost daily having interesting conversations about them. And we are fortunate to have world-leading collections of footwear on our doorstep, at Northampton Museum and at the Museum of Leathercraft. So, having worked for a long time on the subjects of masculinity and the body in the Georgian period, and having developed an interest in material culture, shoes were the obvious next port of call.

If the book feels inevitable, that does not mean that the process of writing it was straightforward, and I have many people to thank. As any student of material culture will know, studying objects is heavily reliant on the generosity of museum curators, who give their time and expertise to enable scholars to access their collections. I should particularly like to thank Tim Crumplin, Vikki Green, Graham Lampard, Victoria Mulford, Nikki Ritson, Calum Robertson, Elizabeth Semmelhack, Rebecca Shawcross, Emily Taylor, Oliver Walton and Philip Warner. Much of this research was conducted during and after the COVID-19 pandemic, which (among other things) was a difficult time for the museum sector. I am doubly grateful that curators were able to accommodate me when they were having to deal with closures, furloughs, social distancing and other challenges. It was not an easy time to carry out material culture research, since object handling was not something that could be 'moved online' like a lot of other academic research activity. Special thanks go to Andy Burke, who also helped me at this challenging time, and who not only made me a wonderful pair of shoes but also shared his knowledge and extended his hospitality.

I should also like to thank many historians for their advice and feedback over the course of the project. I am wary of naming names for fear of missing anybody out, but I should particularly like to thank Hilary Burlock, Arthur Burns, Elaine Chalus, Elizabeth Craig-Atkins, Petra Dotlacilová,

Christopher Fletcher, Sarah Fox, Sarah Goldsmith, Karen Harvey, Ceri Houlbrook, Catriona Kennedy, Rachel Moss, Mark Philp, Matthew Roberts, Mark Rothery, Tim Reinke-Williams, Gillian Russell, Jon Stobart, John Styles, William Tullett, Emily Vine and Gillian Williamson. Thank you to my students for indulging my material culture obsessions and sharing interesting thoughts about it and, in particular, to my PhD students Ruth Barton, Martyn Green, Kerry Love and Kathrina Perry for offering comments on chapter drafts. Audiences at numerous conferences and seminars have given me generous feedback, and the British Society for Eighteenth-Century Studies, in particular, has heard nearly all of the chapters at its annual conferences.

This project would not have been possible without research funding. The research involved a lot of travelling and I am grateful to the Georgian Papers Programme and the Society of Antiquaries London for funding portions of this research. I should like to thank Bloomsbury, the Pasold Foundation and the University of Northampton for providing funding towards the image costs in this book. I am grateful to many institutions for giving me permission to reproduce images: these are listed in full in the captions accompanying the figures. Every effort has been made to trace and properly acknowledge the owners of the images reproduced here, but please contact me if there have been any omissions. I should like to thank the following publishers for permission to reproduce material that has appeared in print before: Manchester University Press for Chapter 2, which is adapted from 'Embodying the History of Footwear: Shoes and Gender in Britain, 1700–1850' in Elizabeth Craig-Atkins and Karen Harvey (eds), *The Material Body: Embodiment, History and Archaeology in Industrialising England, 1700–1850* (Manchester: Manchester University Press, 2024); Routledge for Chapter 3, which is adapted from 'Wooden Shoes and Wellington Boots: The Politics of Footwear in Georgian Britain' in Christopher Fletcher (ed.), *Everyday Political Objects: From the Middle Ages to the Contemporary World* (London: Routledge, 2021); and Routledge for Chapter 4, which is adapted from 'Boots, Material Culture and Georgian Masculinities', *Social History* 42, no. 4 (2017). I should like to thank everyone at Bloomsbury for their fantastic work on the book, and particularly Frances Arnold for taking it on.

Finally, I should like to thank my friends and family. Thank you Amy for your advice, love and support. I promised the boys a book each and, ever since I dedicated the last one to Toby, Joey has asked fairly regularly when I would finish this one. So here it is.

Introduction

> *The covering of the foot, or the shoe, is a part of the dress more deserving of attention than any other, for its improper application is more productive of pain and uneasiness than any other part of dress . . . On no part of the body, however, have fashion and caprice exerted their influence more than here, and the shape of the shoe alters with every whim of the day.*[1]

Shoes have a close relationship with the body. As this medical treatise of 1801 by William Nisbet noted, they arguably have the greatest impact of any item of clothing, given their potential to inflict pain and restrict movement. Shoes bear the whole weight of the body, so they affect how that body stands and moves. They enable the wearer to do certain things, or prevent them from doing others, so they say a great deal about the wearer's occupation or the role that they have in society. For this reason, shoes are loaded with social meaning. As Giorgio Riello and Peter McNeil note, they have for centuries 'given hints about a person's character, social and cultural place, even sexual preference'.[2] This book explores the significance of footwear for men at a time when these meanings were particularly powerful and were undergoing vital changes. The position of men and women in Georgian society related to shifts in the styles of shoes, but the importance of this went deeper than visual appearance; it was fundamentally about shoes' physical properties and the effect that they had on their wearers' bodies.

Shoes and the Georgian Man therefore thinks about shoes as material objects in conjunction with the gendered physical bodies that wore them. Because shoes support the weight and movements of the body, they endure great stresses. They have to be made in a particular way to withstand this, which is why shoemaking has historically been such a skilled and specialized business. They also have to be made from particular materials. Before the advent of rubber and plastics, the only material that was sufficiently hardwearing, flexible and waterproof was leather. Leather has its origin in skin, so shoes become a kind of second skin, an adjunct to our bodies. When we wear shoes, they mould to our foot and our way of walking. They may be uncomfortable at first but they gradually 'wear in' and become softer and more flexible. The more we wear them, the more comfortable they become, until they ultimately 'wear out'. The way they wear, however, is unique to the wearer. You cannot wear in a pair of shoes for anybody else, since they mould to the unique shape of your feet. For this reason, it is difficult to wear someone else's shoes. Nowadays 'most people resist wearing second-hand shoes, perhaps because of their close association with their former wearers', although we shall see that the sheer cost of shoes in the eighteenth century meant that acquiring them second-hand was more common.[3] Stories such as Cinderella attest to the way that shoes were thought only to fit their rightful owner. In Samuel Richardson's *Pamela*, the heroine's master gives her some fine silk shoes that belonged to her late mistress; they fit exactly, indicating that Pamela fits the role of the lady of the house.[4]

Shoes therefore tell us about their wearer. Because they wear out in a unique way, the shoe retains an imprint of their owner.[5] It is possible to detect the shape of their foot, the nature of their gait, and even what they used the shoes for, in their stretches, stains, scratches and scuffs. We shall see in Chapter 2 that some shoes even retain traces of bodily material from their wearer, such as sweat and blood. For this reason, it has been said that the shoe is 'the mirror of the foot in action'.[6] Worn shoes provide us with a ghostly trace of the wearer's body; from the historian's point of view, this means that the shoe is a primary source for a historical human being. No other garment provides us with an imprint of the body in this way, even those that fit close to the body; the closest examples are probably whalebone corsets, which shaped themselves around the body (in a way that later metal stays did not), but they did not bear the whole body so were not reconstituted to the same extent as shoes. It is the wear that makes shoes interesting. For this reason, curators of shoe collections in museums tend not to prefer 'perfect' examples, and many historic shoes are in heavily worn condition (Figure 0.1).

Figure 0.1 *Man's straight black leather shoe, 1760s. Image courtesy of the Alfred Gillett Trust.*

Shoes stand in for their wearer. As well as retaining visible traces of their wearer – and perhaps because of this – they have historically been identified with their wearer in other ways too. Proverbs attest to the common identification of shoes with their wearer. To 'step into another's shoes', to 'walk a mile in their shoes' or to 'wait for dead men's shoes' suggest that shoe and owner are synonymous. The shoe becomes 'an extension of the subject rather than mere object'.[7] Historically, worn shoes have often been seen to retain something of the soul of their owner. Hilary Davidson argues that shoes are 'supernatural vessels' since they 'hold the soul' of their former wearer.[8] A host of superstitions have been attributed to footwear. In particular, there was a common folk practice in eighteenth- and nineteenth-century Britain whereby shoes were ritually concealed in houses. A worn shoe might be secreted beneath a floorboard or in a wall, typically at thresholds such as doors or chimney breasts, in order to bring good luck or to protect the house against evil spirits. In a practice of what Ceri Houlbrook terms 'ritual recycling', the worn shoe represents the wearer, so wards off evil or acts as a 'lighting conductor' to draw it away from the house and its inhabitants.[9] The precise meanings of this folk practice are obscure, since there are virtually no written sources about it; the only source we have are the shoes themselves. These artifacts are doubly interesting for historians because of their ritual significance, and because these are often plebeian shoes that would not otherwise have survived.

Shoes tell stories. They are sometimes kept by family members as a keepsake, to remember a loved one or a special occasion like a wedding, suggesting that they are bound up with emotions and personal identity.[10] They evoke memories, tell us about people and their lives, and often have stories to tell of their own. A recent book on women's shoes in eighteenth-century America takes a biographical approach, using the evidence of material culture to explore the lives of their wearers.[11] This approach is also increasingly reflected in the way that shoes are displayed in museums. Traditionally shoes were organized by style and period, with more of a focus on the way that they were produced than the way that they were consumed. But newer shoe exhibitions try to understand what the shoes tell us about the people who wore them, in terms of their identities and their life stories. Visitors are then encouraged to think about their own shoes and what they mean to them.[12] A shoe might be memorable because it was worn on an adventure, which may be visible in the condition of the shoe itself. Shoes may also evoke darker memories. The poet William Cowper (1731–1800) recalled his school days when he was bullied by an older boy: 'he had by his savage treatment of me imprinted such a dread of his very figure upon my mind that I well remember being afraid to lift my eyes upon him higher than his knees, and that I knew him by his shoe buckles better than by any other part of his dress'.[13] A pair of Cowper's shoes from later in life are preserved in the Metropolitan Museum of Art (Figure 0.2).

Shoes therefore have huge potential to tell us about history. They may be functional objects but they are replete with meanings, which tell us a great deal about the past society in which they were

Figure 0.2 *Shoes owned by William Cowper, late eighteenth century. The Metropolitan Museum of Art, New York City: Gift of Charles Ryskamp, 2002.*

made and worn. *Shoes and the Georgian Man* explores the powerful significance that shoes had for men in the eighteenth century. Men's shoes from this period have been studied less than women's.[14] Eighteenth-century men's shoes were increasingly plain and uniform, and tended to be of black leather, in contrast with the attractive colours and fabrics used in women's shoes of the period, and they have perhaps been less appealing for historical study for this reason. Because they were more utilitarian, they were more likely to be worn until they fell apart, so they were less likely to be kept than the fancier women's examples. Museum collections of shoes tend to skew towards elite and female, as these are more visually striking and more likely to have survived. There are far fewer men's shoes from the eighteenth century in museums, and fewer still plebeian examples. It is worth studying those that have survived, however, since they tell us much about men's lives at a time when new ideas about masculinity and men's role within society were coming to the fore. As well as being symbolic, the functional nature of footwear contributed to men's experience of the world in a practical and physical way. Studying surviving examples of shoes as material objects therefore helps historians to understand the embodied experience of living in the past.

Shoe histories

Shoe history is an established field. Traditionally, histories of footwear documented changing styles in a chronological way, with reference to social history and to changing methods of manufacture.[15] Some key works on shoe history were written by museum curators, often focusing on the specific collections in the museums where they worked.[16] There is also a large literature on shoe manufacturing in professional publications such as trade journals, which sometimes feature historical studies.[17] More generally, shoes have been studied within the field of dress history. This had its origins in art history as a means to date paintings from costume, so was 'a useful tool in processes of authentication and connoisseurship'.[18] As such, early studies tended to focus on the details of dress styles in a fairly descriptive way. Until the later twentieth century, shoes and other items of dress tended to be studied by those with a professional interest in them; academic historians dismissed them as 'trivial', in contrast with the weightier matters that they considered their stock in trade.[19] Fashion was a feminine domain, in contrast with the masculine worlds of politics and war that dominated historical studies.

More recently, dress history has developed into fashion studies. This is a vibrant interdisciplinary field incorporating insights from right across the arts and social sciences, including sociology, literary studies, art history and cultural history.[20] Within this field, shoes have been a favourite focus because of their psychological and symbolic interest. Shoes have been explored in terms of sexuality, identity, race, emotions and the body, among other approaches. In this way, they have been the focus of topics as rich and diverse as fetishism, cinema, dance, modernism, remembrance and fairy tales.[21] Ellen Sampson wonders whether this focus on what the shoe represents serves to obscure the material thing: 'the shoe that is missing is the real shoe; the habitual shoe; the shoe as a worn and bodily object'.[22]

The eighteenth-century shoe has received scholarly interest. Given the interdisciplinary appeal of shoes, they are a fitting topic for eighteenth-century studies, since this is a century where scholars have often worked across disciplinary boundaries. Giorgio Riello has typified this approach in his work on the long eighteenth century, since he has studied shoes from a range of perspectives including economic history, material culture and cultural history.[23] Since the 1980s, economic historians have shifted their focus from production to consumption, from the industrial revolution to the consumer revolution.[24] The shoe was therefore a consumer object and one that had important implications for social status. In the eighteenth century, social standing was increasingly defined in terms of appearance and performance, rather than its traditional markers. Mastery of 'politeness' involved bodily cultivation, refined conversation and the right clothes, and shoes contributed to one's appearance, posture and movement.[25] Hilary Davidson has explored shoes in terms of the wider dress ensembles for men and women in Regency England, in a range of locales including the home, the country, the city and the empire.[26] The importance of shoes in the Atlantic World has also been examined by Kimberly Alexander, who has highlighted the complex relationship between the London fashion market and the American colonies in the years before and after the revolution.[27]

This new work on the eighteenth century has often focused on gender. As we shall see in Chapter 1, changing shoe styles for men and women over the course of the eighteenth century map onto the divergence of their gender roles in that period. Elite shoes for men and women were visually fairly similar at the beginning of the century, but by the end of the century they were quite different. Men were wearing leather boots that empowered them to move around the public sphere, whereas women's flimsy fabric shoes suggested their suitability for domestic roles; their footwear signalled their social roles in both symbolic and practical senses. Women's historians used to discuss this shift in structural terms, as 'the emergence of separate spheres'.[28] This interpretation has since been substantially critiqued, but historians do still tend to argue that notions of gender diverged over the course of the long eighteenth century. Historians need a way to conceptualize men's increasing monopoly of the public world during the Enlightenment; and thinking about this in terms of material artefacts and embodied experience helps to map the theory of gender exclusion onto everyday practice.

Our focus here is men's shoes and it is worth dwelling on masculinity, as it is a key consideration in the book. The history of masculinity explores what it meant to be a man in different times and contexts. It is not a history of men as such, in the way that women's history sought to write the untold histories of women, since men have hardly been neglected in the historical record. Rather, it has sought to understand ideas, practices and experiences of masculinity, and how these have changed over time. It emerged from the development of gender history, since it argued that masculinity and femininity need to be studied in relation to each other, and that these notions are fluid rather than historically fixed.[29] It was a pro-feminist history rather than a backlash, since it argued that notions of masculinity have been oppressive to men and women alike; indeed, some early practitioners sought to reform damaging patriarchal norms through therapy and left-wing activism.[30]

The first works on masculinity in British history were on the Victorian period, thinking about 'manliness' as a powerful moral ideal and the ways that it was inculcated in institutions like the public school.[31] John Tosh's pioneering work on the middle-class family demonstrated the importance of domesticity for men, challenging the assumption that men and women lived in 'separate spheres' and that the home was feminine.[32] By contrast, work on the eighteenth century tended to emphasize more public and ebullient masculinities, focusing on issues such as sociability, violence and national identity.[33] This was possibly due to the importance of politeness in the eighteenth century, which wove masculine behaviour into the fabric of public life.[34] It was also a reflection of the nature of Georgian masculinities themselves, which tended to prioritize the outward ways that masculinity was performed rather than the interior moral values that preoccupied the Victorians.[35] We shall see that this shift from outer display to inner morality was manifested in changing shoe styles and the wider dress ensemble over the course of the eighteenth and nineteenth centuries, and how this related to ideas about masculine virtue and men's public image.

A gender perspective also helps historians to think about the body. Histories of the body emphasize that, rather than being a constant of human life, notions and experience of the body can be cultural and therefore subject to change over time. There has been a huge amount of historical work on the body in recent years, but much of it has been oddly disembodied, focusing on representations of the body rather than the physical body itself.[36] The wider 'embodied turn' across the arts and social sciences has, however, engaged with the corporeal and the material to a much greater extent. Fields such as fashion studies, disability studies and archaeology necessarily have these as a focus, and there is much that historians can learn from these approaches.[37] For example, this book draws on work by archaeologists. Some of the historic shoes that I studied were retrieved from digs, and archaeological approaches to material artefacts and the human body informed my own. Paleopathologists study disease and injury in skeletal remains, and this enables them to think about the impact of material artefacts on the body even where the artefacts themselves do not survive. For example, studying the bones of the foot for evidence of *hallux valgus* (or bunions) can highlight the injurious effect of shoe styles such as narrow toes or high heels.[38] The final chapter of this book also draws on insights from experimental archaeology, in reconstructing and testing a historical artefact in relation to the body.[39]

In particular, this book thinks about shoes as examples of material culture. The history of material culture involves using objects as primary sources, which is an unusual approach for historians who tend to prioritize source materials that are 'on the page', namely texts, images and statistics. This study employs a wide range of those source types as well but, where possible, it has taken the object as a starting point and has used it to drive the analysis. As Adrienne Hood notes, rarely do historians '*begin our research with objects or use them as an integral form of evidence*'.[40] As well as using and prioritizing material sources, the history of material culture emphasizes that objects have agency and that they have an effect on the people who encounter them.[41] So material culture history is not just interested in the objects for their own sake or as evidence of a past society, but also in terms of the cultural work that they were performing. This approach has proved to be particularly productive for historians of gender and the body. Some gender historians had expressed frustration with the cultural turn in history, arguing that its focus on representation was taking us away from the reality of social experience.[42] Engaging with objects has enabled gender historians to re-engage with the physical realities of practice and, in particular, that of the gendered body. My own work has taken this course, since my early work on masculinity was informed by the linguistic turn. My subsequent project on *Embodying the Militia in Georgian England* tried to get at the ways that masculine citizen soldiering was represented and practised in the eighteenth century, but the book was divided in two and dealt with these questions in separate sections.[43] I hope that the present work integrates these perspectives more fully.

Much of the research for this book has taken place in museums.[44] I have handled around 150 shoes or pairs from the long eighteenth century, a large majority of which were men's. I have also viewed many more examples in public museum displays and handled various other related items such as pattens, buckles and lasts. Given the low rates of survival for men's shoes from this period, I aimed to study a good proportion of those that still exist. When studying a shoe, I documented its key features and measurements, making handwritten notes and taking photographs: many of the shoes I studied are reproduced in these pages. I also spent time reflecting on the shoe and what it would have been like to wear. In part this was a practical exercise, assessing physical properties such as weight, flexibility, shape and suppleness, and thinking about the impact that this would have had upon the body and the walking gait. But there is also a sensory and affective aspect to encountering a past object. Objects convey non-verbal things that a written source never could, such as texture and smell.[45] And whereas it is not possible to re-experience that which is described in a written primary source, an object can be experienced first-hand.

There is, of course, a danger of anachronism in this encounter, since a twenty-first-century academic sitting in a museum will bring an entirely different frame of reference to an object than its original owner would have done. Nevertheless, the unique capacity of the worn shoe to retain a record of its wearer means that the encounter can be peculiarly evocative. Bethan Bide advocates the benefits of 'slow looking' as an approach to objects, which shifts the focus 'from the study of material objects as representations of broader historical narratives towards the minute details that reveal how clothes were used and experienced'.[46] I also became aware that the research activity was a very embodied experience, as I handled heavy and delicate objects, tried to get awkward camera angles, carried large acid-proof boxes around museum stores and employed my senses to analyse the shoes. Embodiment therefore became part of the process as well as the focus.

Shoes and the Georgian man

Shoes were an important part of male dress in the long eighteenth century. In order to set up this exploration of the Georgian male shoe, the opening chapter introduces the ways in which they were constructed, manufactured and consumed. It is also necessary to trace the changing nature of shoe styles between the seventeenth and the nineteenth centuries, and to situate these in terms of the wider dress ensemble. Shoes were a key element of the uniform of the patrician man in this period and were all the more striking because they were fastened with a decorative buckle. The story of the rise and fall of the shoe buckle tells us a great deal about the century with which it is associated and so is worth exploring in detail.

The relationship between shoes and the body is a key theme of the book, and Chapter 2 explores this in detail. By examining writings by chiropodists, physicians and shoe wearers themselves, alongside examples of worn shoes, it explores the impact of the body on shoes, and the impact of shoes on the body. Shoes might seem to be an unlikely topic for political history, but Chapter 3 shows how shoes were highly politicized in this period. Since shoes were an important marker of social class, gender and national identity, they had a big impact on the political world at a time when the social definition of the citizen was being reworked. Leather footwear played an important role in constructions of Britishness and was commonly juxtaposed with the 'wooden shoe' that stood for poverty, oppression and 'Frenchness'. The types of footwear worn by different social classes also had political connotations, such as the clogs proudly worn by working-class radicals or the Wellington boots sported by late-Georgian statesmen.

Thereafter the chapters focus on particular types of footwear and the types of men who wore them. Chapter 4 focuses on the boot. Men's boots are generally regarded today as practical articles with a utilitarian function, but this chapter shows how they could have very different meanings in the eighteenth century. Boots were initially for riding rather than walking, although their high heels and shiny leather gave the wearer an impressive bearing when standing. Their association with equestrianism linked them with social elites and the military, so they projected a particular masculine image. They came into fashion for general wear in the war decade of the 1790s and supplanted the aristocratic shoe-and-breeches ensemble with a look that was more democratic and energetic. The chapter concludes with a case study of the eponymous boot designed by the Duke of Wellington, which suited the sober and businesslike public men of his era.

Shoes can also help us to think about ill health and disability. Eighteenth-century Britain witnessed an epidemic of gout, since the propertied classes lived sedentary lifestyles and consumed copious amounts of alcohol and rich food. Although women and humbler classes also suffered from gout, it was primarily known as a 'gentleman's disorder' so is significant in terms of masculinity. Since podagra creates a painful swelling of the foot and lower leg, conventional footwear cannot be comfortably worn, so Georgians used a range of alternatives including outsize 'gout shoes', adapted footwear and flannel 'bootikins'. Chapter 5 therefore uses the material culture of gout to shed new light on a disorder that was very characteristic of the age.

Shoes affect the way that the body moves. Heavy outdoor footwear for activities such as riding impede movement, but light and supple shoes can enhance it. Chapter 6 focuses on the shoes that were worn by men for dancing, which had soft uppers and flexible soles. These suited the dances of the eighteenth century, which emphasized the movement of the legs and often required the dancer to bounce on tiptoe. This chapter therefore contributes to our understanding of dance as a physical and material practice, and also enables us to think about the nature of 'polite' masculinity and the contemporary male bodily ideal. Finally, Chapter 7 focuses on a category of men who had good reason to value their footwear. Common soldiers in the eighteenth century marched huge distances, from the militiamen who traversed the country, to regulars who trudged across Spain during the Peninsular War. Soldier's memoirs often dwelt on the nature of their shoes and the painful foot complaints that they endured, and commanders appreciated the strategic significance of regular supplies of adequate footwear. The large-scale manufacture of shoes for the military also informed modern footwear practices, such as standard sizing and mass production techniques.

Throughout the book, examples of historic shoes are studied to shed light on the embodied experience of wearing them. In order to answer many of the questions I had about this, I would ideally have put them on, but clearly this is not possible with fragile and irreplaceable artefacts. The concluding section of the book therefore records an experiment, whereby I commissioned a pair of replica eighteenth-century shoes and wore them for an extended period of time. Drawing on approaches including auto-ethnography, experimental archaeology and re-enactment, I sought to reconstruct the experience of wearing Georgian shoes. This enabled me better to understand the shoes that I was studying in museums and also debunked some of the myths and questionable prescriptions in the written primary sources. The book therefore concludes by drawing together the themes of material culture and embodiment.

Notes

1. William Nisbet, *A Practical Treatise on Diet, And on the Most Salutary and Agreeable Means of Supporting Life and Health, by Ailment and Regimen* (London, 1801), 30–1.

2. Giorgio Riello and Peter McNeil (eds), *Shoes: A History from Sandals to Sneakers* (Oxford: Berg, 2006), 3.

3. Margo DeMello, *Feet and Footwear: A Cultural Encyclopedia* (Santa Barbara, CA: Greenwood Press, 2009), xxi.

4. Alicia Kerfoot, 'Virtuous Footwear: Pamela's Shoe Heel and Cinderella's "Little Glass Slipper"', *Eighteenth-Century Fiction* 31, no. 2 (2019): 343–71 (349).

5. Hilary Davidson, 'Holding the Sole: Shoes, Emotions, and the Supernatural', in *Feeling Things: Objects and Emotions through History*, ed. Stephanie Downes, Sally Holloway and Sarah Randles (Oxford: Oxford University Press, 2018), 75.

6. A. W. Swallow, 'Interpretation of Wear Marks Seen in Footwear', *Museum Assistants' Group Transactions* 12 (1973): 28–32.

7. Janice West, 'The Shoe in Art, the Shoe as Art', in *Footnotes: On Shoes*, ed. Shari Benstock and Suzanne Ferriss (New Brunswick, NJ: Rutgers University Press, 2001), 41–57 (49).

8. Davidson, 'Holding the Sole', 72, 93.

9. Ceri Houlbrook, 'Ritual, Recycling and Recontextualization: Putting the Concealed Shoe in Context', *Cambridge Archaeological Journal* 23, no. 1 (2013): 99–112 (107).

10. Alison Fairhurst, 'Eighteenth-Century Women's Shoes: A Valuable Historical Resource', *Costume* 53, no. 1 (2010): 20–42 (33).

11. Kimberly Alexander, *Treasures Afoot: Shoe Stories from the Georgian Era* (Baltimore, MD: Johns Hopkins University Press, 2018).

12 Matthew McCormack, 'A Pair of Shoe Exhibitions: Northampton Museum and Art Gallery and "Shoephoria!" at Bath Fashion Museum', BSECS Criticks (31 August 2021): https://www.bsecs.org.uk/criticks-reviews/a-pair-of-shoe-exhibitions-northampton-museum-and-art-gallery-shoephoria-at-bath-fashion-museum/ (accessed 23 May 2023).

13 William Cowper, *The Letters and Prose Writings of William Cowper: Volume 1,* Adelphi *and Letters 1750–1781*, ed. James King and Charles Ryskamp (Oxford: Clarendon Press, 1979), 5.

14 Recent studies of eighteenth-century women's shoes include: Alexander, *Treasures Afoot*; Fairhurst, 'Eighteenth-Century Women's Shoes'; Kerfoot, 'Virtuous Footwear'.

15 For example: Anon., *A Brief History of Shoe Fashion Through the Ages* (Leicester, 1930); Iris Brooke, *A History of English Footwear* (London: St Giles, 1948); Turner Wilcox, *The Mode in Footwear: From Antiquity to the Present Day* (London: Charles Scribner's Sons, 1948); Eunice Wilson, *A History of Shoe Fashions* (London: Pitman, 1969).

16 Lucy Pratt and Linda Woolley, *Shoes* (London: V&A Publications, 2000); June Swann, *Shoes* (London: Batsford, 1982); Rebecca Shawcross, *Shoes: An Illustrated History* (London: Bloomsbury, 2014).

17 Such as the *Journal of the British Boot and Shoe Institution*.

18 Christopher Breward, *The Culture of Fashion: A New History of Fashionable Dress* (Manchester: Manchester University Press, 1995), 1.

19 Giorgio Riello, *A Foot in the Past: Consumers, Producers and Footwear in the Long Eighteenth Century* (Oxford: Oxford University Press, 2006), 3.

20 Joanne Entwhistle surveys this field in *The Fashioned Body: Fashion, Dress and Modern Social Theory* (Cambridge: Polity Press, 2000).

21 As just one example, these topics are among those addressed in Benstock and Ferriss (eds), *Footnotes*.

22 Ellen Sampson, *Worn: Footwear, Attachment and the Affects of Wear* (London: Bloomsbury, 2020), 30.

23 Riello, *Foot in the Past*; Giorgio Riello, '*La Chaussure à la Mode*: Product Innovation and Marketing Strategies in Parisian and London Boot and Shoemaking in the Early Nineteenth Century', *Textile History* 34, no. 2 (2003): 107–133. His wider work on the history of shoes includes Riello and McNeil (eds), *Shoes*.

24 Neil McKendrick, John Brewer and J. H. Plumb, *The Birth of a Consumer Society: The Commercialisation of Eighteenth-Century England* (Bloomington: Indiana University Press, 1982).

25 Lawrence Klein, 'Politeness and the Interpretation of the British Eighteenth Century', *The Historical Journal* 45, no. 4 (2002): 869–98 (882–3).

26 Hilary Davidson, *Dress in the Age of Jane Austen: Regency Fashion* (New Haven, CT: Yale University Press, 2019).

27 Alexander, *Treasures Afoot*; Kimberly Alexander, 'Shoes and the City: Shoes and Their Sphere of Influence in Early America, 1740–1789', in *The Routledge History Handbook of Gender and the Urban Experience*, ed. Deborah Simonton (London: Routledge, 2017), 296–308.

28 Amanda Vickery, 'Golden Age to Separate Spheres? A Review of the Categories and Chronology of English Women's History', *The Historical Journal* 36, no. 2 (1993): 383–414.

29 Laura Lee Downs, *Writing Gender History* (London: Hodder Arnold, 2004), ch. 6.

30 Victor Seidler (ed.), *Men, Sex and Relationships: Writings from* Achilles' Heel (London: Routledge, 1992).

31 J. A. Mangan and James Walvin (eds), *Manliness and Morality: Middle-Class Masculinity in Britain and America, 1800–1940* (London: Palgrave Macmillan, 1987).

32 John Tosh, *A Man's Place: Masculinity and the Middle-Class Home in Victorian England* (New Haven, CT: Yale University Press, 1999).

33 For example, the essays collected in Michèle Cohen and Tim Hitchcock (eds), *English Masculinities, 1660–1800* (London: Longman, 1999).

34 Philip Carter, *Men and the Emergence of Polite Society: Britain, 1660–1800* (London: Longman, 2001).

35 John Tosh, 'Gentlemanly Politeness and Manly Simplicity in Victorian England', *Transactions of the Royal Historical Society* 12 (2002): 455–72.

36 As argued by Karen Harvey, 'Men of Parts: Masculine Embodiment and the Male Leg in Eighteenth-Century England', *Journal of British Studies* 54, no. 4 (2015): 797–821 (800).

37 See, for example, the collaboration between Karen Harvey and Elizabeth Craig-Atkins on the British Academy-funded project, 'The Material Body: An Interdisciplinary Study Using History and Archaeology'.

38 S. A. Mays, 'Paleopathological Study of Hallux Valgus', *American Journal of Physical Anthropology* 126, no. 2 (2005): 126–39.

39 Hilary Davidson, 'The Embodied Turn: Making and Remaking Dress as an Academic Practice', *Fashion Theory* 23, no. 3 (2019): 329–62 (338).

40 Adrienne Hood, 'Material Culture: The Object', in *History Beyond the Text: A Student's Guide to Approaching Alternative Sources*, ed. Sarah Barber and Corinna Peniston-Bird (London: Routledge, 2009), 176.

41 Karen Harvey (ed.), *Material Culture: A Student's Guide to Approaching Alternative Sources* (London: Routledge, 2009), 6.

42 John Tosh, 'The History of Masculinity: An Outdated Concept?', in *What is Masculinity? Historical Dynamics from Antiquity to the Contemporary World*, ed. John Arnold and Sean Brady (Basingstoke: Palgrave, 2011), 17–34.

43 Matthew McCormack, *Embodying the Militia in Georgian England* (Oxford: Oxford University Press, 2015).

44 The Alfred Gillett Trust (Street, Somerset), the Bata Shoe Museum (Toronto), Bath Fashion Museum, Chatham Historic Dockyard, Platt Hall Costume Museum (Manchester), Museum of Leathercraft (Northampton), National Museum of Scotland (Edinburgh), National War Museum (Edinburgh), Northampton Museum and Art Gallery, Trowbridge Museum and Castle Museum (York).

45 Katherine Ott, 'Disability Things: Material Culture and American Disability History, 1700–2010', in *Disability Histories*, ed. Susan Burch and Michael Rembis (Urbana: University of Illinois Press, 2014), 120–2.

46 Bethan Bide, 'Signs of Wear: Encountering Memory in the Worn Materiality of a Museum Fashion Collection', *Fashion Theory* 21, no. 4 (2017): 449–76 (454).

1
Georgian men and their shoes

Great Britain is the most wealthy, and, politically speaking, perhaps the most powerful kingdom upon earth. Considered from a domestic point of view, here are thousands of large and affluent families; it follows of course that there is scarcely a young man who enters upon life without being able to furnish himself with shoes. Nay, most have an opportunity of gratifying their tastes and passions in the purchase of a great variety; and I am greatly deceived if experience does not prove, that much more than half the miseries of the world arises either from ill-directed tastes in the purchase of shoes, or the entire want of them.[1]

This commentator from 1825 emphasized the importance of shoes for British men entering public life. The article is likely a satire as the case is comically over-stated, but it nevertheless highlights the many ways in which shoes were important for Georgian patrician men. A good pair of shoes provided comfort and mobility, and allowed refined deportment and gait, thence enabling the wearer to embark on a career in the public sphere. Choice of shoes also had a moral dimension, hinting at the taste and character of the wearer, and thence the private virtue that was expected to underpin the public virtue of late-Georgian statesmen. They therefore had implications for masculinity and national identity, since they shod the intrepid men who led 'the most powerful kingdom upon earth'. It was vitally important to choose the right shoes since they accompanied and supported the man through his trials and triumphs. The 'SHOE of a good man is his most constant and useful companion': it is 'THE MEDICINE of the SOLE'.

This chapter introduces the Georgian male shoe and thinks about its significance for men. It will begin by focusing on the shoe itself, and the ways in which it was constructed and manufactured. Shoes in this period were designed and made in a particular way, which had important implications for what they were like to wear and the impact that they had upon the wearer's body. We then shift our focus from production to consumption, thinking about the relationship between the maker and the wearer: patrician men shod in bespoke shoes had a very different relationship with the making process to working men, who made do with ready-made or second-hand footwear, and this impacted the shoes they wore and their experience of them. The chapter will then focus on a characteristic component of the Georgian shoe, the detachable buckle, and will conclude by thinking about how footwear styles changed over the course of the long eighteenth century, and the implications that this had for the wider dress ensemble and for notions of gender difference.

In common with the rest of the book, this chapter therefore works across several fields of historical investigation: in this case the histories of material culture, consumerism, fashion and masculinity. The history of masculinity sheds light on the study of objects, and vice versa. There is now a large literature on the emotional power of objects, which often have implications for gender in an affective and psychological sense.[2] Material culture can also inform the bodily experience of gender, although some recent studies of the body still tend to read objects in terms of representation, so do not fully engage with body or object in a physical way.[3] Footwear, on the other hand, has huge potential in this regard. Since it is worn on the body and affects its movements, footwear has a closer relationship with the body than most other types of object. The study of shoes as worn material articles enables us to locate ideas about masculinity in the physical realities of men's bodies and their social experiences.

The Georgian shoe

The basic male shoe of the Georgian period took a fairly standard form and changed only in style between the mid-seventeenth century and the mid-nineteenth. Sometimes known as the 'common shoe', it shod ordinary Britons for two centuries (Figure 1.1). Wealthier men would wear shoes of finer craftsmanship and more stylish shapes, with expensive details and linings, made from finer materials and a wider range of colours, but the basic pattern was the same. The shoe was of fairly simple construction. The uppers usually consisted of three pieces of leather: a large piece to form the forward portion of the shoe, known as the 'vamp', and two 'quarters' to form the rear of the shoe, which included long straps that could be fastened together with a buckle. More expensive shoes would be lined, but cheaper ones would probably only have a lining at the heel to prevent rubbing on the rear seam. The sole would also be made of leather, but of a thicker and harder variety than the uppers. Finally, the heel was constructed by stacking offcuts of sole leather, which were attached to the sole with nails or wooden pegs.

A distinctive feature of shoes in this period was their shape. They were straight lasted, so a pair of shoes were symmetrical rather than being shaped around the left and right foot (Figure 1.2). Nearly all shoes in the seventeenth and eighteenth centuries were made this way, whereas prior to this they had been 'handed': in Shakespeare's *King John* (written in the 1590s) a character puts them on the wrong way round, 'falsely thrust on contrary feet'.[4] The reason for the adoption of straights in the early seventeenth century is obscure, and shoe historians are undecided about the reason for it. June Swann

Figure 1.1 *Man's black leather shoe with silver buckle, 1790s. Image © 2024 Bata Shoe Museum, Toronto, Canada.*

suggests that the manufacturing process for heeled shoes lent itself to straight lasts with squared toes, and that this continued until shoes with lower heels became fashionable at the end of the eighteenth century.[5] Others argue that they were simply quicker to produce, were a conscious fashion choice, or were a logical outcome of the wide Tudor styles.[6] Whatever the reason, straights were worn until handed shoes returned in the early nineteenth century. One might assume that straight-lasted shoes would be uncomfortable, but wide-squared toes could accommodate either foot, and the uppers were supposed to mould to the foot with wear.

Leather was the key material for making shoes. Other materials could be used to make the uppers: textiles such as silk, linen or wool would be used for more decorative shoes, particularly those worn by women or, less frequently, elite men.[7] But these offered little protection against the elements and could easily become spoiled, so pattens or overshoes might be worn when venturing out to raise the shoe above the dirt. Even shoes that appear to be made of fabric often had a layer of leather underneath, providing the uppers with some strength and structure: this is sometimes visible in shoes in museum collections where the outer fabric has worn or decayed (Figure 2.4). Leather could itself be decorative and fine leathers could be had in a range of bright colours, but men's shoes were predominantly black.

Figure 1.2 *Sole of straight shoe, 1760s. Image courtesy of the Alfred Gillett Trust.*

Leather in its natural state is brown, so the leather was dyed black as a deliberate stylistic choice. Soles, too, were generally made from leather, although we shall see in the following chapters that wooden soles were often worn by working people.

There were many reasons why shoes were made from leather, including its appearance and abundance, but it was fundamentally because of its material properties. Leather can be flexible, hardwearing and waterproof. Shoe materials have to be flexible in order to accommodate the motions of the foot, which bends at the toes and the ankle as you walk. Most materials are either too rigid to accommodate this, or would be quickly broken down by the movements and pressures exerted upon them. Nowadays synthetic materials derived from petrochemicals can be used for the purpose, but these essentially mimic the properties and appearance of leather, compared to which they are generally less hardwearing, repairable or breathable (and are much more damaging in their environmental impact). Leather possesses these properties because of its origins in animal skin. It therefore provides an ideal protective layer to the skin of the human foot, with which it shares many attributes.

Animals were generally not farmed for their skins, since leather was a by-product of the meat industry.[8] Shoe leather was usually cowhide and eighteenth-century Britons ate a great deal of beef, so the raw materials were widely available. The tanning process was however lengthy and complex, so good shoe leather was not cheap. Rawhide had to be stripped of flesh and hair, and then softened and expanded, with malodorous and polluting chemical processes. (Indeed, it smelled so strongly that tanners and shoemakers were known to lose their sense of taste and smell.) Hide was then tanned for a long period in a vegetable 'ooze' made from bark. The tanning process prevented leather from putrifying and made it supple, hardwearing and visually appealing. The Leather Act of 1563 decreed that leather should be tanned for at least a year; and the fact that this was still in force in the later eighteenth century shows how traditional the methods were in this industry.[9]

The process for making shoes was as follows. Sheets of leather had to be cut into the correct shapes for the uppers and soles, in a process known as 'clicking' because of the noise of the knife on the block. This was skilled, intricate work, which required great strength, a keen eye and a very sharp knife. It also carried great responsibility, since leather was expensive, and clickers had to get the maximum number of pieces from a skin to minimize waste. The next stage was 'closing', whereby the pieces of the upper were stitched together. Third came 'making', where the upper and sole were attached together, around a wooden last in the shape of the foot (for which straight lasts had a symmetrical toe section). A leather welt would be used to enable the two elements to be stitched together tightly with waxed linen thread, thus ensuring that the bond was secure and waterproof. The welt also allowed the sole to be removed and replaced when it wore out. 'Finishing' would tidy up the work and clean the shoes so that they would be presentable for sale. This method changed very little between the early seventeenth century and the later nineteenth, when the arrival of sewing machines and other machinery sped up parts of the process: prior to that, all of these tasks were all carried out by hand.[10]

There were divisions within the trade. In the eighteenth century, 'cordwainers' made new shoes, whereas 'cobblers' repaired them. Cordwainers were skilled artisans who enjoyed certain privileges and protections, whereas cobblers were humbler workers who might work from a street stall or from home (Figure 1.3). Cobblers were not allowed to work with new leather, so used old leather to carry out repairs: even a worn-out shoe could therefore be recycled as there was a thriving trade in leather parts. This helps to explain why there are so few surviving plebeian shoes from the period, as they would be worn until they could be no longer and were then repurposed. In addition to this, 'translators' could refurbish a used shoe to make them appear as new, which was also a way to fence stolen footwear.[11] In practice, these divisions were blurred and difficult to enforce, and in the nineteenth century they broke down altogether.[12]

Because shoemaking was skilled and specialized, it largely avoided the revolutionary changes that impacted manufacturing in Britain during the Georgian period. Shoemaking often took place at home or in small workshops and, even when manufacturers started to concentrate workers into factories, these were relatively small scale and relied on out-work. As with many industries in this period, shoemaking became concentrated in particular localities, and shoemakers were originally associated

Figure 1.3 *Anon., Cobler's Hall (c. 1793). Image courtesy of the Lewis Walpole Library, Yale University.*

with London, Staffordshire and Northamptonshire. Gradually, Northampton and its surrounding towns and villages became the centre of the British shoe industry. This was partly due to the area's natural advantages, as it had rich pasture for cattle and forests of oak that produced bark for tanning: it was a centre for tanning so leather was readily available.[13] It was also accessible to the London market, while undercutting its wages, and the arrival of the canals and later the railways enabled Northampton to sell its goods further afield. As we shall see in Chapter 7, the key factor was the French Wars from the later eighteenth century, which gave Northampton manufacturers the opportunity to take on large military contracts, driving the expansion and consolidation of the industry. The 1831 census shows that, by the end of our period, a third of men in the town were employed in the shoe trades.[14]

The key difference with factory shoemaking was that the various processes were carried out by different people, rather than by a single cordwainer. Workers would be known as 'clickers', 'closers' and so on, according to the process they performed. Shoemaking developed a highly gendered division of labour, whereby men would perform the skilled and high-wage tasks such as cutting, and women would perform lower-wage tasks. This was reflected in the distinctive architecture of shoe factories, where the genders were segregated and the shoe made its way from the top of the building to the bottom, with a different process taking place on each floor. Victorian factories were often on the corners of streets, connected by the terraced dwellings that housed their workers.[15]

Buying shoes

Our attention now switches from production to consumption. This echoes the shift in emphasis within social and economic history in recent decades. Traditionally, the story of this period was told in terms of the first industrial revolution, as the increasing use of mechanization and the concentration of workers into factories increased productivity and drove down costs. The extent to which industrialization was indeed 'revolutionary' has since been debated and, while sectors such as textiles are still regarded as having undergone big changes, shoe manufacturing only partially followed these trends, as we have seen.[16] More recently, the focus of historians has been on consumption, thinking about the ways that goods were bought and used. Instead of industrial revolution, historians think about the eighteenth century as a time of 'consumer revolution'.[17] Not only were there many more types of goods to be purchased – made with new manufacturing processes or imported from further afield – but the ways in which they were consumed were new.

Originally shoes would have been made and sold in the same workshop, but as the eighteenth century progressed some shoemakers began to sell their wares at dedicated premises.[18] The eighteenth century witnessed an urban renaissance, where towns were remodelled as places of pleasure and polite sociability, and shopping became a pleasurable activity in its own right.[19] Shopkeepers became adept at the culture of politeness in order to appeal to potential customers: the painting of the Norwich shoe merchant 'Black Charley' depicts him in fine clothes that would not look out of place on his patrons (Figure 1.4). Shops were remodelled with large windows, counters and luxurious furnishings, and so were attractive places to be. It was therefore in this period that shoe shopping became modern. By the middle of the eighteenth century some shoemakers were seeking to create a brand: paper labels on the inside of shoes indicated the maker and the location of their shop.[20]

The stereotypical consumer of the eighteenth century was a propertied woman. Women of this class were supposed to spend money rather than earn it, and it was women who generally controlled household budgets. Women were also thought to take pleasure from acquiring material goods and from the process of shopping itself. The culture of sensibility emphasized that refined women had heightened nervous sensitivity, so were attuned to the sensory experience of shopping and were adept at assessing the material properties of things.[21] This contributed to the misogynist caricature that women were preoccupied with spending and acquiring. The feminist Mary Wollstonecraft was critical of the frivolous

Figure 1.4 *John Dempsey,* Black Charley, Shoemaker at Norwich *(1823). Collection: Tasmanian Museum and Art Gallery.*

way that women were supposed to live, and of her female contemporaries who were complicit in it: she despaired 'of those English women whose time is spent … shopping, bargain-hunting, etc. etc.'[22]

Within this model it is difficult to conceive of the male consumer and, indeed, male consumerism in the eighteenth century has often been neglected by historians. Margot Finn has studied men's diaries from the period and has concluded that there was no shortage of 'highly acquisitive men', noting that they disproportionately spent money on textiles and personal possessions.[23] Claire Walsh agrees and notes that, whereas women bore the brunt of the household shopping, men's consumerism 'was more frequently pleasurable than women's'.[24] Shoe shopping might well have come under this category of pleasurable shopping, since these were expensive, fashionable articles that propertied men would be buying for themselves. Shopping for footwear was a very sensory experience, as consumers would assess the material properties of the shoe through touch, assessing the qualities of the leather and the construction, the suppleness of the uppers, the flexibility of the sole and the weight of the whole (in much the same way as I have assessed historic examples in museums). If they tried a shoe on, they would require the senses of touch and sight to assess whether they were a good fit. They would also have deployed their noses, since leather and polish have distinctive smells that would have been amplified in the confines of a shoemaker's shop.

There were two ways to buy new shoes: bespoke and ready-made. These provided very different consumer experiences as well as finished products. Those who could afford it bought bespoke shoes, as these would be designed to their requirements and would be made to measure, so would be a good fit. These were much more expensive than ready-made and would typically be bought on credit. We can get an insight into the bespoke relationship in the correspondence of Hampton Weekes (1780–1855), a surgeon at St Thomas's Hospital. His correspondence with his family in Sussex when he was a young man reveals an intense interest in dressing well and making a good appearance in London society. In October 1801 he was particularly concerned with acquiring a good pair of boots. He repeatedly asked his father to arrange for the local shoemaker, John Randell, to make him a pair of 'buck boots' and, not being there in person, specified them at great length in his letters: 'If you were to desire him to make me a pair, stiff in the Leg & pretty high up, long in ye. foot with seams on each side of the Leg instead of behind'. A subsequent letter included a sketch of the style he desired: his ability to describe what he wanted in visual and anatomical terms possibly owed something to his occupation. He continued, 'Now for buck boots, crimping at the instep is quite out of fassion, neither do they have any tongues at the instep quite plain, & stiff Legd, tell Randles to make them round toed & rather long in the Foot than my last Shoes for they were too short'. A week later he urges, 'be pleased to send them soon, for I have walked to day almost upon my Toes it being so very dirty'. Alas, his father replied on 18 November: 'Randles has declind making your buck boots says he dont know how therefore wish you to get a strong pair in London tell them they must be stout and the Soal good'.[25] Getting shoes in the size, style and fit that you wanted was therefore a lengthy and complex business, involving detailed knowledge of the product and its vocabulary, and a two-way relationship with the producer.

By contrast, ready-made shoes were cheaper, so were the recourse of ordinary people. They did not have the credit with tradesmen that the wealthy enjoyed, so they paid for their goods up-front. In urban areas, shoes could be bought in 'Shoe Warehouses', which sometimes stocked a single maker but more usually distributed a range of suppliers. Lucy Pratt and Linda Wooley note that they were popular with the middle classes as they could acquire fashionable looks at a fraction of the price. In this way, the culture of politeness was socially accessible and potentially a threat to the social order, since anyone with ready money could visually pass themselves off as being more wealthy and respectable than they really were. Humbler consumers could buy shoes from markets, itinerant pedlars or fairs: the annual Boughton Green Fair outside Northampton allowed consumers from far and wide to acquire shoes from the local shoemakers.[26] Buying ready-made shoes presupposed that a range of sizes would be available; and we shall see in chapter 7 how the practice of bulk-buying for the military introduced the modern practice of standard sizing. Nevertheless, buying ready-made shoes was a compromise where size was concerned, and plebeian consumers would be fortunate indeed if their shoes were a good fit.

If you could not afford new shoes, you could buy second-hand. Beverly Lemire has argued that we need to think about a two-tier clothing market in the eighteenth century, whereby wealthier consumers would buy new fashions, which would make their way down to poorer people through second-hand consumption.[27] It was common for servants to receive hand-me-downs from their masters and mistresses, and we have seen how cobblers and translators would repair and repurpose used footwear for humbler consumers. There were therefore a range of ways that people could acquire shoes according to their means. We should not assume that the poor were excluded from the world of fashion, since the availability of recycled, repaired, second-hand and ready-made goods meant that they engaged with it in distinctive ways.[28] Indeed, visitors from abroad typically remarked on the good quality of footwear worn even by poorer Britons.[29]

Buckles

An important feature of the eighteenth-century shoe was its buckle. Shoes were constructed with two long straps that needed to be fastened together, and they did not come with fastenings, so the buckle had to be purchased separately. Shoe buckles were widely adopted from the 1690s and quickly went out of fashion in the 1790s. They epitomize many features of the intervening period. They were an essential part of fashionable dress for both men and women, but their significance goes deeper than this.[30] Their satisfying intricacy and their monetary value – combined with their detachability and portability – made them a desirable consumer good, and one that could be loaded with personal meaning. They also offered an opportunity for decoration, especially for men, whose shoes were increasingly to be had only in plain colours and uniform styles.

The buckled shoe became central to the dress ensemble of the eighteenth century. Patrician men dressed in their uniform of jacket, waistcoat and breeches, with a stockinged leg terminating in a buckled leather shoe. The look drew attention to the classical proportions of the body and the shapeliness of the leg, which was a particular sign of male beauty.[31] One gentleman was known for his 'handsome foot and ancle', which he displayed to the greatest advantage with 'the most brilliant and costly buckles':

> 'Don't you admire my buckles?' he cried.
> 'I was just admiring,' said my lively friend, 'not your *buckles*, but your *policy*, in making your heels the object of attraction rather than your head.'[32]

Women's buckles were less visible than men's, since they were generally smaller and could be concealed under long skirts, but this made the flash of a jewelled buckle all the more tantalizing.

Early shoe buckles were fairly simple articles, with a prong that pivoted on a central bar. The first time you attached a buckle to a shoe, you would have to pierce the leather in just the right place, to create a hole that you would use every subsequent time: this was a complex manual operation that you would learn with practice. As time went on, they became more elaborate. By the mid-century, one commentator noted that 'they began to increase in size, their designs displayed a greater degree of taste, and their workmanship a greater degree of elegance'.[33] The metal ring could be adorned with jewels and decorative motifs, or even symbols to denote the wearer's political allegiance.

Buckles were also part of the culture of mourning. They could be had japanned in black, to be worn as part of the mourning outfit. While ostensibly unshowy, they are still striking articles, with a shiny surface and even black jewels (Figure 1.5). In March 1788, Prince William wrote to his brother, George, asking for 'two mourning frocks and three pair of mourning buckles' so that he might be properly attired.[34] The correspondence of the Prince of Wales shows that he often sent buckles as gifts. Because they were small, attractive and potentially expensive – and would fit almost any shoe – they made excellent presents. They could also be personalized with initials or inscriptions, so were meaningful objects with strong emotional associations. Buckles often appear in wills, a sign both of their expense and their value to family members.[35] Their monetary value also meant that they were an asset to sell, which was particularly useful to groups with limited access to property, such as women and minors.

The 1770s and 1780s marked the height of shoe buckles' size and extravagance. The 'Artois' buckles were named after the Comte d'Artois, who was known for his lavish tastes. These huge buckles could be wider than the shoe they were fastening, so were heavy and impractical, but certainly made a striking visual impression (Figure 1.6). The finest buckles were set with diamonds and could cost thousands, and so were a way for the elite to display their wealth and power. Commentators complained that fashionable families were ruining themselves by trying to keep up with the latest buckle fashions, which were constantly changing.[36]

Figure 1.5 *Mourning buckle, 1795. The Metropolitan Museum of Art, New York City: Gift of Frederick Bradbury, 1925.*

If you could not afford diamonds, however, it was possible to achieve a similar look for a lot less money. Many buckles in the later eighteenth century were set with 'pastes', which were glass beads cut like jewels. These could come in many colours but clear pastes were by far the most popular, to emulate the look and glistening effect of diamonds. Semi-precious stones could also be set in buckles, or steel could be cut and buffed to shine like gems. Whereas expensive buckles were made from silver or gold, alternatives were commonly made from white metal or 'pinchbeck', a cheap metal compound with a golden colour. It was, of course, sensible to wear cheaper buckles: since they were worn on the feet, they could easily be lost or broken and, because they were small and detachable, they were vulnerable to theft. Owners of diamond buckles would therefore use cheaper copies for everyday wear but humbler consumers could also copy the fashions of their social betters. Pastes were 'much worn by fops and dandies', including those of modest means.[37] This highlighted the potential for falsity in the culture of politeness. Given that one's social credit could now be achieved through appearance and performance – rather than the traditional markers of personal value and standing – then the fake buckle became the focus of anxieties about the fluidity of the social order. Counterfeit stones were a metonym for the untrustworthiness of the wearer.[38]

Figure 1.6 *Artois buckle, late eighteenth century. The Metropolitan Museum of Art, New York City: Purchase George White Thorne Bequest, 1883.*

Nevertheless, buckles had important roles to play in social interactions. Buckled shoes were part of the formal ensemble that men would wear to dances: indeed, dress regulations at assembly rooms explicitly forbade boots, as they were for riding and were therefore rural outdoor wear. Many Georgian social events took place in the evening, and bejewelled buckles came into their own at candlelit occasions, since their facets reflected the light. Buckles dazzled during a dance, drawing attention to the motions of the feet. They had their disadvantages when dancing – they were prone to breaking, coming off, or catching on a partner's clothing – but the visual effect was worth the risk. In order to understand buckles, therefore, we should not view them in a display case, detached from the body whose shoes they fastened. Rather, we should consider them as worn objects, which moved and glistened, and whose meanings were established in social interactions.

Changing styles for men and women

Although the basic form of the common shoe remained fairly consistent, the style of shoes for both men and women changed over the course of the eighteenth century. Shoe fashions changed in relation to the wider dress ensemble and to ideas about gender. We shall see that men's and women's shoes diverged in style at a time when notions of gender difference were becoming newly polarized. As we saw in the Introduction, shoe designs have historically been highly ideological, since they relate directly to the roles that their wearers hold in society and the roles that they perform. Shoes styles in the eighteenth century were therefore informed by developments in wider fields – such as politics, philosophy, science and the visual arts – and served to ground ideologies of gender in daily physical practice.

At the beginning of the century, shoes for elite men and women were often remarkably similar. Both sexes could wear shoes decorated with brightly coloured and patterned fabrics (Figure 1.7). Neither men nor women from the upper classes were expected to walk any great distance outdoors, where they would be conveyed by carriage or sedan chair, or ride on horseback, wearing boots made specifically for riding rather than walking. Their footwear was therefore not designed to facilitate ambulation, nor to protect against the elements: its very impracticality signalled the elite's social status and political power.

For example, the shoes of elite men and women both typically had a high heel. Although men's tended to have a wider heel of stacked leather, and women's a carved wooden heel, the visual effect was the same.[39] Nowadays the high heel is primarily associated with femininity, as is the distinctive walk and body shape that it promotes. The podiatrist William A. Rossi famously demonstrated that high

Figure 1.7 *Man's silk brocade shoe, c. 1730. Image courtesy of Northampton Museum and Art Gallery.*

heels increase the woman's pelvic angle, accentuates the calves, buttocks and breasts, and increases the motion of the hips when walking.⁴⁰ This exclusive association of heels with femininity, however, has not historically always been the case. Although shoe historians debate the origins of the high heel,⁴¹ in the early modern world it was a sign of class rather than gender, given its associated with equestrianism and with the power of the aristocracy. Men at the court of Louis XIV wore the famous *talons rouges*, to symbolize that they could trample his opponents. The British upper-class male similarly wore red heels in the early eighteenth century, giving him a 'polite' deportment and accentuating his height advantage over his inferiors, above whom he literally towered (Figure 1.8).⁴² The very lack of mobility permitted by heels emphasized that the wearer did not perform manual labour, an enduring association that would later attach to women.⁴³

The heeled shoe was an important element of the early-Georgian dress ensemble. David Kuchta has shown how the three-piece suit came to be the uniform of the British gentleman – and arguably remains so to this day.⁴⁴ The men who gathered at court and parliament were dressed in this common way, emphasizing that they were members of the political club. These suits could be very colourful and were made from the finest fabrics, with bejewelled accessories such as buttons and swords: they were therefore an outward projection of the wearer's wealth and refinement, and by extension their rank. The attitude of men in this period was, 'if you've got it, flaunt it'.⁴⁵ The early-Georgian three-piece suit consisted of breeches, a buttoned waistcoat and a long frock coat (Figure 1.9). At the top of the

Figure 1.8 *Men's shoes with red heels, 1740–79. Brooklyn Museum Costume Collection at the Metropolitan Museum of Art, New York City: Gift of the Brooklyn Museum, 2009; Gift of Mrs Clarence R. Hyde, 1928.*

Figure 1.9 *William Hogarth, The Strode Family (1738). Alamy stock photo.*

ensemble was a wig and sometimes a hat, and at the bottom were heeled shoes: the heels gave the body its distinctive deportment, and decorated buckles drew attention to the feet. Aileen Ribeiro notes that 'the solidity of the footwear complemented the general heaviness of the outline'.[46]

Historians often argue that it was over the eighteenth century that modern, binary schemes of gender difference emerged, positing that men and women had different bodies that befitted them for different spheres of activity. Gender difference certainly existed prior to the eighteenth century, but it was relatively fluid and was not grounded in sexual anatomy to the same extent: Thomas Laqueur argues that men and women shared a common 'one sex' body. Over the course of the eighteenth century, however, men and women came to be seen as different creatures with distinct anatomies and social roles: gender came to be conceived of in more binary terms as it was increasingly grounded in the 'two sex' body. Crucially, Laqueur argues that political considerations rather than medical 'discoveries' were the drivers of the process, as women's place in society came to be a focus of the Enlightenment.[47] This argument has been widely debated,[48] as has the 'separate spheres' interpretation in women's history that complements it in many ways,[49] but historians agree that gender roles were reformulated over the course of the eighteenth century. Not coincidentally, the styles of men's and women's shoes diverged at this time. Given the impact that shoes have on the appearance of the body and its capacity to carry out certain tasks, shoes were arguably integral to this process. Although shoes today are instantly recognizable as being 'male' or 'female', and women's feet are on average smaller than men's, differences in shoe styles are not down to anatomical differences. Rather, shoes have become a site for the construction of gender difference.[50]

As the century wore on, men's and women's shoes went their separate ways. Men's shoes became plainer in style and their heels lowered (Figure 1.1). Heels now carried the taint of the aristocracy and 'polite' manners came under attack for their insincerity and effeminacy. Lower shoes did not seek to deceive and placed their wearers on a level with one another, so were symbolic of equality in the Age of Revolutions.[51] Increasingly, men's shoes were only to be had in black (or, occasionally, brown) and in generic styles. The only source of decoration was the buckle but these, too, fell foul of the new values of the 1790s and men adopted laces instead. 'From the era of the REVOLUTION in FRANCE, we have to lament the decline of the BUCKLE manufactory', noted one British commentator, 'and from the ultimate triumph of Jacobinism in that unhappy land, the almost total extinction of those elegant ornaments, Shoe Buckles, in this nation.'[52] In a period of war, many men adopted the military fashion for boots, and Chapter 4 will show how these were increasingly made from supple leather with a low heel, and so could be worn for walking as well as riding. They therefore enabled men to conduct their business and suited the serious attitude of the day.

These new footwear styles were an important part of the dress ensemble at the end of the eighteenth century, as the three-piece suit was reworked in order to project a very different image. Boots or laced shoes would be paired with trousers or pantaloons (another fashion from the military), which emphasized the length of the leg and the classical proportions of the body, underlining the wearer's civic virtue. Men stopped wearing wigs, too, in the 1790s, partly because of the tax on hair powder but mostly due to a preference for wearing hair in a natural style. In the later eighteenth century the culture of 'politeness' came under attack for its falsity, and Georgians instead celebrated the culture of 'sensibility' which prided genuine emotional expression. The flamboyant clothes from earlier in the century therefore became problematic as men sought a less showy and elitist style. Masculine virtue was increasingly judged, not by the outer display of wealth and refinement, but by the inner qualities of a man's soul.[53]

By contrast to men, women came to be seen as sensual and irrational over the course of the Enlightenment, and their footwear followed suit.[54] Whereas men's shoes were usually made of leather, women's were typically made from silk or wool.[55] By the end of the eighteenth century, fashionable women were wearing delicate fabric pumps tied with ribbons, which wore out so quickly they bought several pairs at once (Figure 1.10). Boots were available for walking or riding but, unlike men's, these were for a specific purpose and were not for general wear. In the 1800s, half-boots were fashionable among female walkers, but even these were narrow and relatively flimsy, being made from kid leather or cotton.[56] So, whereas men's shoes were avowedly practical articles that equipped them for mobility within the public sphere, women's footwear restricted them to domestic arenas and roles.

As we approach the Victorian period, there was a proliferation of new shoe styles available for men. Many of our modern shoe styles date from this period, such as the Oxford shoe or the Derby boot. These smart but understated black shoes and a black top hat bookended a sober three-piece suit, which was itself often black (Figure 1.11). Colour disappears from the male wardrobe in general by the Victorian period. Historians have conventionally argued that this constituted a 'renunciation' of bodily display, which smoothed over distinctions between propertied men, giving them a common identity and a moral justification for their collective power.[57] Far from being dull or self-abnegating, some recent commentators have pointed out that sartorial blackness could in fact be very showy, and made a collective statement about men's 'standing, goods [and] mastery'.[58] Black was expensive to buy and maintain, and the well-to-do had an army of servants, tailors, laundresses and bootblacks to help them achieve the look. Humbler men also wore plain clothes and shoes as a mark of respectability, but the cut, quality and *blackness* of these would be visibly inferior to those of their betters. The Derby boot and the brogan had the same basic construction, but the former was visibly the boot of a gentleman. Moreover, its close fit, thin sole and supple construction would have enabled a refined and quiet walking gait, signalling the rank and virtue of the wearer.

Figure 1.10 *Women's slippers, 1805–15. Brooklyn Museum Costume Collection at the Metropolitan Museum of Art, New York City: Gift of the Brooklyn Museum, 2009; Gift of Herman Delman, 1954.*

Figure 1.11 *Théobald Chartran, Edwyn Burnaby, MP, Vanity Fair, 10 March 1883. Yale Center for British Art: Gift of Michael H. LeWitt, Peter A. LeWitt and Erwin Strasmick, B1979.14.371. Public domain.*

Shoes, therefore, have important implications for gender and the body. Because they are worn articles, they have a close relationship with the body and its motions, affecting what the wearer can do. They are, therefore, highly ideological objects, which have historically been the focus of discussions about social class, gender and national identity. This was no truer of any period than the eighteenth century, since the Enlightenment sought to justify the position of people in society in new ways. In particular, new ideas about masculinity and femininity, and the proper roles of men and women, informed the styles of shoes. In turn, shoes grounded these ideologies in the practice of everyday life, affecting the way that men and women of different classes moved and dictating what they could do, and where. This chapter has considered the shoe as a physical artefact and a consumer good, as well as a powerfully ideological fashion item. It is necessary to outline this context in order to set up the more exploratory chapters that follow, but it is also important to underline the materiality of the shoe, since this is fundamental to understanding it.

Notes

1 'The Street Companion; Or, The Young Man's Guide and the Old Man's Comfort, in the Choice of Shoes. By the Rev. Tom Foggy Dribble', *London Magazine and Review* n.s. 1 (January–April 1825): 73–77 (73, 77).

2 Stephanie Downes, Sally Holloway and Sarah Randles (eds), *Feeling Things: Objects and Emotions Through History* (Oxford: Oxford University Press, 2018).

3 For example, Joanne Begiato, *Manliness in Britain, 1760–1900: Bodies, Emotion, and Material Culture* (Manchester: Manchester University Press, 2020), 16.

4 Act 4, scene 2: William Shakespeare, *King John* (*c*. 1595), ed. John Tobin and Jesse Lander (London: Bloomsbury, 2018), 206.

5 Swann, *Shoes*, 32.

6 Wilson, *A History of Shoe Fashions*, 186; Vivi Lena Anderson, 'Old Shoes in a New Perspective – Fashioning Archaeology', *Fashion Practice* 9, no. 2 (2017): 168–82 (178); J. H. Thornton, 'Left – Right – Left', *Journal of the British Boot and Shoe Institution* 7, no. 4 (1959): 164–70.

7 Alexander, *Treasures Afoot*, 111.

8 Giorgio Riello, 'Nature, Production and Regulation in Eighteenth-Century Britain and France: The Case of the Leather Industry', *Historical Research* 81, no. 211 (2008): 75–99 (77).

9 Ibid., 85.

10 Christopher Breward, 'Fashioning Masculinity: Men's Footwear and Modernity', in *Shoes: A History from Sandals to Sneakers*, ed. Giorgio Riello and Peter McNeil (Oxford: Berg, 2006), 223.

11 Eric Hobsbawm and Joan Scott, 'Political Shoemakers', *Past & Present* 89, no. 1 (1980): 86–114 (101).

12 Fairhurst, 'Eighteenth-Century Women's Shoes', 32.

13 Roy Church, 'Gotch & Sons, Kettering, Tanners, Curriers, Boot and Shoe Makers, 1797–1888', *Journal of the British Boot and Shoe Institution* 7, no. 11 (1957): 479–88 (480).

14 Victor Hatley, 'Shoemakers in Northamptonshire, 1762–1911: A Statistical Survey', *Northampton Historical Series* 6 (1971): 1–13 (5).

15 See, for example, the street layout of areas of Northampton such as the Mounts.

16 David Cannadine, 'The Present and the Past in the English Industrial Revolution 1880–1980', *Past and Present* 103 (1984): 131–72.

17 McKendrick, Brewer and Plumb, *The Birth of a Consumer Society*.

18 Pratt and Woolley, *Shoes*, 66.

19 Peter Borsay, *The English Urban Renaissance: Culture and Society in the Provincial Town, 1660–1770* (Oxford: Oxford University Press, 1991).

20 Alexander, 'Shoes and the City', 299.

21 Serena Dyer, 'Shopping in Georgian London', *History Today* 65, no. 3 (2015): 30–6.

22 Mary Wollstonecraft, *A Vindication of the Rights of Woman*, ed. Janet Todd (1792; Oxford: Oxford University Press, 2008), 147.

23 Margot Finn, 'Men's Things: Masculine Possession in the Consumer Revolution', *Social History* 25, no. 2 (2000): 133–55 (135, 139).

24 Claire Walsh, 'Shops, Shopping and the Art of Decision Making in Eighteenth-Century England', in *Gender, Taste and Material Culture in Britain and North America, 1700–1830*, ed. John Styles and Amanda Vickery (New Haven, CT: Yale University Press, 2007), 151–77 (164).

25 James Ford (ed.), *A Medical Student at St Thomas's Hospital, 1801–1802: The Weekes Family Letters* (London: Wellcome, 1987), 55, 61, 74, 77. I am grateful to Gillian Williamson for this reference.

26 Pratt and Wooley, *Shoes*, 68.

27 Beverley Lemire, 'Consumerism in Preindustrial and Early Industrial England: The Trade in Secondhand Clothes', *Journal of British Studies* 27, no. 1 (1988): 1–24.

28 John Styles, *The Dress of the People: Everyday Fashion in Eighteenth-Century England* (New Haven, CT: Yale University Press, 2007).

29 Aileen Ribeiro, *Dress in Eighteenth-Century Europe, 1715–1789* (London: Holmes & Meier, 1985), 63.

30 Matthew McCormack, 'So Manly and Ornamental: Shoe Buckles and Britain's Eighteenth Century', *The English Historical Review* 138, no. 592 (2023): 474–96.

31 Harvey, 'Men of Parts', 797–821.

32 *Literary and Fashionable Magazine* (1809), 301.

33 Joseph Moser, 'The Revolution in Shoe Buckles', *The European Magazine*, June 1807, 424.

34 Prince William to Prince George, 10 March 1778: A. Aspinall (ed.), *The Correspondence of George, Prince of Wales 1770–1812: Volume 1: 1770–1789* (London: Cassell, 1968), 268.

35 Bernard Hughes and Therle Hughes, *Georgian Shoe Buckles* (London: Greater London Council, 1972), 6.

36 Brooke, *A History of English Footwear*, 70.

37 Vivienne Becker, *Fabulous Fakes: The History of Fantasy and Fashion Jewellery* (London: Grafton, 1988), 32.

38 Alicia Kerfoot, 'Declining Buckles and Movable Shoes in Frances Burney's *Cecilia*', *The Burney Journal* 11 (2011): 55–79.

39 Swann, *Shoes*, 20.

40 Federico Bondi and Giovanni Mariacher, *If the Shoe Fits*, trans. Jane Chisholm (Venice: Cavallino, 1979), 166.

41 Elizabeth Semmelhack, 'A Delicate Balance: Women, Power and High Heels', in Giorgio Riello and Peter McNeil (eds), *Shoes: A History from Sandals to Sneakers* (Oxford: Berg, 2006), 224–49 (225).

42 Matthew McCormack, 'Tall Histories: Height and Georgian Masculinities', *Transactions of the Royal Historical Society* 6, no. 26 (2016): 79–101.

43 Christopher Breward, 'Men in Heels: From Power to Perversity', in *Shoes: Pleasure and Pain*, ed. Helen Persson (London: Victoria & Albert Museum, 2015), 128–39 (134).

44 David Kuchta, *The Three-Piece Suit and Modern Masculinity: England, 1550–1850* (Berkeley: University of California Press, 2002).

45 Paul Langford, 'Politics and Manners from Sir Robert Walpole to Sir Robert Peel', *Proceedings of the British Academy* 94 (1997): 103–125 (109).

46 Ribeiro, *Dress*, 31.

47 Thomas Laqueur, *Making Sex: Body and Gender from the Greeks to Freud* (Cambridge, MA: Harvard University Press, 1990).

48 For example: H. King, *The One-Sex Body on Trial: The Classical and Early Modern Evidence* (Farnham: Ashgate, 2013).

49 For example: Vickery, 'Golden Age to Separate Spheres?'

50 Giorgio Riello and Peter McNeil, 'Footprints from History', *History Today* 57, no. 3 (March 2007): 30–6 (30).

51 Elizabeth Semmelhack, *Standing Tall: The Curious History of Men in Heels* (Toronto: Bata Shoe Museum, 2016), 42.

52 Moser, 'The Revolution in Shoe Buckles', 426.

53 Tosh, 'Gentlemanly Politeness and Manly Simplicity'.

54 Elizabeth Semmelhack, *Shoes: The Meaning of Style* (London: Reaktion, 2017), 170–2.

55 Swann, *Shoes*, 29.

56 Pratt and Woolley, *Shoes*, 61.

57 J. C. Flügel, *The Psychology of Clothes* (London: Institute of Psycho-Analysis and Hogarth Press, 1930); Kuchta, *The Three-Piece Suit*; T. King, *The Gendering of Men, 1600–1750: Volume 1: The English Phallus* (Madison: University of Wisconsin Press, 2004).

58 J. Harvey, *Men in Black* (London: Reaktion, 1995), 10.

2

Shoes and the body

John Gay's satirical poem, *Trivia: Or the Art of Walking the Streets of London* (1716), described the many hazards that the pedestrian might encounter and how best to avoid them. It began by advising the reader on appropriate footwear:

> Let firm, well-hammer'd Soles protect thy Feet
> Thro' freezing Snows, and Rains, and soaking Sleet.
> Should the big Laste extend the Shoe too wide,
> Each Stone will wrench th' unwary Step aside:
> The sudden Turn may stretch the swelling Vein,
> Thy cracking joint unhinge, or Ankle sprain;
> And when too short the modish Shoes are worn,
> You'll judge the Seasons by your shooting Corn.[1]

Well-made shoes protected feet against the elements, as well as other contemporary urban dangers mentioned in the poem, such as mud, overflowing gutters and the contents of chamber pots. They were therefore essential apparel for the early-Georgian *flâneur*. As Gay reminds us, however, ill-fitting shoes hold dangers of their own, resulting in injuries, accidents and medical complaints. Other items of clothing impact on the human body but shoes do so in a unique way. Shoes have to bear the body's entire weight and the considerable stresses imposed by walking, while supporting the delicate structure and sensitive skin of the foot. Furthermore, the forces imposed on shoes leave an indelible impression of their wearer, giving an insight into the shape, size and motions of their bodies. No other garment does this. Footwear therefore has the potential to tell us a great deal about the human body.

This chapter makes a case for an embodied history of shoes, which thinks about shoes as material articles that had a close and reciprocal relationship with past physical bodies, allowing the historian to shed new light on both. To date, histories of gender and the body have had little to say about the history of shoes, and vice versa. While recent years have seen an increasing interest in the social and cultural history of shoes, the focus tends to be on shoes themselves rather than what they tell us about the bodies of their wearers.² The one historical field that has systematically thought about shoes as objects that relate to bodies is archaeology. For example, studies of footwear remains have demonstrated changing patterns of wear over a long period or across social classes, suggesting differences in the way that people walked.³ Alternatively, evidence of human bones has allowed archaeologists to speculate about the nature of footwear where no such evidence has survived.⁴ In general, shoes retrieved from archaeological digs are in poor condition: leather is only preserved in specific conditions, so the evidence tends to be scraps that are heavily decayed and very fragile.⁵

This chapter will instead focus on examples of footwear from museum collections. The condition of these vary, but particular attention has been paid to worn examples as it is these that tell us most about the bodies of their wearers. Because of shoes' vital practical function, it is important to engage with them as objects in order to get a sense of their materiality. Studying their shape, weight, texture and flexibility gives an insight into what they would have been like to wear, and examining patterns of wear on the soles, heels and uppers tells us about their wearer. So, whereas the current study of material culture encompasses a range of approaches – including the subjective, the emotional and the economic – this study will prioritize the practical physicality of the object itself. As Ulinka Rublack has argued, material articles like shoes need to be studied as 'real-life objects in use'.⁶

As well as using material evidence from museums, this chapter will explore writings from the time about feet and footwear. Some of this writing is medical, often by writers who were keen to establish chiropody⁷ as a respectable medical discipline, and who were anxious to distance themselves from the corn doctors and barbers who were notorious for butchering people's feet (Figure 2.1). Lewis Durlacher paraded his credentials as 'Surgeon-Chiropodist to Her Majesty the Queen and the Royal Family'.⁸ Other writings focus on clothing, but these too were concerned with health and hygiene: a novel and distinctive focus for the eighteenth century. This scientific emphasis might appear neutral, but Peter McNeil and Giorgio Riello argue that it continued the centuries-old debate about the expense and morality of fashion, and that shoes were 'at the center of such debate'.⁹ Attention is also paid to life writing, in order to get an insight into how people from the time articulated their experience of wearing shoes.

The chapter will begin by thinking about the impact that the body has upon shoes, and the way in which the body is therefore visible in worn footwear. As well as providing historians with concrete, physical evidence of the wearer, this also highlights the very individual relationship that people have with their shoes, something that is perceptible in a range of cultural practices across our period. It is also revealing to think about the requirements that shoes have to fulfil and the materials that they are made from in order to achieve this. The focus will then be reversed, as the chapter thinks about the impact of shoes upon the body. It will explore how the design of shoes affects the experience of wearing them, and the influence that this has upon the wearer's bodily health, posture and mobility.

Figure 2.1 Anon., The Corn Doctor *(1793)*. Wellcome Collection.

The impact of the body on shoes

Shoes commonly bear tell-tale signs of their owner. Look at the insole of any used pair of shoes and you will likely see the outline of a footprint, with indentations marking where the heel, midfoot and toes have exerted repeated pressure on the sole. The term 'footprint' is commonly used today to signify the impact of human activity, but in the case of shoes this literal footprint is a record of a human being. In addition to the footprint, wear to the sole and heel provide evidence of how the wearer moved in their shoes, and stretches in the upper record the outline of their foot. Shoes in museum collections rarely come with a provenance and, although it is possible to infer things about the owner from the design of the shoe, patterns of wear are often the only direct record we have of them. For example, we do not know who owned these Wellington boots in Northampton Museum (Figure 2.2): the style dates from around 1820 and the quality of the materials and workmanship tells us that the owner was well-to-do. By studying the

Figure 2.2 *Wellington boots, 1800–25. Image courtesy of Northampton Museum and Art Gallery.*

boots, however, we can see that they have stretched in order to mould to the foot. Wellingtons like this were made of supple leather and were bespoke articles, since before the availability of elastic they had to fit exactly, but it was fashionable in this period to wear tight boots in order to give the impression of slender feet. To judge by the stretching – which extends beyond the outline of the sole – and also by the long cut that has been made to the leg in order to get them on and off, this pair were made too small. The owner could afford to wear footwear that fitted but chose not to in order to achieve a certain appearance.

Footwear therefore has a unique relationship with its owner. Bespoke footwear is directly manufactured for a particular owner, but even shoes that were made in generic sizes gradually mould to the foot through wear and adaptation. The ghostly outline of the absent foot has encouraged various cultures to identify the worn shoe with the soul of its original owner. Impromptu monuments of empty shoes can convey loss; and soldiers who looted boots from the fallen on the battlefield would leave their own worn-out pair as a mark of respect.[10] The folk practice of concealing shoes within the house in order to protect it against evil spirits suggests that the shoe magically retains the power of its owner. As June Swann notes, the shoe is 'the only garment we wear which retains the shape, the personality, the essence of the wearer'.[11] Many people resisted buying second-hand shoes for this reason, a practice that was often regarded as being unlucky. Contemporaries also highlighted the medical dangers of wearing used shoes, which retained bodily traces of their former owner: Christian Struve warned that a boy contracted scarlet fever 'by wearing the boots of a patient labouring under that disease'.[12] Writers like this showed little sympathy for working people who had no choice but to wear second-hand or cast-offs. In practice, shoes were often acquired used due to their expense.[13]

The structure of the human foot places certain requirements upon shoes. Humans are bipeds and so place the entire weight of their bodies upon their feet. Primates have an opposable big toe but, as human feet are just used for walking, their toes have shortened and have largely lost the ability to grab.[14] Human feet are plantigrade, since humans stand and walk on flat feet rather than upon their toes. Their feet therefore developed an arch, to bear the weight of their bodies and the forces imposed by locomotion. The renowned surgeon, Sir Charles Bell eulogized that 'there is nothing more beautiful than the structure of the human foot'. He praised its structure in architectural terms:

> The foot has in its structure all the fine appliances you see in a building. In the first place, there is an arch ... so that, instead of standing, as might be imagined, on a solid bone, we stand upon an arch composed of a series of bones, which are united by the most curious provision for the elasticity of the foot; hence, if we jump from height directly upon the heel, a severe shock is felt; not so, if we alight upon the ball of the great toe, for there an elasticity is formed in the whole foot, and the weight of the body is thrown upon this arch, and the shock avoided.[15]

In total, the foot consists of twenty-six bones, thirty-three joints and dozens of ligaments (Figure 2.3). When stressed in the right way, they can withstand great forces, but the foot is also extremely fragile

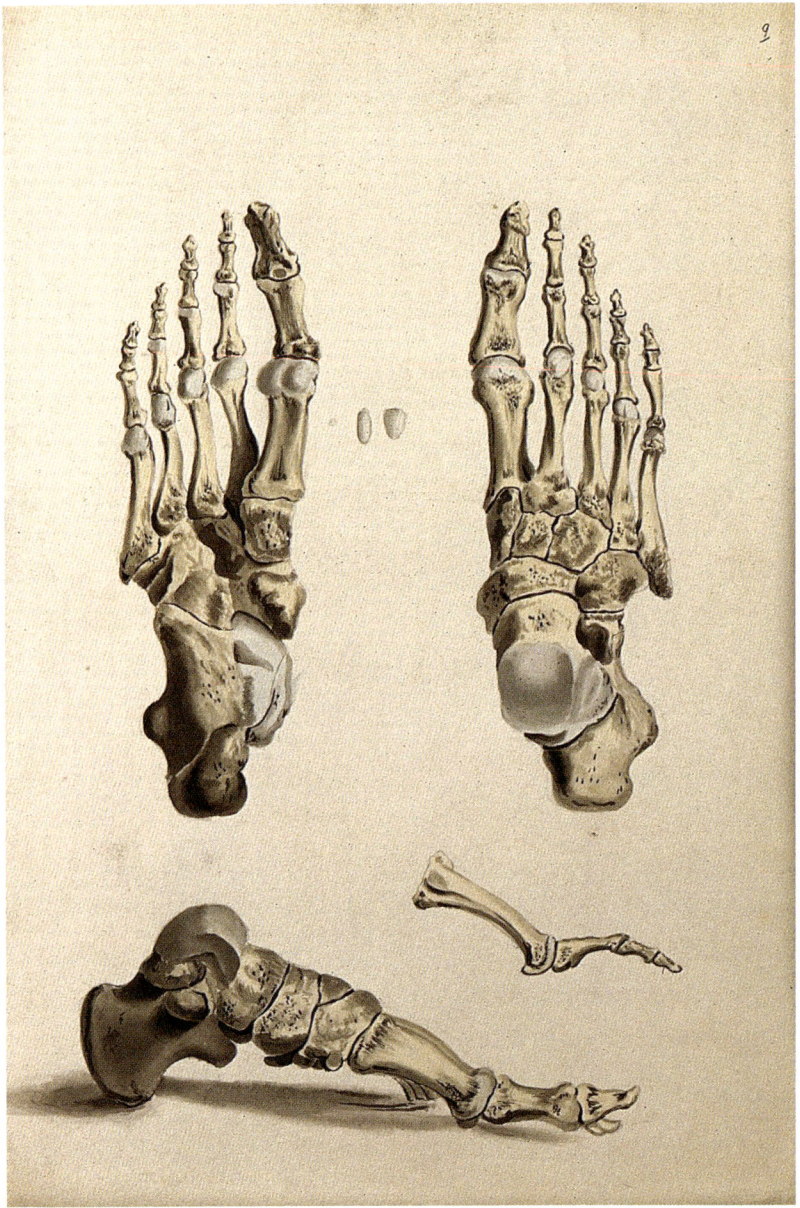

Figure 2.3 *The bones of the foot (1830), after William Cheselden (1733). Wellcome Collection.*

at certain points and angles. (England football fans may remember how their hopes in the 2006 World Cup hinged on the fourth metatarsal in Wayne Rooney's right foot.) For this reason, shoes should ideally offer a measure of protection and support in their uppers as well as their soles.

Shoes therefore have to fulfil various requirements. These requirements are exacting and often in opposition to one another: shoes have to endure great forces and yet also protect a sensitive and vulnerable part of the body; they therefore have to be strong and hardwearing, at the same time as being soft and flexible. Additionally, they have to be waterproof. Gay reminds us that shoes protect us against the elements; and Richard Weekes wrote to his brother in October 1801 to suggest that he 'wear a flannell waistcoat. gett a pair of Buck boots. directly and wear them. for the wet weather is coming on'.[16] As we saw in Chapter 1, shoes have for this reason historically been manufactured from leather. With the exception of wooden clogs, all of the examples examined here were leather shoes. Even fine silk brocade shoes for indoor wear were based upon leather, with a layer of fabric on top (see Figure 2.4).

Leather is strong, durable, flexible, breathable and waterproof. Before the vulcanization of rubber in the 1840s, and the later invention of petrochemical plastics, any material article that required these properties was typically made from it. William Nisbet noted that the 'materials of which the shoe is formed' are fundamental to its design:

> The substance, along with softness and pliancy, should possess the particular quality of excluding moisture. Leather is generally preferred, and by preparing it with a composition of oil, wax and turpentine, till the leather is fully saturated, it becomes impervious to the access of the wet of any kind. Thus by a shoe ... made of a soft, pliable material, rendered impervious to moisture, an easy motion of the whole foot will be permitted.[17]

Figure 2.4 *Slip-on man's shoe, 1700. Image courtesy of Northampton Museum and Art Gallery.*

Leather has these properties because of its origins in skin, and shoe leather tended to be made from cowhide.[18] After butchering, the flesh and hair are removed and the leather is soaked, dried and stretched. The tanning process alters the protein structure in the leather, to make it more durable and retard putrefaction. It remains a changing organic material, however, and needs to be 'fed' with polish if it is going to retain its flexibility, impermeability and longevity, not to mention its shiny appearance. Eighteenth-century household manuals abounded with recipes for bootblack, and servants spent much of their time polishing shoes: one gentleman lamented that his refused to do it anymore until they got a pay rise, 'wh. measure we were obliged to come into'.[19] Given the expense of shoes in this period, it was essential that they were maintained so as to last as long as possible. Because they were made from skin, shoes – and other leather articles like breeches and waistcoats – became a kind of second skin to the wearer, raising the question of where the boundaries of the body begin and end.[20] Moulding to the body and complementing the function of the wearer's own skin, the wearing of shoes was fundamentally an embodied experience.

A further characteristic of the wearer's skin that affects the shoe is its tendency to sweat. The combination of moisture, acid and heat darkens the leather, so sweat marks are visible on shoes in museum collections. This provides a lasting physical trace of their wearer and potentially biological material: there is a large forensic literature on how to obtain biological traces from clothing, although this decreases with the age of the object.[21] Alison Fairhurst notes that sweat also damages the shoe, causing leather to curl at the edges and the glue to degrade.[22] Georgians believed that sweat had a corrosive effect on skin – which, of course, includes leather – but they were more concerned about its effect on the body than the shoe. A 1797 treatise on healthy clothing noted that 'there is not a greater and more important emunctory [that is, an organ with an excreting function] in the whole human system than the feet' and that 'free perspiration from the feet' was essential.[23]

Eighteenth-century medicine was still informed by the ancient humoral understanding of the body, which conceived of a fluid economy that needed to be regulated by purging in order to stay healthy. A chiropody treatise of 1785 blamed corns on 'obstructed perspiration' – rather than what we would today identify as a protective layer of hard skin formed in response to the rubbing of the shoe – since trapped sweat becomes 'so acrid and corrosive as to occasion the most painful inflammations'.[24] As Kevin Siena notes, blockages that caused fluids to stagnate 'provided common explanations for early modern diseases'.[25] Despite the sweat and smell of feet, another writer cautioned against bathing them too frequently, since 'it is apt to attract a greater flow of humours to the spot, and thus increase, perhaps bring on, a morbid perspiration'.

For this reason, much medical writing on feet focused on socks, not so much for their ability to prevent blisters, but for the breathability and dryness of their material. Cotton socks, oddly, were universally condemned for their tendency to absorb sweat, 'thus confining the feet in a bath of cold perspirable matter'.[26] Furthermore, 'cotton saturated with the sweat of the feet (and cotton can contain more than linen), soon rots'. Instead, wool was recommended. Podiatric writers lauded wool for its ability to prevent 'humidity and smell'.[27] Soldiers who had to march long distances were issued with woollen socks, and the many treatises on foot health that appeared during the First World War continued to recommend them.[28] This suggests that a concern with healthy perspiration outlived the humoral body, as we can see in Joseph Sparkes Hall's treatise of 1847:

> The pedestrian well knows the difference on a long day's walk, between a cotton or linen stocking and one of wool; he knows that the former soon becomes hard, damp and chilly, with the moisture of the foot, whereas the latter enables him to bear fatigue, defends the foot from the friction of the shoe, secures it from blisters, and in every way ministers to his comfort.

Note how the intrepid pedestrian who could endure a 'long day's walk' was conceived of in the masculine: podiatric writers tended to adopt a masculine universal unless specifically talking about women, assuming that only men would need to wear shoes for a utilitarian purpose.

As well as being strong, flexible and sweaty, feet are also delicate. Whereas walking barefoot hardens the sole, this does not happen when the foot is shod. Shoes therefore create their own necessity: wearing shoes makes the foot soft and delicate, which, in turn, means that shoes have to be worn to protect this vulnerable extremity. Writers at the time noted that 'feet are peculiarly exposed to injury from the delicacy of the skin'.[29] In particular, this delicacy was described in terms of the nerves (Figure 2.5). Nisbet noted that feet, like the hands, 'are endowed with much sensibility, by the large share of nerves they visibly possess. In covering them, therefore, particular regard should be had that no interruption take place to these purposes of nature.' Shoes should therefore possess 'pliancy' and allow the wearer to feel what they are coming into contact with.[30] This abundance of nerves also explained the pain caused by ill-fitting footwear and the complaints that resulted from them. Corns led to the 'desiccation of the nervous *fibrialle* of the skin; and the pain they communicate is like that which we experience in walking with gravel or small stones in our shoes'.[31]

As we have seen, this emphasis on the nervous body coexisted with an older vision of the body, which excreted and rotted. This is important for the history of gender, since the supposed decline of the humoral body is often central to accounts of how gender roles diverged over the course of the eighteenth century. As we saw in the previous chapter, Thomas Laqueur argues that a flexible 'one sex' vision of the body (where men and women shared a common body governed by the four humours) was replaced by a 'two sex' body (where men and women had utterly different physiologies that equipped them for separate social roles).[32] The embodied history of shoes shows how multiple visions of the body existed alongside one another in the eighteenth century, and that these had a practical and physical dimension as well as a theoretical medical one. This approach therefore offers a critical perspective on some of our key narratives of gender change in this period.

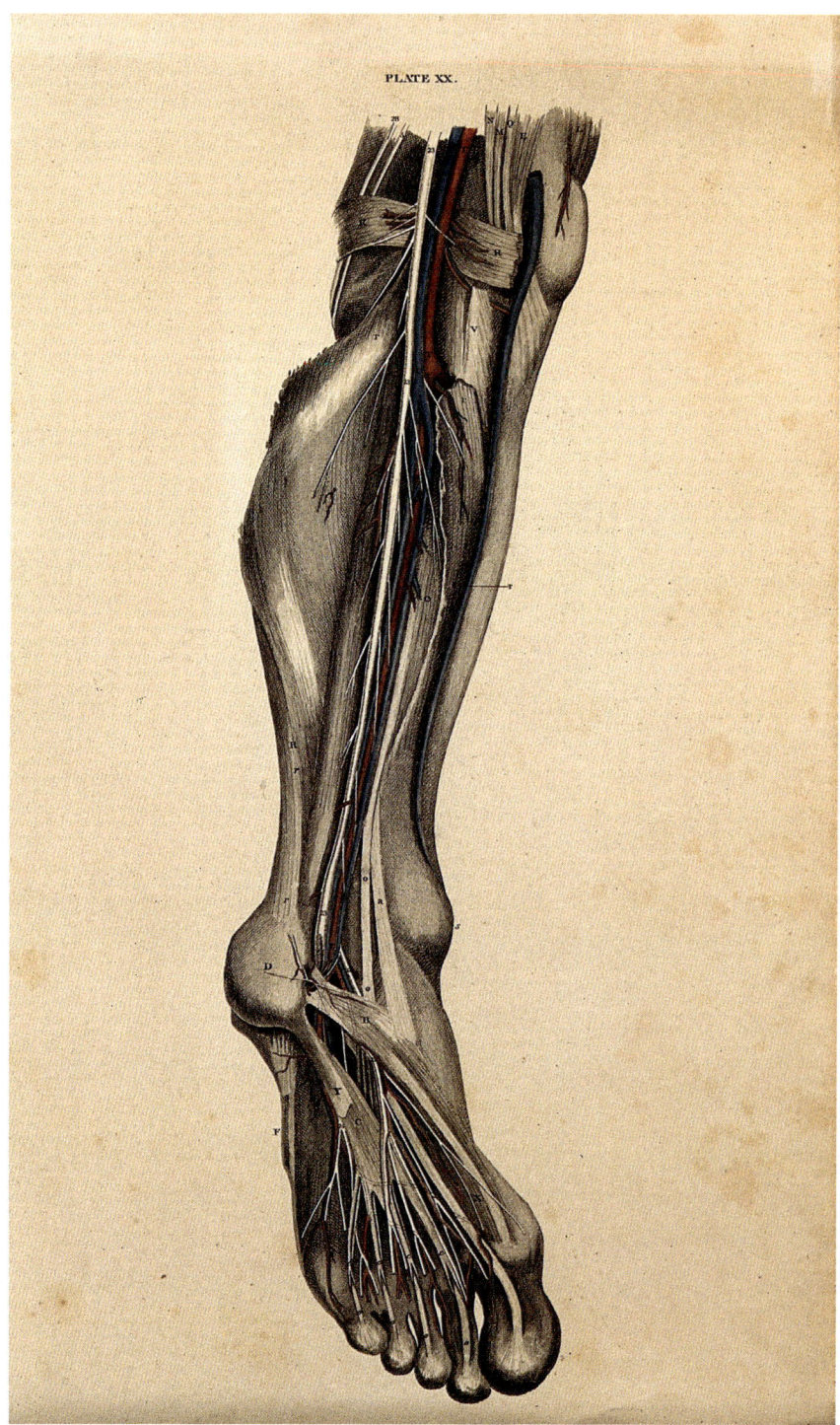

Figure 2.5 *W. H. Lizars,* Leg and foot: dissection, with blood vessels and nerves … *(1822). Wellcome Collection.*

The impact of shoes on the body

Shoes are unique among garments in that they support the whole body. As well as affecting the feet and the legs, their role in absorbing shock, bearing weight and enabling mobility impact upon body parts higher up such as the hips, the spine, the shoulders and the neck. Contemporary medical writings emphasized that ill-fitting footwear, and the complaints they caused, were a factor in the body's general health. As Durlacher explained, 'these local complaints, when neglected, injure the general system by preventing the body from obtaining that natural and indispensable exercise, so conducive to health'. He therefore urged that patients seek the 'proper attention' of a professional chiropodist, rather than cutting their feet with 'razors, knives and other unwieldy instruments'.[33]

Choice of footwear affects the body's entire posture and gait. A 1792 translation of the German Bernhard Faust's *Catechism on Health* by the Scottish physician James Gregory emphasized the importance of the foot's natural structure for standing and walking:

> Q. 108. What is the form of the human foot?
> A. At the toes it is broad, the heel small, and the inside of the foot is longer than the outside.
> Q. 109. Why does it take this form?
> A. That a man may walk and stand with ease and firmness, and move his body freely.

The writer was not just using the masculine universal here: he was specifically describing the way that patrician men were expected to stand and move in this period. The next question concerned the type of shoe that should facilitate this, and the answer was one that has 'the same form as the foot'.[34] At the time of writing, this was a pointed remark, since shoes did *not* take the form of the foot, as we shall see. Even half a century later, Durlacher bemoaned that choice of footwear was impairing people's mobility:

> Few adults possess that firmness of step and ease of walking which Nature intended, in consequence of the confined and compressed condition in which their feet have been placed, by the unyielding material and bad shape of their shoes; the consequence is, that the natural spring and muscular action of the foot are lost, and they are deprived of the assistance that would be rendered by the action of the toes in progression.[35]

Placing 'Nature' in opposition to fashion and the trappings of civilization was a common trope in these writings. On the one hand, this was characteristic of the Enlightenment; on the other, it expressed anxieties about modernity itself.

Studying texts like these and shoes themselves helps us to understand how people walked in the past. McNeil and Riello argue that attitudes and practices around walking changed over the eighteenth century. The early eighteenth-century city was not easy to move around and there are few references to urban walking.³⁶ Patrician men's shoes from this period were either for indoor wear (Figure 2.4) or for riding: as we shall see in Chapter 4, stiff high-heeled boots were ideal for the stirrups but unwieldy for walking. Walking was therefore for plebeians, whereas Gay notes that those who could afford it travelled by horse, carriage or sedan chair.³⁷ Changes to the urban environment over the course of the century, however, made walking a more viable and pleasurable pursuit. The parks, promenades, squares and pavements of the urban renaissance facilitated urban walking. Diaries from the second half of the eighteenth century by the likes of John Wilkes and James Boswell record how often they travelled around the metropolis on foot.³⁸ From the later eighteenth century, men's footwear became more suitable for perambulation. Heels lowered, soles were more flexible, and the leather was thinner and more supple (Figure 2.6). As well as a different type of shoe, walking on hard pavements required a different type of walk: Durlacher noted that persons from the country noted that 'they suffer more from corns when in the town, owing probably to the flat surface of the pavement causing an equal degree of pressure, to which they had not previously been accustomed'.³⁹

Walking was not universally accessible, however. The increasing normativity of walking among late-Georgian men – facilitated by new styles of footwear such as the Wellington boot – highlighted the many people in contemporary society who were not able to walk easily for reasons of disability, illness or age. As the chiropodist D. Low blithely noted:

Figure 2.6 *Man's shoe, 1828. Image courtesy of Northampton Museum and Art Gallery.*

The blessing of being able to *walk* is seldom much regarded but by those to whom, from whatever cause, that blessing has been denied. By the most trifling accident to the feet ... we may be forced to forgo this noble exercise; and exercise which is of all others the most productive of pleasure to man, and of which the neglect cannot but prove essentially injurious to his bodily health, as well as to the animal spirits, which regulate all his functions.[40]

The writer evokes a noble and vigorous image of the masculine body. The bodily ideal of the late-Georgian man was tall, with shapely and strong legs, and of erect but easy posture. The 'accomplishments' of the polite man included dancing, riding and fencing – activities that required a strong but supple body.[41] If men's shoes were becoming more suitable for these muscular activities, women's shoes were going in the opposite direction. As we saw in the previous chapter, shoes for respectable women were light and flimsy by the end of the eighteenth century, signalling their suitability for domestic roles.

Low continued that the causes of foot complaints that impede walking were clear: 'the use, or rather abuse, of shoes'.[42] The rest of this chapter will therefore focus upon the ways in which contemporary writers critiqued the design of shoes, in terms of their negative effect upon the body. Much of this concern focused on children, since their growing bodies were particularly susceptible to becoming malformed by inappropriate footwear. Philippe Ariès famously argued that, over the course of the early modern period, children ceased to be regarded as little adults and childhood came to be seen as a special life stage.[43] This particularly applied to their dress: writers since Locke emphasized that children should wear loose clothing, to 'Let Nature have scope to fashion the Body as she thinks best.'[44] Faust argued that young children should be dressed in a loose frock and that their shoes should be formed to the shape of their feet. They should not wear heels, since they 'cause the back tendon to shrink and impede the free and easy motions of the body in walking and running'. He continued: 'When children are suffered to walk much, and are bare-footed, they acquire an easy and steady pace. Little children ought not to wear shoes before the eighteenth month; if they do, the soles must be thin and soft, that they may learn to walk easily and well. Boots ought not be worn by children.'[45] Infants should therefore go barefoot, or wear shoes that were sufficiently soft that they would not malform their delicate growing feet.[46]

Surviving examples of children's shoes largely bear out these principles. A box of children's shoes in the Museum of Leathercraft dating from the early nineteenth century are of fine manufacture, indicating their elite origins (Figure 2.7). The leather is notably soft, with supple soles and soft fabric linings. Although the lefts and rights were made the same, the soft leather easily stretched to the shape of the foot. In terms of style, they are strikingly similar to women's shoes of the time. As with petticoats, girls never left them, whereas the transition to masculine youth was often marked by the ceremonial presentation of a first pair of boots.[47]

Footwear writers had several objections to contemporary footwear, in terms of the injurious effect it had on the body. Often it simply did not fit. Few could afford bespoke footwear and those who could

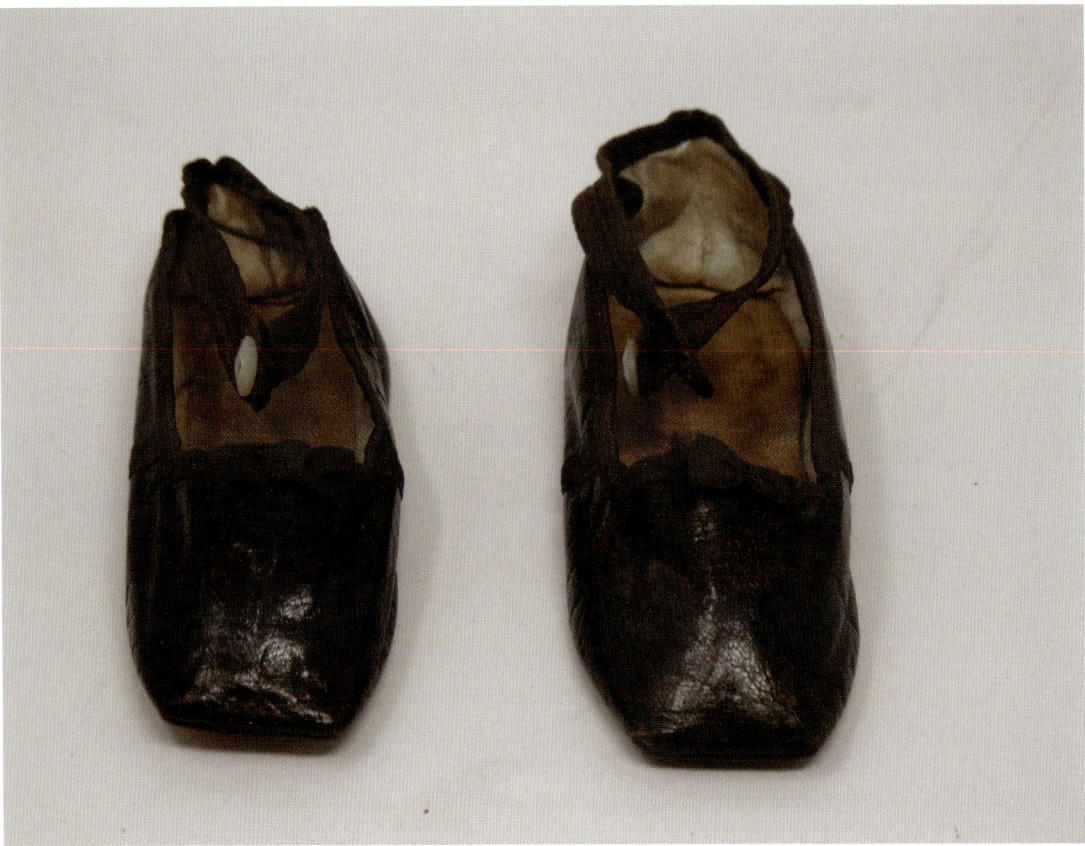

Figure 2.7 *Children's pumps, c. 1830. Museum of Leathercraft.*

not had to make do. Margo DeMello notes that, for much of European history, 'most people were accustomed to wearing shoes that did not really fit their feet'.[48] In the military, shoes for privates were produced in bulk in a range of sizes: this was the origin of standard sizing, and thence the mass ready-to-wear market, where the consumer had no contact with the producer.[49] Prior to this, however, if one wanted shoes to fit well, then they had to be made to measure. Joseph Sparkes Hall bemoaned that shoemakers use 'some old misshapen pieces of wood, that perhaps did service to their fathers and grandfathers', instead of using proper lasts. He urged that everyone 'who wishes to be comfortably fitted, should have a pair of lasts made expressly for his own use' – something that would have been accessible only to the wealthy.[50] Easy mobility in shoes was therefore the preserve of those who could afford footwear that fitted, suggesting that different classes moved differently.

As well as being the wrong size, footwear writers complained that shoes were the wrong shape. Virtually all shoes produced in the seventeenth and eighteenth centuries were straight lasted, and this exercised medical writers on feet and footwear. Several treatises included images of a human foot superimposed on a straight-lasted sole, protruding beyond its edges in order to demonstrate the lack of fit.[51] Shoes should have 'the true shape of the foot, which at the toes is broad, the heel small, and the length of the inside is greater than the outside. They should be made from two lasts, as the shape of the feet indicates.' Only by wearing these 'natural shaped shoes' would foot complaints such as corns be cured.[52] In the meantime, most people continued to wear straights; and in theory you could swap your shoes daily to prevent them wearing unevenly, so they would last longer.[53] This was contrary to the medical advice, which urged people never to do this.[54] After about 1790, shoes were increasingly lasted to the right and left feet, but this did not necessarily mean that they fitted better. In this period, it was fashionable for men and women alike to have the appearance of small feet so shoes were commonly worn too small. As we have seen, this is visible in stretching and damage to shoes in museum collections. This was accompanied by a shift from wide to pointed toes. 'Square toes' became an insult to suggest that somebody was old-fashioned.[55]

The fashion for tight, short, pointed shoes was blamed for a wide range of foot complaints in the early nineteenth century, including corns, calluses, blisters and bunions. Samuel Cooper noted that corns 'are usually owing to wearing tight shoes, and consequently women and genteel persons are more frequently afflicted than the lower classes'.[56] Bunions or 'onions' were so called because of the spherical swelling on the joint of the great toe. Durlacher provided illustrations for this (Figure 2.8) and blamed bunions on 'the wearing of shoes too short, and with a narrow sole, so that the feet are subjected to an undue degree of pressure'.[57] In modern terms, hallux valgus is caused by a misalignment of the first metatarsal and the proximal phalanx, by forcing the big toe inwards.[58] Paleopathologists have reported high prevalence of *hallux valgus* in premodern populations who wore pointed, high-heeled footwear, and that it is also an outcome of female footwear today.[59]

Footwear in the eighteenth and early nineteenth centuries came in for so much criticism that writers repeatedly evoked the value of going barefoot. As well as being recommended for children, walking barefoot was lauded for its naturalness, in contrast with the unnaturalness of wearing restrictive footwear. Some writings take an ethnographic turn at this point, lauding the noble savage 'who never wear[s] shoes', who has much greater mobility and can use their toes to perform 'delicate operations'.[60] These sources exhibit a tension between admiring this ability and curiosity at the different bodies of other races. Edward Swaysland suggested that the 'Hindoo shoemaker' does not himself wear shoes, so he can use his feet as 'auxiliary hands' to assist his labours.[61] As one chiropodist argued:

> Without shoes, the most delicate feet, far from being injured by fatigue, would be more and more hardened and invigorated by it; and for the truth of this remark, let us turn our eyes to various countries yet uncivilised, in which the *luxury* of wearing a SHOE is still unknown, and in which is likewise still unknown the *pain* which results from a CORN.

Here we see not just a critique of shoes but of modern civilization in general, where the 'tyrant FASHION' requires Britons to wear shoes that are uncomfortable and emasculating.[62] Arguably, this

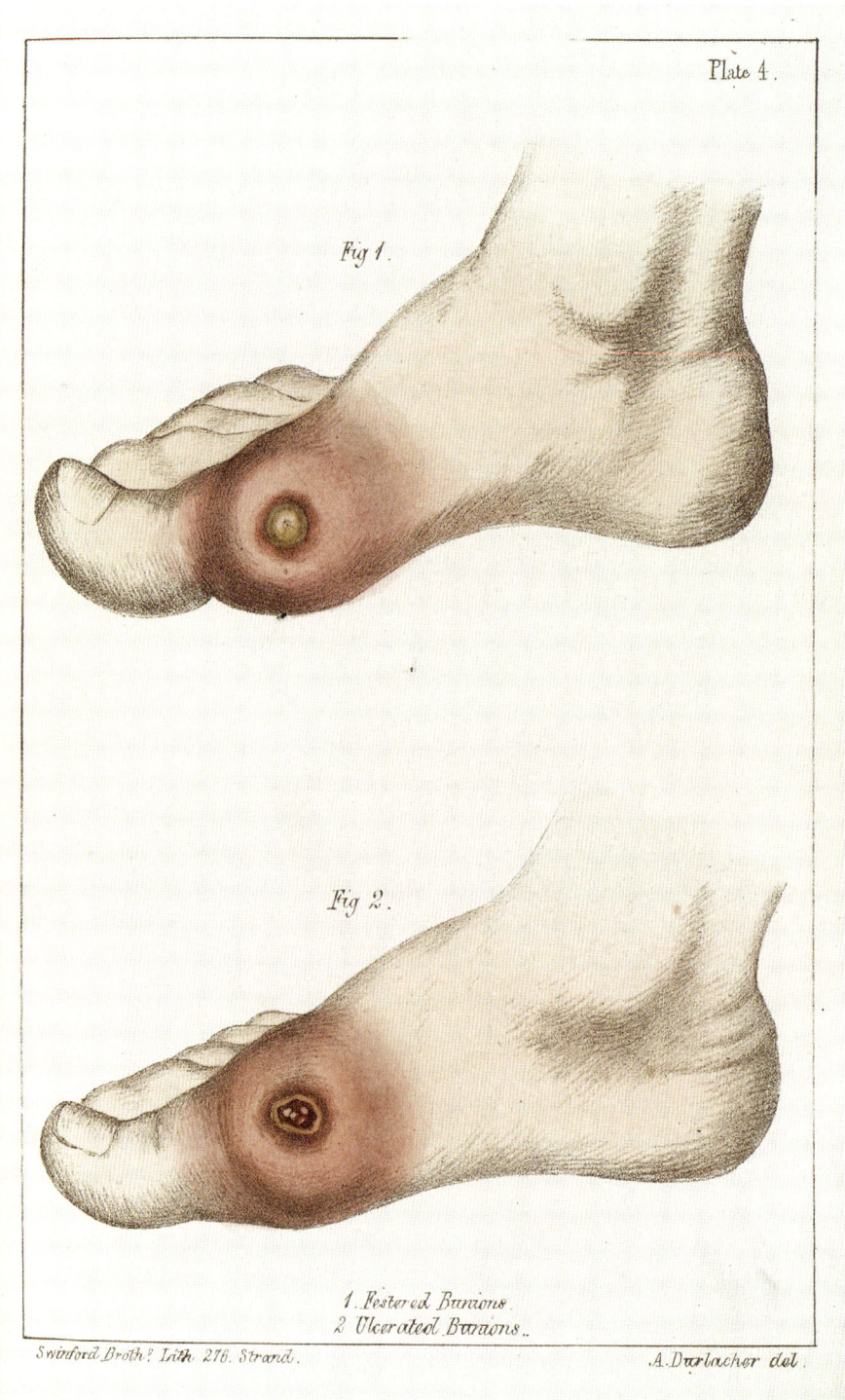

Figure 2.8 *Lewis Durlacher, plate 4 from* A Concise Treatise on Corns, Bunions and the Disorders of Nails *(London, 1845). Wellcome Collection.*

particularly applies to men, since Christopher Forth argues that modern masculinity revolves around a fundamental tension: as men become 'civilized' they become detached from the conditions of struggle that constitute authentically 'masculine' habits and practices.[63] Luxury was often accused of corrupting the body politic in the eighteenth century by rendering men weak and effeminate, and sapping their native qualities of independence and public spirit.[64] Shoes help us to understand how this process could be seen as directly corrupting the *physical* body, by impairing men's mobility, hardness and physical health.

Shoes, therefore, give us a fundamental insight into gender and the ways in which it was embodied in the Georgian period. Bodies impacted on footwear, providing a lasting record of that body that is unsurpassed by any other physical source, bar human remains themselves. And as we have seen, footwear impacted on bodies, affecting its posture and mobility, and causing a range of ailments. Writings from the time reveal an intense interest in the close relationship between shoes and bodies. Whereas some of this writing is blandly practical, it is also evident that there were important political agendas in the background: to create chiropody as a respectable medical profession; to justify the roles of the sexes and their relative position in society; and to grapple with the contradictions of consumerism and western modernity. Shoes therefore supported not only the physical body, but a whole host of contemporary ideologies.

Notes

1 John Gay, *Trivia: Or the Art of Walking the Streets of London* (London, 1716), 2–3.

2 A notable exception is Peter McNeil and Giorgio Riello, 'The Art and Science of Walking: Gender, Space and the Fashionable Body in the Long Eighteenth Century', *Fashion Theory* 9, no. 2 (2005): 175–204.

3 Anderson, 'Old Shoes in a New Perspective'; A. Trujillo-Mederos *et al.*, 'Hallux Valgus among an 18th Century Population of the Canary Islands', *International Journal of Osteoarchaeology* 24, no. 5 (2014): 590–601.

4 Mays, 'Paleopathological study of Hallux Valgus'.

5 As noted by Maya Veres, 'Introduction to the Analysis of Archaeological Footwear', *Australian Historical Archaeology* 23 (2005): 89–96.

6 Ulinka Rublack, 'Matter in the Material Renaissance', *Past and Present* 219, no. 1 (2013): 41–85 (85).

7 Until recently, physicians in Britain who specialised in feet were known as chiropodists. The term podiatrist is more commonly used today, which is more in line with international usage.

8 Lewis Durlacher, *A Concise Treatise on Corns, Bunions and the Disorders of Nails* (London, 1845), frontispiece.

9 McNeil and Riello, 'Art and Science of Walking', 194. See also Aileen Ribeiro, *Dress and Morality* (London: Bloomsbury, 1986).

10 Semmelhack, *Shoes*, 320, 120.

11 June Swann, 'Shoes Concealed in Buildings', *Costume* 30 (1996): 56–69 (56). See also Houlbrook, 'Ritual, Recycling and Recontextualisation'.

12 Christian August Struve, *A Familiar Treatise on the Education of Children, during the First Period of Their Lives* (London, 1802), 343–4.

13 Vivienne Richmond, *Clothing the Poor in Nineteenth-Century England* (Cambridge: Cambridge University Press, 2013), 91.

14 P. J. Fernández *et al.*, 'Evolution and Function of the Hominin Forefoot', *Proceedings of the National Academy of Sciences of the United States of America* 115, no. 35 (2018): 8746–51.

15 Quoted in Joseph Sparkes Hall, *The Book of the Feet: A History of Boots and Shoes, with Illustrations* (New York, NY, 1847), 96–7.

16 Richard Weekes to Hampton Weekes, 14 October 1801, in Ford (ed.), *Weekes Family Letters*, 53.

17 Nisbet, *A Practical Treatise on Diet*, 32.

18 Riello, 'Nature, Production and Regulation'.

19 Hampton Weekes to Richard Weekes, 18 October 1802, in Ford (ed.), *Weekes Family Letters*, 218.

20 Lynn Festa, 'Personal Effects: Wigs and Possessive Individualism in the Long Eighteenth Century', *Eighteenth-Century Life* 29, no. 2 (2005): 47–90 (48).

21 V. Sterzik *et al.*, 'Visualizing Old Biological Traces on Different Materials without Using Chemicals', *International Journal of Legal Medicine* 132, no. 1 (2018): 35–41.

22 Fairhurst, 'Eighteenth-Century Women's Shoes', 34.

23 Anon., *On Clothing* (Manchester, 1797), 15, 17.

24 D. Low, *Chiropodologia, Or, A Scientific Enquiry into the Causes of Corns, Warts, Onions and Other Painful or Offensive Cutaneous Excrescences* (London, 1785), 31, 29.

25 Kevin Siena, *Rotten Bodies: Class and Contagion in Eighteenth-Century Britain* (New Haven, CT: Yale University Press, 2019), 21.

26 Anon., *The Art of Preserving the Feet; Or, Practical Instructions for the Prevention and Cure of Corns, Bunnions, Callosities, Chilblains, &c.* (London, 1818), 208, 214.

27 The writer even suggested knitting toe socks, since it is between the toes that 'the more fluid part of the sweat being absorbed, leaves the gross and glutinous part to accumulate and putrefy': Anon., *On Clothing*, 16, 18.

28 Cecil Webb-Johnson, *The Soldier's Manual of Foot Care and Foot Wear* (London: Dryden Pub. Co., 1916), 28–9.

29 Hall, *Book of the Feet*, 129, 103.

30 Nisbet, *A Practical Treatise on Diet*, 31.

31 James Gregory (trans.), *The Catechism of Health: Selected and Translated from the German of Dr Faust* (Edinburgh, 1797).

32 Laqueur, *Making Sex*, 8.

33 Durlacher, *Concise Treatise*, x.

34 Gregory, *Catechism of Health*, 35.

35 Durlacher, *Concise Treatise*, 18–19.

36 McNeil and Riello, 'Art and Science of Walking', 178.

37 Gay, *Trivia*, 28–9.

38 Robin Eagles (ed.), *The Diaries of John Wilkes, 1770–1797* (Oxford: Boydell & Brewer, 2014); Frederick Pottle (ed.), *Boswell's London Journal, 1762–1763* (New Haven, CT: Yale University Press, 1950).

39 Durlacher, *Concise Treatise*, 31.

40 Low, *Chiropodologia*, ix.

41 Matthew McCormack, 'Dance and Drill: Polite Accomplishments and Military Masculinities in Georgian Britain', *Cultural and Social History* 8, no. 3 (2011): 315–30.

42 Low, *Chiropodologia*, x.

43 Philippe Ariès, *Centuries of Childhood: A Social History of Family Life*, trans. Robert Baldick (New York, NY: Vintage, 1962).

44 John Locke, *Some Thoughts Concerning Education* (London, 1693), 10.

45 Gregory, *Catechism of Health*, 37.

46 Struve, *Familiar Treatise*, 304; Michael Underwood, *A Treatise on the Diseases of Children, with Directions for the Management of Infants*, 3 vols (London, 1805), vol. 3, 183–4.

47 Semmelhack, *Shoes*, 95.

48 DeMello, *Feet and Footwear*, 283.

49 Riello, *A Foot in the Past*, 212.

50 Hall, *Book of the Feet*, 108, 104.

51 Plate II from Gregory, *Catechism of Health*.

52 Anon., *On Clothing*, 19–20.

53 Bennett Cuthbertson, *A System for the Complete Interior Management and Oeconomy of a Battalion of Infantry* (Dublin, 1768), 135.

54 Nisbet, *A Practical Treatise on Diet*, 32.

55 Anon., *Art of Preserving the Feet*, 96.

56 Samuel Cooper, *Practice of Surgery: Being an Elementary Work for Students and a Concise Book of Reference for Practitioners* (Hanover, NH, 1815), 145.

57 Durlacher, *Concise Treatise*, 65.

58 Trujillo-Mederos *et al.*, 'Hallux Valgus', 590.

59 Bertrand Mafart, 'Hallux Valgus in a Historical French Population: Paleopathological Study of 605 First Metatarsal Bones', *Joint, Bone, Spine* 74, no. 2 (2007): 166–70.

60 Anon., *On Clothing*, 18–19.

61 Edward Swaysland, *Boot and Shoe Design and Manufacture* (Northampton, 1905), 14.

62 Low, *Chiropodologia*, xi.

63 Christopher Forth, *Masculinity in the Modern West: Gender, Civilization and the Body* (Basingstoke: Palgrave Macmillan, 2008), 4–5.

64 Philip Carter, 'An "Effeminate" or "Efficient" Nation? Masculinity and Eighteenth-Century Social Documentary', *Textual Practice* 11, no. 3 (1997): 429–44.

3

Shoes and politics

One of the most striking passages in Jonathan Swift's *Gulliver's Travels* (1726) is where Lilliput's principal secretary explains the politics of the kingdom. In what is clearly a satire of contemporary Britain, he notes that the two rival parties were distinguished 'from the high and low Heels on their Shoes'. The 'low Heels' (the Whigs) were favoured by the present king (George I), whereas his successor (the future George II) supposedly had divided loyalties: 'we can plainly discover one of his Heels higher than the other; which gives him a Hobble in his Gait'.[1] Literary scholars have debated the significance of this joke: high and low may refer to their religious leanings, or to foreign affairs, since high heels was a French fashion and the Whigs favoured a bellicose policy. Either way, shoes could have political meanings in the eighteenth century.

Shoes may not seem to be an obvious topic for political history, but shoes were highly politicized in Georgian Britain. As expensive consumer articles, which were key markers of social status and gender identity, shoes were 'political' in the indirect sense of being bound up with social power, but this chapter will make the case that shoes were political in the more direct sense of the operation of power within the state. Shoes were an important component of the uniform worn by the class of men who wielded power at court, in parliament and in the localities. Footwear can help us to think about the precise ways in which their masculinity was embodied and lived, since it has an important impact upon the body in terms of its appearance, its posture and its ability to move. Work on political masculinities has emphasized the importance of the body in terms of rhetorical performance and the projection of a political personality.[2] Shoes were also an important topic of political discussion: they were at the centre of moral debates about consumerism and luxury, which dominated political culture in the eighteenth century. Their very importance for notions of class and gender implicate them in debates about citizenship, given that this was a period when the lines of political inclusion were being redrawn in those terms. This everyday object can therefore contribute to our understanding of the new public sphere that was created in the eighteenth century, as well as the social world of high politics. Changes in shoe design, and the differences in the footwear worn by different social classes, shed light on the types of masculinity that came to be privileged within the political cultures of the day.

If political history has had little to say about shoes, it is also the case that shoe history has had little to say about politics. Whereas work on material culture has highlighted the political significance of other articles of clothing, Kimberly Alexander has noted that the 'signifying role' of shoes has been left out of such interpretations.[3] As we have seen, studies of shoes have employed a wide range of approaches and have focused on many aspects but, to date, politics has not been one of them.

This chapter therefore makes a case for a political history of shoes, by bringing together these two rich fields. It will begin by thinking about the nature of political culture in the eighteenth century, where political virtue was evaluated in highly moral and gendered terms, and where shoes became the focus of debates about masculinity and citizenship. It will then turn its attention to citizenship in a national sense, to think about how certain types of leather shoes came to be seen as synonymous with Britishness, and how wearing them informed what it meant to live as a 'Briton'. Debates about politics and gender were inseparable from those on social class, and shoes worn by different social classes were loaded with political meaning. They also give us an insight into how people from different social classes moved and comported themselves. Focusing on the history of shoes in these ways can therefore show how embodiment should be central to our understanding of the practice of politics in eighteenth-century Britain.

Gender and politics

Where historians have considered the political importance of shoes, it has tended to focus on shoemakers as a group. Shoemakers have historically had a reputation for political radicalism. Their patron saints, the twins Crispin and Crispinian, were shoemakers who helped the poor and preached unorthodoxy and so were martyred by the Romans. Like other manufacturing occupations, they were militant on trade matters and prone to strike – particularly cordwainers who were keen to protect their hard-won privileges – but historians have noted that they were also militant in their politics.[4] They were prominent in wider movements of social and political protest: many shoemakers were arrested for rioting during the early stages of the French Revolution; and they were numerous among the Chartist movement. Shoemakers were prominent at events as diverse as the Swing Riots of 1830, the German Revolution of 1848 and the Paris Commune of 1871. Furthermore, Eric Hobsbawm and Joan Wallach Scott note, 'as worker-intellectuals and ideologists shoemakers were exceptional'.[5]

There were several possible reasons for this. Shoemakers were traditionally self-employed, so had a strong sense of masculine independence. Cobblers were often itinerant, so were well-travelled and had a wider life experience than many working men (Figure 3.1). Traditionally, their trade was more accessible than others, so was an avenue for the poor to improve themselves, and the lowly status of those who worked with leather and shoes may have fostered resentment. It may also have been the

Figure 3.1 The Elected Cobler, *from M. Darly,* Macaronies, Characters, Caricatures, etc. *(London, 1772). Image courtesy of the Lewis Walpole Library, Yale University.*

nature of the work, which was 'sedentary and undemanding' and also relatively quiet, so lent itself to 'thinking and discussing while working'.[6] Henry Mayhew noted that 'the solitude of their employment' developed their 'internal resources', making them 'a stern, uncompromising and reflecting race'.[7] They were therefore key figures in rural political life and often participated in the life of the pub, where the lines between work, leisure and politics were blurred.[8] The proverb 'shoemaker stick to your last' suggests that shoemakers had a reputation for expressing opinions on topics beyond their trade.

Shoemakers could therefore be highly politicized, but it is also worth focusing on the shoes they made and the political significance that they had for those who wore them. We saw in Chapter 1 how shoe styles for men and women diverged over the course of the eighteenth century, and how this was significant in terms of men's and women's social roles. Shoes were therefore important in terms of gender politics, but this also impacted the shape of the political world in a more direct way. Over the course of the Enlightenment, the position of men and women in society and politics were rethought and justified in new ways. Women's subordinate position in society and their exclusion from formal politics was justified in terms of 'nature', since their physiologies equipped them for maternity. Their weaker physiques and delicate sensibility supposedly meant that they were vulnerable and suited to the domestic sphere. The increasing flimsiness and impracticality of footwear for propertied women reflected these new ideals, and also ensured that they were put into practice, given the very direct way that footwear has an impact upon what the wearer is able to do.

By contrast, men's footwear became plainer and more practical. Shoe heels lowered, making them more suitable for perambulation. Whereas boots had formerly only been worn for riding, they became fashionable for general wear at the end of the eighteenth century, and their newly supple uppers and flexible soles meant that they could be worn for both riding and walking. Men's footwear therefore met the requirements for mobility and activity within the public sphere, equipping them for the roles for which their larger, sturdier bodies were apparently suited. Whereas access to the political world had formerly been assigned according to rank, over the course of the Enlightenment political inclusion was increasingly conceptualized in terms of gender.[9] Only men possessed the independence, rationality and physical strength to participate in the public world and, as such, they should be appropriately shod.

This divergence of gender roles was relevant to the politics of the century; and recent historians have shown how Georgian political culture was fundamentally gendered.[10] The primary critique of the establishment was known as 'Country patriotism', which alleged that the Hanoverian monarchs and their governments were not ruling in the interests of the people. Derived from neoclassical republicanism, it believed in the power of propertied citizens, whose virtue and independence allowed them to speak out against the corrupt oligarchy.[11] The power of this appeal rested on nationalism and gender. Country thought pitted the patriots and 'the people' against an establishment that they alleged was culturally foreign. The polite classes' desire for foreign luxuries – such as food, art and fashion – was taken to be evidence of their lack of patriotism and moral fibre. Worse, in the neoclassical tradition, 'luxury' was a source of corruption in the body politic: it upset the constitution, both in the sense of the individual's bodily health and in terms of the political system.[12] As we shall see, expensive consumer articles like shoes could therefore be the focus of anti-establishment political critique. As well as being unpatriotic, their targets were 'effeminate', suggesting that they lacked the moral qualities of true men. In opposition to this, the patriots revelled in a culture of sturdy masculinity, which celebrated physical strength, direct manners, simple tastes and rural virtue.

The political subject of the Georgian period was a male head of household, who governed and represented those who depended upon him, on the model of a Roman citizen. This political celebration of virtuous masculinity evolved over the course of the century. In the later eighteenth century, radicals who sought to reform the political system usually made their case within this tradition, arguing that the establishment was morally and politically corrupt, and that ordinary men deserved citizenship rights on the basis of their masculine independence. This involved organizing citizenship along gendered lines, since women, children and any man who did not meet the required masculine standard were excluded from political rights.[13] Radicals, too, celebrated a muscular, assertive vision of masculinity and politicized the ways in which that body was clothed, as we shall see.[14] It was therefore not the case that men's claims to political citizenship were based upon disembodiment or 'renunciation', as the corollary to women's exclusion on bodily grounds. On the contrary, men's political claims were highly corporeal, based upon a particular vision of the virtuous body.[15]

In this context, the masculine body was politicized and particular attention was paid to what men wore on their feet. As a commentator of 1825 noted: 'Religion, patriotism, public and private virtue, pure and fixed principles of taste, intellectual and corporeal refinement, all – all depend upon the choice of *shoes*.'[16] Shoe leather itself could even be said to be a masculine material, given its toughness, dull colours and earthy smell. It comprised an area of consumerism that included breeches, luggage and other safely masculine accoutrements.[17] Real men wore leather shoes whereas women, foreigners and the poor often did not, highlighting how notions of manhood were constructed in terms of gender, race and class in this period.

Shoes and the nation

The consumption of foreign goods and styles could be highly politicized in the eighteenth century. As a first example, let us return to John Gay's *Trivia* (1716), a satirical poem about walking the streets of London. The fact that the narrator is walking is itself pointed, since the fashionable elite come in for criticism in the poem for not doing so. The fashionable lady whose feet are bound in 'braided Gold' travels by coach or chair: 'Her shoe disdains the Street'. By contrast, the narrator offers advice to the manly urban walker:

> Then let the prudent Walker Shoes provide,
> Not of *Spanish* or *Morocco* Hide;
> The wooden Heel may raise the Dancer's Bound,
> And with the 'scalloped Top his Step be crown'd.[18]

Gay condemns these fine soft leathers from abroad, which were both culturally suspicious and not up to the rigours of a London winter. Instead, Gay recommends 'firm, well-hammer'd Soles': Aileen Ribeiro notes that such shoes would have been made from 'sturdy English cowhide with well-nailed soles'. Unlike dancer's shoes, these would have modest heels and would be wide at the front and fitted at the back, so as to be suitable for walking.[19] The discussion of shoes throughout *Trivia* has a political focus. Gay associated with Tory writers and was critical of the Hanoverian establishment. Whereas Whig writers like Joseph Addison and Richard Steele promoted 'polite' urban behaviour, Gay celebrated the sturdy indigenous culture of the lower and middling sorts.[20]

Gay's focus on footwear in the poem was quite deliberate, since shoes were redolent with national symbolism. It was partly a question of supporting indigenous manufacturers, on mercantile grounds. In Britain there were regular drives to buy home-produced goods and to reject foreign luxuries. This also worked against Britain, since British imports had a changing meaning in the American colonies as the century wore on. Kimberly Alexander has shown how London shoes went from being a sign of sophistication to an unpatriotic attachment to British rule. Instead, pro-revolution propagandists promoted the 'virtue' of local manufacture, and political leaders made a powerful political statement by sporting homespun styles.[21]

The connection between shoes and Englishness went deeper, however. Most shoes were made from cowhide, which was a by-product of the meat industry.[22] Beef was, of course, synonymous with Englishness, being associated with strength and prosperity: cartoonists celebrated it as John Bull's favourite dish, and Hogarth's *O the Roast Beef of Old England* (1748) suggested that it was the envy of the French in particular (Figure 3.2). If food symbolism could be deployed to suggest that other nations were poorer and less free, then so could leather and the articles manufactured from it. Leather, too, was a product of the English landscape, which provided rich pasture for grazing cows and also materials such as bark and acorns (from the symbolically redolent oak) that were used in the tanning process. Edmund Burke famously used the image of 'thousands of great cattle, reposed beneath the shadow of the British oak' to signify the silent majority who rejected revolution and radicalism in the 1790s.[23] Leather was therefore of 'the country' in an organic way and leather shoes mediated between the wearer and the land on which he trod. Clothes' proximity to the body make them expressive of the politics of the wearer but, given that leather articles like shoes function as a 'literal second skin', they embody that connection in a particularly direct way.[24]

If sturdy English footwear connected the wearer to their country, then footwear or styles from abroad represented a form of contamination. Critics of the elite noted that they were corrupted by the experience of the Grand Tour, where they acquired foreign clothes, tastes and manners. The 'macaroni'

Shoes and Politics 61

Figure 3.2 *William Hogarth,* O the Roast Beef of Old England *(1748). Tate Britain. Image of an engraving reproduced from the painting courtesy of the Lewis Walpole Library, Yale University.*

was the man who brought effeminate manners back home with the pasta dish, and became a stock figure in prints, satires and on the stage. Gay condemned the 'Fop, of nicest Tread' who sported his 'red heel'd Shoes' on the streets of London: *talons rouges* originated in the court of Louis XIV (r. 1643–1715) and were copied by fashionable and Francophile Englishmen.[25] Historians debate whether the fop was a sexual or a social figure: did he represent a queer sexuality, or was he a heterosexual figure who took 'polite' manners too far?[26] Either way, Peter McNeill and Giorgio Riello argue that he 'undermined social hierarchy and the English pragmatic sense of style'.[27] The cartoon, *Welladay, is this my Son Tom* (1774) juxtaposes the fop with his father, a farmer who has come to town and is shocked at his attire (Figure 3.3). The fop's tiny slippers with fancy buckles contrast with the farmer's top-boots, which are bulky in order to protect the leg while riding, and which are fitted with spurs. Their

Figure 3.3 Welladay, is this my Son Tom (1774). Image courtesy of the Lewis Walpole Library, Yale University.

masculinities are embodied in their contrasting postures, since the fop's refined step contrasts with his father's broad gait. This relates to their choice of footwear, since the fop's heeled slipper lent itself to a refined, toe-first step, whereas the farmer's riding boots would have fostered a broad-legged stride.

As well as providing a means to satirize the foreign tastes of English elites, footwear also served to characterize foreigners themselves. 'Wooden shoes' came to symbolize poverty, oppression and foreignness. A poem of 1734 condemned the '*Wooden Shoe,* that *Type* exotick / Of *Tyranny* and *Pow'r Despotick*'.[28] In particular, it was used by the English to caricature the French. This symbolism was widely employed in the politics of the 1670s when Charles II was criticized for allying with the French against the Protestant Dutch. In 1673, a wooden shoe was placed in the speaker's chair, bearing the arms of Charles on one side and the king of France on the other.[29] As one satirist put it:

When the English Prince shall Englishmen despise,
And think French only loyal, Irish wise;
Then wooden shoes shall be the English wear,
And Magna Carta shall no more appear;
Then th' English shall a greater tyrant know
Than either Greek or Gallic stories show.[30]

Forcing Englishmen to wear 'wooden shoes' meant imposing French-style absolutism upon them. James Gillray satirized the prejudices of 'patriot' politicians in his print *Independence* (1799). It depicted the backbencher, Sir Thomas Tyrwhitt Jones (1765–1811), ranting to an empty House of Commons about foreigners, non-Anglicans and corruption, amongst other things: 'I don't like Wooden Shoes! no Sir, neither French Wooden Shoes, no nor English Wooden Shoes neither!' Jones is presented as a John Bullish squire, of sturdy build and clothed in dishevelled rural attire, including bulky leather riding boots (Figure 3.4).

Throughout the eighteenth century, 'wooden shoes' stood for the footwear supposedly worn by the French. Gay noted that, in Paris, 'Slav'ry treads the Streets in wooden Shoes' – in contrast to the comfortable and expensive leather shoes worn by his English narrator.[31] Leather shoes permit an easy freedom of movement that clogs do not, so footwear can relate to notions of liberty in a direct, corporeal sense. The availability of such shoes was a direct consequence of the political system: before the revolution, the French leather industry was tightly controlled and heavily taxed, so France suffered from 'an endemic absence of leather' whereas Britain was more successful at meeting demand.[32] During the revolutionary wars, leather was required for the military, so clog-wearing became even more common and the *sabot* became a revolutionary symbol. In the 1790s, British caricaturists depicted bloodthirsty *sans-culottes* either in wooden shoes or barefoot. In James Gillray's *Un petit Souper a la Parisienne, or, A Family of Sans-Culotts refreshing after the fatigues of the day* (1792), their huge clogs emphasized their emaciated frames, and contrasted with the buckled leather shoe and shapely leg of the murdered aristocrat under the table (Figure 3.5).

Figure 3.4 *James Gillray,* Independence *(1799). Alamy stock photo.*

Figure 3.5 *James Gillray,* Un petit Souper a la Parisienne, or, A Family of Sans-Culotts refreshing after the fatigues of the day *(1792). Image courtesy of the Lewis Walpole Library, Yale University.*

Class and the politics of the body

In reality, of course, many British people wore wooden shoes as well. This only serves to demonstrate how notions of nation intersected with those of class in this period. Working people in Britain commonly wore clogs.[33] They were widely worn in the Lancashire mill districts, for example, where clog fighting or 'purring' was a violent popular pastime. Northern radical politicians were aware of the class connotations of the wooden shoe. George Williams (1765–1850) was a former soldier, who supported universal suffrage and the ballot, and opposed slavery and the Corn Laws. He stood for Ashton-under-Lyne when the borough got its first parliamentary seat as a result of the 1832 Reform Act. A deputation from the town found him working on his farm 'with a spade in his hand and good strong clogs on his feet', which apparently confirmed his radical credentials. After his victory,

Figure 3.6 *Clogs, early nineteenth century. Image courtesy of Northampton Museum and Art Gallery.*

he was presented with 'a pair of clogs strong enough to trample a score of boroughmongers to the dust'.[34]

Rather than being fully wooden shoes, these clogs commonly had thick leather uppers on wooden soles. Wooden soles were cheaper than leather and wore out much less quickly. Thick leather uppers were nailed to the wooden sole, so they were sturdy and quick to produce. The disadvantages of wooden soles are their lack of flexibility and their weight. A pair of crudely constructed clogs from the early nineteenth century in Northampton Museum are notably heavy, with soles that are a minimum of fifteen millimetres thick (Figure 3.6). Leather shoes provide a very different sensory and corporeal experience to wooden ones. Leather soles mould to the insole, providing comfort that unyielding wood does not. They also become flexible and sympathetic to the motions of the foot, allowing the wearer to walk with a smooth gait. By contrast, clogs are noisy and cumbersome, and promote an inelegant walking style. In terms of the body's appearance, they exaggerate the size of the foot, which would have had particular class connotations in the early nineteenth century when it was fashionable to have the appearance of small feet. Footwear can therefore help us to understand how social class manifested itself in bodily terms in the past.

Many working people in Britain did wear leather shoes, but these, too, could be signifiers of class. Shoes were expensive consumer articles in the Georgian period. Before the introduction of sewing machines and new welting techniques in the 1840s, shoes were very labour-intensive to produce and were therefore a significant purchase. Whereas the elite could afford bespoke footwear that was made to measure, others had to make do with ready-made footwear that was only available in a few sizes. As Margo DeMello notes, most people in this period therefore wore shoes that did not really fit.[35] As well as having implications for comfort, it will have affected how large numbers of people walked and comported themselves. Working people commonly made do with cast-off or second-hand shoes, which could be uncomfortable if they had moulded to the foot of their previous owner. Shoes were also repaired and adapted, to eke out as much wear in them as possible. An early nineteenth-century ankle boot from the Museum of Leathercraft has clearly been cut down from a riding boot: this adaptation will have given the boots a new lease of life, possibly for a humbler consumer than the original (Figure 3.7).[36]

Whereas the elite could afford several pairs of shoes in a range of shapes and colours, working people typically only had one or two pairs in much more generic styles. The divergence of men's and women's styles was far less pronounced among working people than it was for their social betters: linking shoe design to widening sexual difference only works to an extent, since social class also needs to be taken into account. Working-class footwear gravitated around particular styles, such as the

Figure 3.7 *Man's cut-down leather boot, early nineteenth century. Museum of Leathercraft.*

Blücher boot, a laced ankle boot that shod private soldiers and working men in the early nineteenth century. A lower quality version was the brogan, which often had wooden soles and 'stiff leather that dug into the skin of the wearer'. Cheapest of all was the 'Negro brogan', which was exported to America to be worn by enslaved people.[37] A common feature of working people's footwear was hobnails. Hobnails added to the durability of the sole and also provided grip when walking on muddy ground: they were therefore useful for private soldiers and working people, but rarely appeared on elite footwear. Hobnails had the disadvantages of being noisy and unyielding on hard ground, and were notorious for causing leaks when the nails fell out.[38]

Shoes were therefore highly symbolic of social class. Although sumptuary laws that restricted certain clothes to certain classes had been repealed in 1604, the exigencies of economics and culture were almost as effective at prescribing footwear styles. Rebecca Earle notes that 'a deep sartorial gulf … separated the rich from the poor' by the nineteenth century.[39] In today's parlance, to be 'well heeled' implies wealth and station, whereas to be 'down at heel' is its opposite. In the eighteenth century, these phrases were not yet proverbial: they could be used to comment on someone's shoes, but the social comment was only implied.[40] For example, at a criminal trial in 1784, a witness described a defendant as having 'one of his shoes down at heel'.[41] This was a comment on the shoe rather than the man, although it was in keeping with his shabby appearance. In the nineteenth century, however, these phrases took on their modern meaning as describing the person themselves, implying a close identification between clothing and its wearer.

All of this has wider implications for the nature of social identity. Dror Wahrman argues that the 'modern self' emerged over the course of the eighteenth century, and that clothes became detached from it, as one would see through them to perceive the real self.[42] Earle agrees that clothing 'was no longer considered a racial characteristic' by the nineteenth century.[43] As we have seen, however, shoes became *more* important to the ways in which their wearers were socially classified. Perhaps more than any other item of clothing, shoes are synonymous with their wearer: they are identified *with* the body rather than merely being an adjunct to it.

It is therefore worth concluding by focusing on elite men's footwear and their implications for politics. We have noted how, over the course of the century, men's shoes became plainer and lower-heeled. The shoe remained an important part of the elite male ensemble, however. As McNeill and Riello note: 'The male shoe also acted as a type of emphatic punctuation stop at the end of silk-stockinged legs, which marked out his gender distinction from young boys and women, and his class distinction from working men wearing leather or cloth protective leggings, ragged shoes, and clogs.'[44] As Karen Harvey has noted, apparel such as leather breeches emphasized the shapeliness of the leg and the prominence of the genitals, so was highly sexualized.[45] It was therefore men's very *bodiliness* that marked out their status in society and the public sphere. Although shoes were usually plain, one opportunity for decoration was the buckle. These went out of fashion in the 1790s when they became a politicized symbol of the aristocracy, along with the stockings-and-breeches ensemble. Nathaniel Wraxall noted in his diary that, in 'the era of Jacobinism and equality', men's dress was characterized by 'pantaloons, cropped hair and shoe strings, as well as the total abolition of buckles and ruffles'.[46]

As we shall see in the next chapter, boots came into vogue in the 1790s and remained central to the gentleman's wardrobe for decades to come. The adoption of trousers had implications for shoe fashions, since trousers and pantaloons would typically be worn with boots rather than shoes. In 1801, Hampton Weekes wrote from London to his brother in the country to offer him his old silk breeches, since 'I wear my boots and Pantaloons now': he later added, 'indeed it is the wear of all the young Men here'.[47] Given their association with the military and equestrianism, boots are often fashionable in times of war. In the democratic political atmosphere of the time, however, boots became synonymous with public life. Boots suggested energy, activity and a statesmanlike attention to the febrile international situation.

The boot *par excellence* was the Wellington. It was named after the Duke of Wellington (1769–1852), the victor of Waterloo, so its patriotic credentials were never in doubt. In common with other fashionable footwear of the early nineteenth century, the Wellington was cut close and was manufactured from leather that was more flexible than was traditional for riding boots. Examples from museum collections have supple soles and uppers, making them suitable for walking as well as riding (Figure 2.2). It was therefore notable for its adaptability. As Joseph Sparkes Hall noted, 'We go to the ballroom in it, the theatre, the houses of parliament, and even royalty itself is approached in boots!' The 'we' that he referred to were, of course, elite men, and the locations were the centres of the public sphere, where statesmen were expected to dress and move in a particular way. He continued: 'A good Wellington boot of the softest calf leather, the sole moderately thick, the waist hollow and well-arched, firm and yet flexible, cut to go on without dragging all your might with boothooks, and made with an intermediate sole of felt to prevent creaking, is the best boot for general wear that can be made.'[48] The fitted Wellington, whose soft leather hugged the leg, therefore provided a silhouette for elite men that emphasized the contours of their bodies. At a time when men of Wellington's class dominated political life, the Wellington boot underlined their manly qualifications for office. Dandyish but sober, elegant but practical, the Wellington epitomized the balancing act lived by late-Georgian gentlemen, who were expected to embody a refined but moral masculinity. The Wellington, therefore, befitted this transitional period in masculinities, between what John Tosh characterizes as the eighteenth-century 'polite gentleman' and the 'simple manliness' of the Victorian period.[49] Such men were required to be virtuous in both their public and their private lives, to synchronize the 'outer' and the 'inner' man, and footwear – that most liminal of garments – helped them to achieve this.

In conclusion, shoes were loaded with political meaning in the Georgian period. The Wellington boot, the wooden shoe or the women's silk pump all mark out their wearer in terms of class, nation and gender. Shoes were therefore 'political' in the sense that they contributed to the process of classifying people. As we have seen here, however, shoes also had a more direct bearing on the politics of the day and were bound up with debates about political participation in the age of revolutions. The 'wooden shoe' carried connotations of foreignness, poverty and oppression, whereas the leather shoe was replete with masculine and national associations. These were not just symbolic traits, mere facets of representation: rather, these qualities were inherent in the materiality of the objects themselves and the ways in which they were used. If men of a certain class made a case for their right to rule based upon their masculine attributes, then we need to pay attention to the ways in which they mobilized their bodies in order to make this claim. Gentlemen shod in expensive, supple Wellingtons moved and comported themselves in a very different way to a millworker in clogs, or a lady in shoes made from fine textiles. What we wear on our feet therefore helps us to understand the ways in which political cultures have historically been embodied.

Notes

1. Jonathan Swift, *Gulliver's Travels*, ed. P. Turner (1726; Oxford: Oxford University Press, 1971), 35–6.
2. Matthew McCormack, *The Independent Man: Citizenship and Gender Politics in Georgian England* (Manchester: Manchester University Press, 2005), Chapter 2.
3. Alexander, 'Shoes and the City', 306.
4. Eric Hobsbawm and George Rudé, *Captain Swing* (London: Victor Gollancz, 1965), 181.
5. Hobsbawm and Scott, 'Political Shoemakers', 96, 98.
6. Ibid.
7. Henry Mayhew, *The Unknown Mayhew: Selections from the Morning Chronicle, 1849–1850*, ed. E. P. Thompson and Eileen Yeo (London: Merlin, 1971), 279.
8. Peter Denney, 'Clamoring for Liberty: Alehouse Noise and the Political Shoemaker', *Eighteenth-Century Life* 41, no. 2 (2017): 105–21.
9. McCormack, *The Independent Man*.
10. Anna Clark, *Scandal: The Sexual Politics of the British Constitution* (Princeton, NJ: Princeton University Press, 2004); Marilyn Morris, *Sex, Money and Personal Character in Eighteenth-Century British Politics* (New Haven, CT: Yale University Press, 2014); Matthew McCormack, *Citizenship and Gender in Britain, 1688–1928* (Abingdon: Routledge, 2019).
11. Quentin Skinner, *Liberty before Liberalism* (Cambridge: Cambridge University Press, 1998).
12. Carter, 'An "Effeminate" or an "Efficient" Nation?', 429–44; J. Sekora, *Luxury: The Concept in Western Thought, Eden to Smollett* (Baltimore, MD: Johns Hopkins University Press, 1977).
13. McCormack, *The Independent Man*, Chapter 1.
14. Katrina Navickas, '"That Sash Will Hang You": Political Clothing and Adornment in England, 1780–1840', *Journal of British Studies* 49, no. 3 (2010), 540–65.

15 Harvey makes the case for 'embodied citizenship' in 'Men of Parts', 821.

16 'The Street Companion', *London Magazine and Review* n.s. 1 (January–April 1825), 73.

17 Amanda Vickery, *Behind Closed Doors: At Home in Georgian England* (New Haven, CT: Yale University Press, 2009), 124.

18 Gay, *Trivia*, 2.

19 Aileen Ribeiro, 'Street Style: Dress in John Gay's *Trivia*', in *Walking the Streets of Eighteenth-Century London: John Gay's* Trivia *(1716)*, ed. C. Brant and S. Whyman (Oxford: Oxford University Press, 2007), 131–48 (135).

20 C. Brant and S. Whyman (eds), 'Introduction', *Walking the Streets*, 2–26 (8).

21 Kimberly Alexander, 'Footwear, Women's, 1715–1785', in *Clothing and Fashion: American Fashion from Head to Toe: Volume One: Pre-Colonial Times Through the American Revolution*, ed. J. Blanco and M. Doering (Santa Barbara, CA: ABC-Clio, 2015), 110–14 (114).

22 Riello, 'Nature, Production and Regulation', 75–99.

23 Edmund Burke, *Reflections on the Revolution in France*, ed. L. Mitchell (1790; Oxford: Oxford University Press, 1993), 85.

24 Davidson, 'Holding the Sole', 75.

25 Gay, *Trivia*, 15.

26 Philip Carter, 'Men about Town: Representations of Foppery and Masculinity in Early Eighteenth-Century Urban Society', in *Gender in Eighteenth-Century England: Roles, Representations and Responsibilities*, ed. H. Barker and E. Chalus (London: Longman, 1997), 31–57.

27 McNeill and Riello, 'Art and Science of Walking', 187.

28 Anon., *The Secret History of an Old Shoe* (London, 1734), 7.

29 S. Pincus, 'From Butterboxes to Wooden Shoes: The Shift in English Popular Sentiment from Anti-Dutch to Anti-French in the 1670s', *The Historical Journal* 38, no. 2 (1995): 333–61 (344).

30 'Nostradamus' Prophesy', in G. Lord (ed.), *Poems on Affairs of State: Augustan Satirical Verse, 1660–1714: Volume 1* (New Haven, CT: Yale University Press, 1963), 188.

31 Gay, *Trivia*, 5.

32 Riello, 'Nature, Production and Regulation', 99.

33 Riello, *A Foot in the Past*, 34.

34 'Colonel Williams – Obituary', *The Christian Reformer: Or, Unitarian Magazine* 7, no. 74 (February 1851), 126–8 (128).

35 DeMello, *Feet and Footwear*, 283.

36 Man's cut-down leather boot (1820s): Northampton Museum, 1984.1203.

37 Semmelhack, *Shoes*, 100–1.

38 Charles Henderson Melville, *Military Hygiene and Sanitation* (London: E. Arnold, 1912), 308.

39 Rebecca Earle, '"Two Pairs of Silk Satin Shoes!!" Race, Clothing and Identity in the Americas (17th–19th Centuries)', *History Workshop Journal* 52 (2001): 175–95 (191).

40 There are twenty-six occurrences of the phrase 'down at heel' and four of the phrase 'well heeled' in the corpus of Eighteenth-Century Collections Online. All of them refer to a shoe itself (or horseshoe, or another material article), rather than a person.

41 E. Hodgson, *The Trial of Kenith McKenzie* (London, 1784), p. 1020.

42 Dror Wahrman, *The Making of the Modern Self: Identity and Culture in Eighteenth-Century England* (New Haven, CT: Yale University Press, 2004), 178.

43 Earle, '"Two Pairs of Pink Satin Shoes!!"', 189.

44 McNeil and Riello, 'Art and Science of Walking', 184.

45 Harvey, 'Men of Parts'.

46 Quoted in Swann, *Shoes*, 34.

47 Ford (ed.), *Weekes Family Letters*, 94, 244.

48 Hall, *Book of the Feet*, 125.

49 Tosh, 'Gentlemanly Politeness and Manly Simplicity', 455.

4

Boots and masculinity

The finest bootmaker in Regency London was George Hoby of St James's Street. He made footwear for royalty and, famously, the Duke of Wellington, for whom he invented the eponymous boot. One chronicler of the time noted that, 'he was so great a man in his own estimation that he was apt to take rather an insolent tone with his customers'. On one occasion, Sir John Shelley went to see Hoby to complain that his top-boots had split in several places. 'How did that happen?' enquired Hoby. 'Why, in walking to my stable', he replied. 'Walking to your stable!' sneered the bootmaker. 'I made the boots for riding, not walking.'[1]

The remark that men's boots were not made for walking is striking to modern readers. Writings about footwear tend to emphasize a fundamental division between those made for men and women: men's footwear is plain, sturdy and functional, whereas women's is decorative, flimsy and impractical. This befits the social roles that the modern world prescribed for men and women: as Giorgio Riello and Peter McNeil note, shoes are instantly recognizable as being male or female, 'not because of functional dissimilarities or anatomical diversities between the sexes, but because shoes are one way by which we construct gender identity'.[2] Shoes are more than just functional objects and have become powerful cultural signs[3] but, paradoxically, one of the key signs of the 'masculine' shoe is its very functionality.

Of all male footwear, boots are typically the plainest, sturdiest and most functional. They are often substantial in construction, offering support to the foot and lower leg, and protecting them against the elements and foreign objects. Boots are the footwear of soldiers, construction workers, hikers or horse riders, which enable them to complete the practical task at hand.[4] Fundamentally, they are outdoor wear. In the polite world of the eighteenth century, indoor shoes for patrician men could be brocaded silk mules or delicate leather pumps with elaborate buckles, shoes that would not be suitable for traversing any great distance or on ground that was uneven, wet or muddy. For elite men, boots were to be worn outside and were specifically prohibited in spaces like court or parliament. The MP Charles Tottenham was fined for wearing top-boots in the House, and commentators from abroad noted that an English gentleman will only wear boots in town if he is carrying a whip, to show that he has been riding. The Bath Assembly Rooms had a rule that 'no gentleman in boots or half-boots be admitted' on ball nights.[5] Riello therefore argues that boots were rustic rather than urbane, the opposite of refined gentility.[6]

In the military world too, boots were for action rather than ceremony. The 1803 standing orders for the garrison of Gibraltar prescribed that officers on duty should wear 'black topped wax leather polished boots': 'When officers go to balls, then, and then only, they will be permitted to appear in Shoes and Stockings.'[7] Northampton Museum has a military dress shoe from 1828 owned by a Lieutenant Norbury (Figure 2.6).[8] Its fine stitching, supple uppers and thin flexible sole would not have held up to wear in the field, but would make it ideal for dancing: as we shall see in Chapter 6, Georgian formal dances often involved bouncing on tiptoe, which would be impossible in a rigid boot.[9] This chapter will consider both the civilian and military worlds, since this was a period when there was considerable overlap between the two.[10] Military and civilian styles informed one another: uniforms often followed civilian fashions, and military styles such as the Hessian and the Wellington achieved vogue in times of war. Furthermore, distinctions of rank in dress echoed those of social class. Whereas shoes for the men would be provided in bulk, officers were expected to buy their own uniforms and would acquire bespoke riding boots from a bootmaker in much the same way that a gentleman would in civilian life.[11] A pair of military riding boots in the National Army Museum, for example, bear Hoby's label, and display stitching and workmanship that is notably fine.[12] It is often difficult to tell military and civilian boots apart in museum collections, unless they come with a clear provenance, so it is practical to consider them alongside one another.

In this chapter, I want to nuance this stereotype of the plain and functional male boot. I shall do this by exploring the complex symbolic associations of the boot from the early eighteenth to the early nineteenth centuries, and the significance that they had for the gendered lives of men. It will use visual and textual sources from the time in order to learn about the significance that footwear had for their owners and wearers, and to place boots in their historical context, but the key sources are objects from museum collections. It will use boots as examples of material culture. Much of the field is currently concerned with their emotional implications,[13] and shoes were personal effects to which people were peculiarly attached. Lieutenant Colonel Kelly of the First Foot Guards died 'in endeavouring to save his favourite boots' from a burning building, and memoirs from the Napoleonic Wars attest to the value that common soldiers placed on their footwear when on long marches.[14]

The primary focus, however, is the effect that the boots would have had upon the bodies that wore them. Articles that are worn provide distinctive sensory experiences and can even affect the body itself. Tailored clothing can shape the frame, as well as altering its outward visual appearance, and can thence bestow self-confidence or social status upon the wearer.[15] Shoes can be a source of comfort or pain, of warmth or exposure, of dryness or damp, and can support or distort the motions of the body. Factors such as suppleness, shape or heel height can affect the posture or the walk. In handling the objects, therefore, I sought to establish the physical effect that the footwear would have had upon the wearer, as well as evaluating issues such as style and visual impact.

In order to conduct such a study, you need surviving examples, and the small number of these goes some way to explain why the study of men's footwear from the eighteenth century is such a compact field. We have seen that museum collections are dominated by fancier examples and, therefore, female and elite.[16] Plain and functional footwear – and, in particular, those belonging to working people – were worn until they could no longer be repaired and were then discarded or recycled. This means that, despite the millions of common soldiers' boots that were produced during the Napoleonic Wars, virtually none have survived. The boots studied here are therefore largely high-quality items belonging to patricians and commissioned officers, although some may have been worn by plebeians in equestrian occupations, such as coachmen or cavalrymen, who may not have owned them directly. Their relationship with their expensive boots was one of 'involuntary consumption', John Styles's characterization of how groups such as servants engaged with the consumer culture of the eighteenth century.[17] Again, this reminds us that, in order to understand an object, it needs to be placed fully in context rather than merely experienced first-hand.

Boots and the body

In the Georgian period, boots and shoes were more distinct than they are today. They had different functions and would be worn in different situations. In terms of manufacture, bootmaking and shoemaking were separate trades, requiring different skills.[18] Whereas there was a large ready-made trade in shoes, bootmaking was more likely to be bespoke. As well as being made-to-measure, bespoke goods were of superior quality, and were typically paid for on credit rather than up-front.[19] As we saw in Chapter 1, they also involved a different relationship between producer and consumer. Elite consumers of footwear were very knowledgeable about their production, knew good craftsmen by name and cultivated relationships with them. An anecdote published in *The Spirit of English Wit* (1813) gives us a flavour of this:

> 'Friend, these are handsome boots, Sherry; who made them?' – S. 'Hoby.' – F. 'How did you prevail on him?' – S. 'Guess.' – F. 'I suppose you talked him over in the old way.' – S. 'No, that won't do now.' – F. 'Then when they came home you ordered half a dozen more?' S. – 'No.' – F. 'Perhaps you gave a check on Hammersley, which you knew would not be honoured.' – S. 'No, no, no; in short, you might guess till to-morrow before you hit it. I paid for them.'[20]

It is also worth clarifying where the line was drawn between boots and shoes. Ankle boots, such as those worn by the British infantryman from the Peninsular War onwards (and which are explored in

Chapter 7), would be 'shoes' in military parlance, whereas a 'boot' would typically rise to the calf or the knee. Boots, therefore, used much more leather than shoes, and were typically heavier in construction, so cost considerably more. In 1673 the Duke of Hamilton paid £2 14s. for shoes, and £12 for boots.[21] Even boots for servants could be expensive: the Newdigates of Arbury Hall (who spent a quarter of their clothing budget on livery) spent up to £3 a pair on boots for the stable hands.[22] This was well beyond what servants could have afforded to buy in civilian life, and people often wore shoes with cloth gaiters as a cheaper alternative. Common soldiers did, too, and were expected to black them to give them the appearance of boot leather, unlike their officers who wore the real thing.

Boots were, therefore, a significant purchase, and we have to consider what this tells us about the nature of elite male consumerism. We have seen how men's shopping could be more impulsive and pleasurable than women's; and Margot Finn notes that men 'lavished time, money and signification' on clothes and personal possessions, in particular.[23] Boots were riding equipment. Men's consumption of boots can, therefore, be put in the same category as leather horse tack, which Amanda Vickery suggests was an 'utterly masculine, dark brown territory of goods'.[24] Shoe shopping is one area of consumerism where men will studiedly 'manhandle' a potential purchase: footwear is 'very much the sum of its parts, a physical object whose look, weight, texture and smell bespeak the skill of its maker and point to its intrinsic value'.[25] The same sensory considerations come into play when handling an object in a museum.

Boots are also symbolically distinctive. Boots have a long-standing association with the military and with violence. The verb 'to boot' means to kick; to 'get the boot' or be 'booted out' is to be ejected by force; 'booty' refers to the spoils of war; 'booted up' means ready for action. Johnson's dictionary gives additional contemporary definitions: 'profit; gain; advantage', whereas to be 'bootless' is to be 'useless; unavailing . . . without success'.[26] Valerie Steele suggests that 'boots convey an image of potent masculinity'.[27] Sexual and martial potency go hand in hand. According to oral tradition, the Duchess of Marlborough once declared that, 'the Duke returned from the wars today and did pleasure me in his top-boots'.[28]

Boots' association with the military is underlined by their use in equestrianism, since the horseman was historically a warrior (Figure 4.1). He was also a gentleman, so riding boots connoted social status and authority. In the eighteenth century, mounted soldiers were of higher status, be they cavalrymen or field officers in infantry regiments. Officers rode and soldiers marched,[29] just as gentlemen would not be obliged to walk any great distance in the civilian world. Horse riders require footwear that is stiff and supportive, protecting the lower leg from chafing in the saddle and when riding through scrub. In the dragoons' official Clothing Warrant of 1768, boots were listed with the horse tack rather than with the uniforms: they were equipment rather than clothes as such.[30] The extreme example of this is the huge and heavy postilion's boot, which is reinforced in order to protect the rider at the front of a carriage train from crushing his leg between the horse and wooden shaft (Figure 4.2).

Figure 4.1 *Joshua Reynolds,* portrait of Sir Banastre Tarleton *(1782). Alamy stock photo.*

Figure 4.2 *Postilion's boots with splatterdashes, 1790s. Museum of Leathercraft. @PaulReedPhotography.*

What was good for riding was therefore not good for walking and required a fundamentally different construction, as Hoby's opening remark suggested. Horsemen require footwear with a heel, to sit in the stirrups (Figure 4.3). As we saw in Chapter 1, whereas today heels are associated with femininity, in the early modern world they had different meanings, and were identified with the power of the aristocracy and the equestrian warrior. Such heels gave elite men an impressive bearing and enabled them to tower over their social inferiors.

As such, it is necessary to qualify the statement that men's boots are plain and functional. It is not useful to compare men's boots with women's in the eighteenth century, as women rarely wore them: they were not general wear but were worn for riding, for which women would wear versions of men's.[31] It is more revealing briefly to note the associations that women's boots have had in later periods, since this arguably colours how the boots of the eighteenth century are viewed today. Women's tall boots can be very sexualized, an association played on by dominatrices and drag artistes. Steele suggests that this symbolic power of female boots derives from these historic associations in the masculine world with the military, with violence and with high status. She further notes that the 'rise' of the boot emphasizes that legs are 'the pathway to the genitals, as well constituting an erogenous zone of their own'.[32] This is arguably as true for men as it is for women, and the high-heeled boots of the eighteenth century should be seen in this light. We shall also see how boot design relates to the nature of legwear in this respect, enhancing the male physique in a sexualized way.

This suggests that we need to rethink how we approach, not just boots, but men's dress, in general. As we have seen, historians have conventionally argued that the period witnessed a 'great masculine renunciation', whereby men's dress became plainer and more uniform. The psychologist J. C. Flügel coined the concept in the 1930s, and linked this phenomenon to the great upheavals of the French Revolution and its rejection of social distinctions.[33] Subsequent writers have questioned this interpretation but it continues to be influential.[34] David Kuchta, for example, locates this shift earlier, and in English elites rather than the French middle classes. He argues that the rise of the plain three-piece suit was 'an aristocratic response to the new ideas of manliness legitimated by the culture that emerged after the Glorious Revolution', which was only later appropriated by middling men as they claimed membership of the political class. The renunciation of sartorial display was therefore a conscious form of 'inconspicuous consumption', rather than a lack of showiness as such.[35] As other commentators have noted, the universal adoption of black in the nineteenth century did not equate to dullness or denial.[36]

This ongoing debate has big implications for the understanding of sexual difference. Thomas King argues that 'the "great masculine renunciation" made men and women by promoting an ideology of gendered complementariness': a common sartorial regime ostensibly levelled distinctions between propertied men, consolidating their identity and power as a group.[37] According to this argument, corporeal display came to be identified with femininity: women were increasingly identified with their bodies, and thence maternal roles in the domestic sphere, whereas men's very disembodiedness equipped them for the rational public sphere. As Karen Harvey has noted of men's breeches, though, clothing that served to emphasize the man's anatomy and his very sexual potency can hardly be said to have done this: rather, the bodiliness of men was the basis for a new form of 'embodied citizenship'.[38] Outward signs of male gender took on a renewed significance in a period when political citizenship was increasingly aligning with masculinity. Debates around the franchise, in particular, emphasized that only men could possess the required attributes of independence, rationality and public spirit.[39] There is therefore much at stake in the question of whether men's boots in the Georgian period were plain and functional, or quite the reverse.

As well as having an effect on the appearance of the body, Georgians were aware that boots impacted upon the body itself. McNeil and Riello note that footwear in this period was assessed in terms of its healthiness and physical comfort, within the new scientific discourse of '*hygiène*'.[40] Some medical literature on the subject was anxious about the dangers of wearing stiff high boots: '*Boots* made too small, and of thick hard Leather, are so pernicious to Health, and so disagreeable in Walking, that I wonder any sensible Being should confine themselves in them, for the silly purpose of showing the exact Shape of the Legs.' The author went on to explain that, when the arteries are compressed, 'a *Wasting* or atrophy of the Limb follows'.[41] Coachmen were known to suffer from embolisms from wearing their knee-high boots, probably exacerbated by having to wear them for long periods in a seated position. Eighteenth-century medicine placed great store on the healthiness of free circulation, and the evils of tight footwear came in for particular criticism.

Late-Georgian followers of fashion often wore tight shoes in order to achieve the appearance of small feet. One commentator was horrified that: 'the young and the would-be youthful, should contract their shoes until the members upon which the body rests, and which ought freely to enjoy their own power of motion, have been, as it were, "cribb'd, cabin'd, and confined" in a close prison'.[42] As we saw in Chapter 2, podiatric writers bemoaned that such footwear was the cause of corns, lameness and bone damage, and was particularly damaging to children.[43] Furthermore, the physician William Buchan argued that, in preventing people from walking, such footwear 'may likewise be considered the remote cause of other diseases'.[44] The excesses of fashion were often subject to hostile commentary like this, being a threat to both medical and moral health.[45] The comfort and healthiness of boots are therefore key factors to be considered when examining artefacts from the time. Fashionable boots from the early nineteenth century are notably narrow, with a high instep and pointed toes, and signs of stretching in the uppers suggest that they were too small for their wearer.[46] Alison Matthews David notes that this contrasts with plebeian footwear, which was wide and flat-footed, and therefore designed to be walked in.[47] For this reason, the surgeon Samuel Cooper noted that 'genteel persons are more likely to be afflicted' with corns and other complaints than the lower classes.[48]

The history of the boot in Georgian Britain is a complex one. The boot was suffused with symbolism about gender and class, and came to be the focus of anxieties about political and military power, as well as about bodily and moral health. The meanings of the boot were not static, and there were significant changes in boot design over the course of the century, so it is also necessary to take a chronological perspective. A focus on historical change is particularly apt as far as the history of masculinity is concerned, since the Georgian period is often identified as an important transitional phase in British gender relations. Historians often identify the period after 1750 as being crucial here, be it in terms of the rise of 'separate spheres' for men and women,[49] of binary notions of sexual difference,[50] or even of modern notions of selfhood. Dror Wahrman, for example, argues that the decades around the American Revolution had a crucial role in closing down the fluid and generic personal identities of the early modern world. This was replaced by a sense that individuals were unique and were located within fixed modern categories of gender, race and class.[51] As boots were loaded with meaning in all three respects, it is revealing to consider the significance of changes in boot design across this transformative period in social relations. The focus of this chapter will therefore shift to individual types of boots, exploring how styles changed over the course of the century, and using surviving examples from the museum collections to think about the experience of wearing them.

The jackboot

The jackboot (Figure 4.3) derived from seventeenth-century styles. June Swann notes that the cavalier-style riding boot began to stiffen and straighten after the Restoration and became the 'cavalry boot par excellence'.[52] Riding boots were thereafter made of strong leather with a shiny black wax finish. Of all eighteenth-century footwear, the jackboot is probably the most symbolically redolent. These heavy, over-the-knee boots were a byword for oppression and militarism. When opposition MPs criticized the prime minister, the Earl of Bute in the 1760s, they played on his surname to suggest his despotic nature, and he is instantly recognizable as a 'boot' in caricatures of the time.[53] The jackboot retains this sense to this day, re-emphasized by its association with fascism in the twentieth century. Encountering eighteenth-century jackboots first-hand, it is comprehensible why this should be the case. Their sheer bulk, thickness, hardness and inflexibility, coupled with their shiny black surface and aggressive appearance, makes them fearsome objects to behold. It is therefore important to consider the psychological as well as the physical impact of wearing such footwear: for soldiers, boots can contribute to their 'belligerent attitude' as well as providing an offensive weapon in their own right.[54]

Jackboots got their name from the process of 'jacking', whereby hide was treated with wax and then tar or pitch to make it waterproof. Maintaining this high shine became something of an obsession. In the army, soldiers were required to carry shoe brushes and polish known as 'black ball',

Figure 4.3 *Man's leather jackboot, c. 1720. Image courtesy of Northampton Museum and Art Gallery.*

and footwear was subject to a constant regime of maintenance and inspection.[55] To a certain extent, this was about inculcating discipline and maintaining a uniform appearance, although there was also a practical utility in ensuring that the leather was waterproof, supple and long-lasting. In civilian society, the fetish for blacking was undoubtedly driven by the dictates of fashion, and a whole blacking industry grew up to meet the demand.[56] The unfortunate Lieutenant Colonel Kelly was renowned for his 'brilliant' boots and, after his demise, 'all the dandies [including Beau Brummell] were anxious to secure the services of his valet, who possessed the mystery of the inimitable blacking'.[57]

The jackboot was equestrian wear. Early eighteenth-century jackboots had wide tops (which cavaliers had formerly worn folded down) to protect the lower thigh while riding.[58] Later examples dispensed with these and terminated at the knee, but these were emphatically boots for riding rather than walking. They were often fitted with spurs, and had high heels of stacked leather: the boot pictured in Figure 4.3 has heels of 65 mm. While ideal for the stirrups, and while it would have given the wearer an impressive bearing when standing still, they would have been unwieldy for walking. A colonel asked, 'to what purpose is cavalry loaded with such monstrous heavy boots…? [A] lighter, yet full as strong, and much more serviceable boot might easily be contrived'.[59] The dragoons (mounted soldiers who carried firearms, as distinct from the cavalry who use edged weapons) were originally issued with jackboots, too, but this 'made skirmishing on foot almost impossible'. In the latter stages of the Napoleonic Wars they instead wore short boots, which gave them the flexibility to operate either on foot or in the saddle.[60]

Further factors made jackboots unsuitable for walking. Jackboots were made from hide almost a centimetre thick, which offered excellent protection to the foot and leg but was very heavy and virtually rigid. Several of the jackboots that I handled had no flexibility whatsoever at the ankle, which would impede normal locomotion. This also made them difficult to get on and off. High boots were typically fitted with bootstraps to help pull them up, and a gentleman would require the assistance of a servant to pull them down. The expression 'to boot and saddle' therefore refers to a lengthy process, and the cavalry would be given orders to do this well in advance of an action.[61] Finally, in common with virtually all shoes manufactured between 1600 and 1800, jackboots were straight lasted.[62] Jackboots were symmetrical and had broad square toes, so could be worn on either foot. It was more comfortable to wear them consistently on the left or right, since the boot would mould to the foot, to the limited extent that thick hide would allow. This, however, weakened the stitching and wore out the sole unevenly, so soldiers were under orders to swap them around daily to make them last longer, relying on thick woollen socks to prevent rubbing.[63] Patricians were not quite so cost-sensitive, and there is evidence of consistent wear on some high-end examples.[64] In general, however, the jackboot did not fit around the body: rather, the body fitted around it. Jackboots were, therefore, oppressive to their wearers, as well as to those who beheld them.

The top-boot

The top-boot (Figure 4.4) derived from this equestrian style but was a more wearable proposition. Top-boots started to appear from the 1730s and were fashionable from the 1770s onwards, becoming part of the outdoor uniform of the patrician man. 'John Bull' is invariably portrayed wearing them in caricature, giving them the status of a national style.[65] Top-boots had a shiny black surface and their distinctive 'tops' were created by folding them down so it revealed the contrasting colour of the untreated leather within. In terms of the masculine ensemble, they were worn with breeches that reached to the knee, and a coat and waistcoat: coats shortened over the course of the century, lending to the appearance a long-legged, classical body shape.[66] This created an expanse of leather, from the shiny black of the boots, via the buff of the boot-tops up to the waist, which drew the eye to the shape of the man's leg and the location of the genitals. As Harvey has noted, this very sexualized image of the male body runs counter to the notion that there was a 'renunciation' of showy male dress in the eighteenth century. Rather than being disembodied, the dress of the Georgian man drew attention to his body.[67] By the turn of the century, boots were fitted to the calf and lasted to the left and right foot with a pointed toe, emphasizing the shape of the masculine body where they had formerly concealed it.

Top-boots were cut much more smartly and closely than the jackboot and were fashioned from softer grain leather. Other concessions to comfort included their construction from a single piece of leather, minimizing the number of abrasive seams.[68] Top-boots in museum collections (such as the one pictured in Figure 4.4) are notably more supple and flexible than jackboots, and the heels are much lower, although the soles remain fairly rigid. These could be worn for riding (and are worn by jockeys to this day) but they were also suitable for walking. They shod rural walkers when it became a fashionable pursuit in the Romantic period, and walking around town became a more attractive option when the 'urban renaissance' provided paved streets, promenades, squares and pleasure gardens.[69] In the 1790s, boots became fashionable for general wear, as they often did in times of war, and Riello suggests that they also became 'a sign of democracy and participation in public affairs'.[70] While men's boots were becoming more suitable for rugged outdoor activities, we have seen that women's footwear was going in the other direction. Footwear design, therefore, had a key role to play in this crucial period of realignment in gender relations.

The Wellington boot

The story of the invention of the Wellington is well known. It was developed from the Hessian boot, which had become fashionable around the same time as the top-boot. This was a military style that came to Britain with Hessian auxiliaries during the War of American Independence.[71] Like the

Figure 4.4 *Man's black-and-beige, leather top-boot, 1810–20. Image courtesy of Northampton Museum and Art Gallery.*

top-boot, the Hessian was cut close to the calf, but instead of having folded tops it rose at the front and its decorated top was finished with a tassel. It was worn outside legwear and looked elegant with breeches. It was therefore a rather dandyish style and was favoured by fashionable men such as Beau Brummell (Figure 4.5).[72] As breeches came to be superseded by trousers and pantaloons in male fashion, the tasselled and decorated Hessian posed a problem as it could not be worn under them. Wellington also found that, when on campaign, boots worn outside legwear became damp and difficult to remove, whereas boots worn under overalls stayed dry.[73] He therefore ordered a modified version from Hoby, with a shorter smooth leg and a straight top, and took two pairs with him on the Waterloo campaign. As he wrote from Brussels in April 1815:

Mr Hoby

The last boots you sent me were still too small in the calf of the leg & about an inch and a half too short in the leg. Send me two pairs more altered as I have above described.

    Your most faithfull Servt

      Wellington[74]

They eventually perfected the design, and the victor of Waterloo's footwear became a sensation, becoming a 'virtual national costume'.[75] By the 1830s, boots were the norm among respectable men. One commentator noted 'we are emphatically a booted people' and that, of all boots, 'the Wellington is unquestionably the most gentlemanly thing of its kind'.[76]

The Wellington's great asset was its flexibility. Wellingtons could be worn for riding, formal occasions or general wear. Fitted legwear could be tucked in – as they often were in the military – or they could be worn smoothly beneath trousers or pantaloons, with the strap fitting under the low heel. Christopher Breward notes that the new combination of legwear and footwear was 'a more practical, healthy and aesthetically suitable option for the energetic, bifurcated challenges of modern life'.[77] The Wellington, therefore, befitted late-Georgian masculinities in being elegant but sober and practical, being ideal footwear for the serious statesman, the industrious businessman or the man of action. Wellington boots' combination with trousers underlined their patriotic and manly credentials: trousers had long been worn by common sailors and by the time they entered civilian fashions in the 1800s they were worn by soldiers too.[78] If breeches carried the taint of the old aristocracy, trousers and boots were the uniform of the self-made man.[79]

Wellington boots contrast with their predecessors in their close fit and their suppleness. Without elastic to achieve a close fit, they had to be made to measure, and surviving examples sometimes have cuts in the leg where owners were trying to achieve comfort, or to get them on and off.[80] These were expensive bespoke articles, and the fine leather and detailed stitching reveal their elite origins. As well as having supple uppers, their soles are relatively thin and flexible, suggesting that they could be

Figure 4.5 *Richard Dighton, sketch of George Bryan 'Beau' Brummel (1804). Alamy stock photo.*

Figure 4.6 *Dress Wellingtons, c. 1840. Image © Bata Shoe Museum, Toronto, Canada.*

danced in: one pair that I examined had soles that were only four millimetres thick, which flexed when handling.[81] 'Dress Wellingtons' are especially soft and fine. One example from around 1840 has the deceptive appearance of a laced dancing pump and a stockinged leg (Figure 4.6): these were sometimes known as 'opera boots' as they could be worn at formal occasions. Here, the boot visually becomes part of the body, rather than something that the body wears. Whereas plebeian footwear at the beginning of the Victorian period remained bulky and uncomfortable, the footwear of elite males moulded to their frames, embodying their natural authority in a masculine silhouette.

Figure 4.7 *William Heath,* A Wellington Boot, or the Head of the Army *(October 1827). Alamy stock photo.*

Indeed, in probably the most famous caricature of Wellington, the boot *becomes* his body. William Heath's *A Wellington Boot, or the Head of the Army* (1827) depicts the Duke's head, sandwiched between enormous versions of the two garments with which he was synonymous, the bicorne hat and the Wellington boot (Figure 4.7). As well as signifying his class, the boot signalled Wellington's patriotic and masculine credentials by embodying his many martial achievements. Confident in his situation, he looks at the viewer and wears a satisfied smile. The title refers to his recent appointment as Commander-in-Chief (or 'head') of the Army, but he remains grounded in the realities of warfare. In the background, troops drill outside Horse Guards Parade, not far from Hoby's shop.[82]

Conclusion

Male boots were therefore far from simply being plain and functional items in the Georgian period. Although they clearly did have practical functions – notably, to protect the leg and secure the stirrups while riding – these only served to underline their associations with social status, political authority and military power. In terms of masculinities, their use in outdoor activities contributed to an image that was unrefined to a certain extent, but it would not be correct to pigeonhole them on the 'plain' side of a male/female binary as shoe historians often do. Dandies appreciated the high shine of black leather and the peacock stance fostered by high heels. They may have had to change into shoes in order to dance, but even this was no longer necessary with the arrival of the Wellington, with its soft uppers and flexible sole. Far from witnessing a 'renunciation' in male dress after 1750, the boot becomes increasingly elegant and sophisticated, and more acceptable for fashionable general wear. Furthermore, instead of disembodying the male, changes in styles meant that boots increasingly moulded to the frames of the elite men who could afford bespoke footwear from a fine bootmaker like Hoby. One manufacturer from the 1840s urged that, 'every one who wishes to be comfortably fitted, should have a pair of lasts made expressly for his own use': this takes the bespoke relationship to its logical conclusion, constructing the boot around the actual body shape of the consumer, but was clearly only an option for those who could afford it.[83] The shapely foot and leg permitted by expensive boots was therefore a visual sign of the class of men who possessed social and political authority in the early nineteenth century.

Boots are, therefore, significant in terms of notions of the individual and how that individual relates to society as a whole. As the eighteenth century moved towards fixed modern notions of gender, race and class, high-end boots became more closely personalized to the men who wore them. With the demise of straight lasts, broad, squared toes and thick, wide legs, boots become less generic and more individualized: they shift from being equipment to clothing. An examination of the history of boots supports Wahrman's argument that 'the modern regime of selfhood' arrived at the end of the eighteenth century, as individuals came to possess a unique identity. But, whereas Wahrman argues that clothing comes to be regarded as a mask – something to be 'seen through' – elite footwear in the early nineteenth century serves to reveal the individual's bodily uniqueness rather than to conceal it.[84] Bulky non-elite footwear similarly marked out the wearer in terms of gender, race and (especially) class, but located him as part of a mass rather than as an individual.

Over the course of the eighteenth century, medical understanding of the body shifted from it being flexible and adaptable, to being fixed and suited to its environment.[85] So, whereas in the mid-century, one's body would have to adapt to a rigid symmetrical boot that was not designed for it, by the end of the century the boot was expected to fit around the unique contours and motions of the individual's body. These contours are still visible in surviving examples of boots from the time, given the unique way that leather stretches, scuffs and grains when it comes into contact with the walking foot. The materiality of footwear therefore tells us things about its wearer that visual or textual representations never could.

Notes

1. Rees Howell Gronow, *Captain Gronow: His Reminiscences of Victorian and Regency Life 1810–60*, ed. Christopher Hibbert (London: Kyle Cathie, 1991), 88.
2. Riello and McNeil, 'Footprints from History', 30.
3. Bondi and Mariacher, *If the Shoe Fits*, 164.
4. DeMello, *Feet and Footwear*, 44–6.
5. Southampton's Assembly Rooms were more forgiving, adding 'military gentlemen excepted': John Feltham, *A Guide to the Watering and Sea-Bathing Places* (London, 1806), 33, 295.
6. Riello, *A Foot in the Past*, 70.
7. F. R. T. Trench-Gascoigne, 'Extracts from the Standing Orders in the Garrison of Gibraltar', *Journal of the Society for Army Historical Research* 2, no. 8 (1923): 86–9, and no. 9: 124–9 (125, 127).
8. 'Black patent leather military dress shoe, 1828': Northampton Museum P25/1970.14.
9. Anon., *Art of Preserving the Feet*, 191.
10. David Bell, *The First Total War: Napoleon's Europe and the Birth of Modern Warfare* (London: Bloomsbury, 2007).
11. A regimental bootmaker would make them according to an approved pattern: Hew Strachan, *British Military Uniforms 1768–1796: The Dress of the British Army from Official Sources* (London: Arms & Armour Press, 1975), 70.
12. 'Pair of boots, possibly Light Dragoons, *c.* 1800': National Army Museum 1964-10-32.
13. See, for example: Fay Bound Alberti, *Matters of the Heart: History, Medicine and Emotion* (Oxford: Oxford University Press, 2010); Sally Holloway, *The Game of Love in Georgian England: Courtship, Emotions and Material Culture* (Oxford: Oxford University Press, 2019); Davis Miller, *The Comfort of Things* (Cambridge: Polity, 2008).

14 Gronow, *Reminiscences*, 104.

15 For a study of military uniforms, see Scott Hughes Myerly, *British Military Spectacle: From the Napoleonic Wars Through the Crimea* (Cambridge, MA: Harvard University Press, 1996), Chapter 1.

16 Karen Harvey has noted similar patterns of survival for men's breeches: 'Men of Parts', 804.

17 John Styles, *The Dress of the People*.

18 Riello, *A Foot in the Past*, 40.

19 Ibid., 54.

20 George Cruikshank, *The Spirit of English Wit, or Post-Chaise Companion* (London, 1813), 205.

21 Swann, *Shoes*, 22.

22 I am grateful to Mark Rothery for this information.

23 Walsh, 'Shops, Shopping and the Art of Decision Making', 164; Margot Finn, 'Men's Things: Masculine Possession in the Consumer Revolution', *Social History* 25, no. 2 (2000): 133–55 (139).

24 Vickery, *Behind Closed Doors*, 124.

25 Breward, 'Fashioning Masculinity', 220.

26 Samuel Johnson, *A Dictionary of the English Language*, 2 vols (London, 1792), vol. 1, col. BOO.

27 Valerie Steele, *Shoes: A Lexicon of Style* (London: Scriptum, 1998), 132.

28 E. Knowles (ed.), *The Oxford Dictionary of Quotations*, 6th edn (Oxford: Oxford University Press, 2004), 512.

29 Cecil Lawson, *A History of the Uniforms of the British Army*, 5 vols (London: Kaye & Ward, 1967), vol. 5, 36.

30 Strachan, *British Military Uniforms*, 41.

31 DeMello, *Feet and Footwear*, 47.

32 Steele, *Shoes*, 126.

33 Flügel, *The Psychology of Clothes*.

34 As noted by Karen Harvey: 'Men of Parts', 798–9. For example: Daniel Roche, *The Culture of Clothing: Dress and Fashion in the Ancien Regime*, trans. Jean Birrell (Cambridge: Cambridge University Press, 1994); Kuchta, *The Three-Piece Suit*; Jennifer Jones, *Sexing La Mode: Gender, Fashion and Commercial Culture in Old Regime France* (Oxford: Berg, 2004), 214; King, *The Gendering of Men*; M. Kwass, 'Big Hair: A Wig History of Consumption in Eighteenth-Century France', *American Historical Review* 111, no. 3 (2006): 631–59.

35 Kuchta, *The Three-Piece Suit*, 163, 164.

36 Harvey, *Men in Black*.

37 King, *The Gendering of Men*, 181, 179.

38 Harvey, 'Men of Parts', 821.

39 McCormack, *The Independent Man*.

40 McNeil and Riello, 'Art and Science of Walking', 192–4.

41 Walter Vaughan, *An Essay, Philosophical and Medical, Concerning Modern Clothing* (London, 1792), 44, 57.

42 Anon., *Art of Preserving the Feet*, 197.

43 Vaughan, *Essay*, 46, 65.

44 W. Buchan, *Buchan's Domestic Medicine Modernized; Or, A Treatise on the Prevention and Cure of Diseases by Regimen and Simple Medicine* (London, 1809), 51.

45 Alison Matthews David, *Fashion Victims: The Dangers of Dress Past and Present* (London: Bloomsbury, 2015).

46 For example, 'Man's single black leather boot, early 1800s': Northampton Museum 2000.27.50.

47 Alison Matthews David, 'War and Wellingtons: Military Footwear in the Age of Empire', in *Shoes: A History from Sandals to Sneakers*, ed. Giorgio Riello and Peter McNeil (Oxford: Berg, 2006), 116–37 (130).

48 Cooper, *Practice of Surgery*, 145.

49 Vickery, 'Golden Age to Separate Spheres?'

50 Laqueur, *Making Sex*.

51 Wahrman, *The Making of the Modern Self*.

52 Swann, *Shoes*, 21.

53 Anon., *The Jack-Boot Exalted* (1762): BM Satires / Catalogue of Political and Personal Satires in the Department of Prints and Drawings in the British Museum (3860).

54 A. W. Stokes, *Some Comments on the Design and Construction of Military Footwear* (London: War Office [since 1964 part of the Ministry of Defence], 1960), 3.

55 The 1795 Standing Orders for the 2nd Dragoon Guards provides 'A Receipt [*sic*] for making black balls': Strachan, *British Military Uniforms*, 80.

56 David, *Fashion Victims*, 116.

57 Gronow, *Reminiscences*, 104.

58 'Black leather jack boot with domed toe, 1720': BATA Shoe Museum P94.062.

59 H. H. Pembroke, *Military Equitation: Or, A Method of Breaking Horses, and Teaching Soldiers to Ride. Designed for the Use of the Army* (London, 1813), 29.

60 Charles Oman, *Wellington's Army, 1809–1814* (London: E. Arnold, 1913), 297.

61 B. H. Liddell Hart (ed.), *The Letters of Private Wheeler 1809–1828* (Moreton-in-Marsh: Windrush Press, 1998), 79.

62 Thornton, 'Left-Right-Left'.

63 Cuthbertson, *System for the Compleat Interior Management*, 135.

64 'Pair of boots, possibly heavy cavalry, 1750': National Army Museum 1959-11-59.

65 Swann, *Shoes*, 28.

66 Anne Hollander, *Seeing Through Clothes* (Berkeley: University of California Press, 1993), 225.

67 Harvey, 'Men of Parts', 798.

68 Wilcox, *The Mode in Footwear*, 119.

69 On the parallel phenomenon in France, see L. Turcot, 'The Rise of the Promeneur: Walking in the City in Eighteenth-Century Paris', *Historical Research* 88, no. 239 (2015): 67–99.

70 Riello, *A Foot in the Past*, 71.

71 Wilcox, *The Mode in Footwear*, 120.

72 On Wellington's dandyism, see Harvey, *Men in Black*, 34.

73 Sir William Fraser, *Words on Wellington* (London: J. C. Nimmo, 1889), 56.

74 Quoted in Elizabeth Longford, *Wellington: The Years of the Sword* (London: Weidenfeld & Nicolson, 1969), 409.

75 Breward, 'Men in Heels', 137.

76 Hall, *Book of the Feet*, 124–5.

77 Ibid.

78 Beverly Lemire, 'A Question of Trousers: Seafarers, Masculinity and Empire in the Shaping of British Male Dress, c. 1600–1800', *Cultural and Social History* 13, no. 1 (2016): 1–22.

79 Semmelhack, *Standing Tall*, 45.

80 David, 'War and Wellingtons', 130.

81 'Pair of men's black and red leather dress Wellington boots, 1800–25': Northampton Museum 2000.27.33.1.

82 David, 'War and Wellingtons', 134.

83 Hall, *Book of the Feet*, 104.

84 Wahrman, *The Making of the Modern Self*, 178.

85 Erica Charters, *Disease, War and the Imperial State: The Welfare of the British Armed Forces during the Seven Years' War* (Chicago: Chicago University Press, 2014), 171.

5

Gout shoes and disability

Like many men of his class, the prime minister Lord North (1732–92) suffered from gout. An anecdote of the time tells of how he felt an attack coming on and called for his 'large gouty shoes', which were commonly worn on feet swollen by the condition. His servant discovered that they had been stolen and cursed the thief. 'Poh', replied his Lordship, 'how can you be so ill-natured, John? Now all the harm I wish the poor rogue is, *that my shoes may fit him.*'[1]

Gout was a common subject for humour in the Georgian period but it was no laughing matter for those who endured it. It is not lethal, contagious or permanent, but it is an extremely painful and limiting condition that is disabling in its effect. We know today that gout is caused by too much uric acid in the blood, which can be the result of the kidneys not functioning properly. This can be hereditary and congenital, but is worsened by social conditions, so has reached epidemic proportions at certain times in history.[2] Gout is common in the present day and tends to be associated with lower socio-economic groups since poor diet, alcoholism and lack of exercise are contributing factors. In the eighteenth century it was the elite who ate a meat-heavy diet, drank excessively and enjoyed a sedentary lifestyle. Although gout affected people from all classes, it was predominantly associated with rich men: the wealthy dominated public representations and the attention of physicians, but there were also a range of cultural reasons why it was known as a gentleman's disorder. As today, gout in the eighteenth century could not be cured, so was best managed by a combination of medicine, lifestyle changes and assistive technologies. These included crutches, wheeled chairs, cushions, footstools and various types of shoe.

This chapter will focus upon footwear as part of the material culture of gout, and is therefore a contribution to the history of disability as well as the history of shoes. Disability history has moved beyond the 'medical model' of disability as a problem requiring a solution, and instead seeks to understand the lived experience of disability, as well as the social and cultural factors that informed conceptions of impairment in the past. How disability has been understood has changed through time; and, indeed, the modern notion of 'disability' would have been alien in the eighteenth century. Our focus is on a century of change, from a religious understanding of impairment as immutable, towards a medicalized attitude that it was treatable.³ Since both physical and sensory impairments often involve material intervention and accommodation, disability history has had a productive engagement with the study of material culture. Katherine Ott argues that artefacts 'actively shape and define disability', so there is much to be gained by directly studying the artefacts themselves as material sources.⁴ Disabled people are commonly identified with their assistive technology – such as a pair of spectacles or a wheelchair – and this was true of gout sufferers in the eighteenth century. Of the hundreds of images of gouty people created in the eighteenth century, James Gillray's 'The Gout' (1799) is probably the most famous because it is unique (Figure 5.1). The swollen foot is here presented unclothed and in isolation: we know nothing of its owner, not even their sex, and the viewer is left to imagine what they must be suffering.⁵ In every other picture of gout the condition is signalled by what is worn upon the foot and leg. Shoes are closely identified with their wearer, perhaps more than any other garment. To be 'in my gouty shoe' was to have the gout.⁶

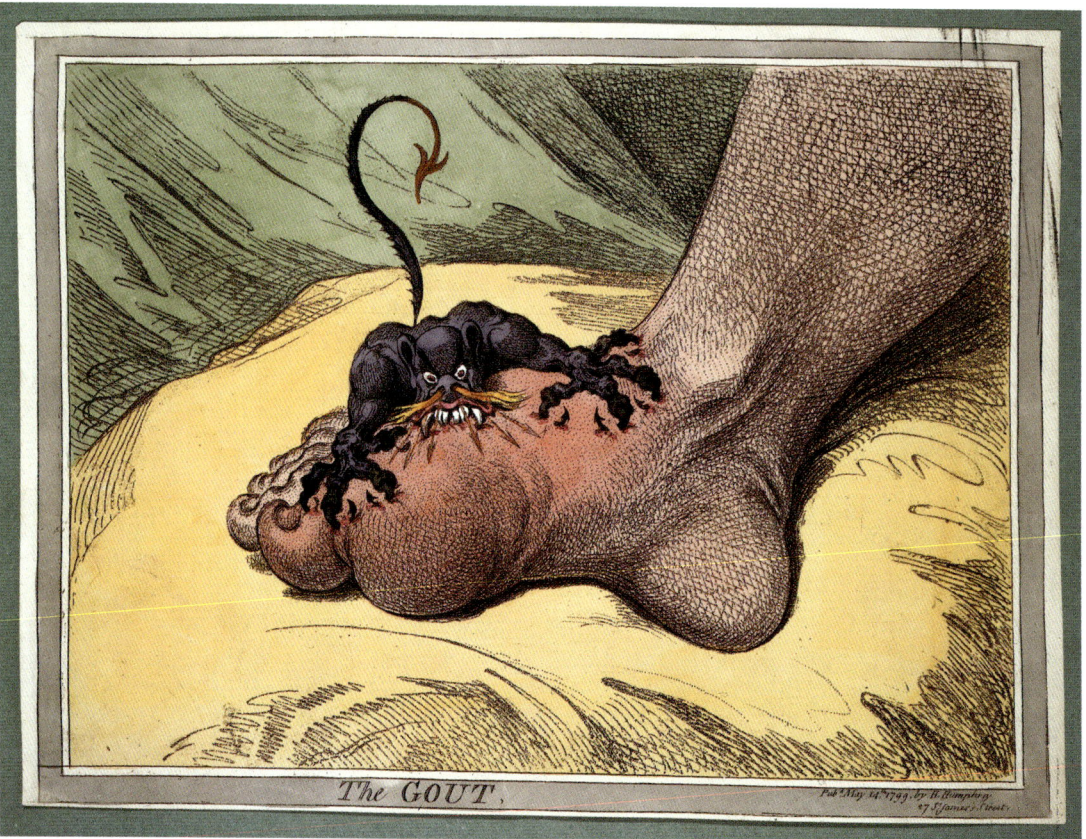

Figure 5.1 *James Gillray,* The Gout *(1799). Wellcome Collection.*

A study of the material culture of shoes would typically proceed by studying surviving objects themselves, but gout shoes present challenges in this respect. Very few survive in museum collections, perhaps because they are not the type of shoe that tended to be preserved. We have seen how shoe collections tend to privilege fancy examples, whereas gout shoes were unattractive, utilitarian articles. A rare example of a gout shoe from the nineteenth century is in Trowbridge Museum (Figure 5.2). It is made of dull brown leather in an unfashionably bulbous shape. This example is quite well worn, with wear to the heel and damage to the stitching: other examples were likely worn until they were no longer usable and then discarded. There are examples retrieved from archaeological digs but these tend to be fragments in poor condition. Gout shoes were also not produced in large numbers. Nicole Belolan notes that before assistive technologies were mass produced people in the past improvised material solutions: they 'commissioned, invented, borrowed and refashioned' objects, which were therefore individual.[7] We shall see how Georgians had shoes made to the size of their swollen feet, or adapted existing footwear by cutting out the uppers or making slits in the leather. This book has argued that shoes have a uniquely close relationship with the body, supporting its entire weight and enabling it to move, while moulding to the shape of the feet. If disability is an 'embodied state', then assistive shoes offer the historian a means to understand this.[8]

Given the lack of physical evidence, this chapter will primarily rely on other source types. There was a plethora of medical writings on gout in the eighteenth century. This was partly because this was a disease of the wealthy, so physicians followed the money, but it is also the case that gout was highly characteristic of many aspects of contemporary thought, from the medical and physiological to the moral and political.[9] Gout often features in social commentary and is also a common feature of personal writings from this period, not least because those confined with the condition had little else to do. Correspondents such as Horace Walpole (1717–97) described their experience of gout in detail, sharing advice and cures with fellow sufferers. The sentimental letter of the eighteenth century was a space for the expression of feeling and the sharing of intimate information, although the urbane Walpole, for one, was cautious of boring his correspondents with his invalidity.[10] Gout sufferers like Walpole created communities of correspondents, which could provide a sort of support group and possibly some compensation for missing out on in-person sociability. It is, therefore, possible to explore the lived experience of disability, at least for the elite classes of society.

Besides textual sources, these is a rich visual heritage of gout. Much of this is satirical and therefore unsympathetic to the sufferer. The eighteenth-century tradition of caricature revelled in exposing folly, so gout was a common means to mock the elderly, the rich and the afflicted, who had apparently brought it upon themselves by their privileged lifestyles. It was also a highly visible condition that was ripe for visual satire. Caricature seeks to make a moral point by exaggerating bodily features in order to expose the soul of its subject, so gout's swelling was part of its symbolic vocabulary.[11] It is, nevertheless, possible to use this material as a visual record of the material culture of gout. Gout shoes,

Figure 5.2 *Pair of gout shoes, nineteenth century. Trowbridge Museum.*

bound legs, crutches and bath chairs abound and, although these are often visually exaggerated for satirical effect, they certainly provide an insight into how the sufferer was culturally constructed by their accoutrements in this period. The chapter will begin by situating the illness within Georgian society and culture and in contemporary understanding of the body. It will then turn to the assistive technology of gout, focusing on footwear in order to shed light on the material and embodied experience of the condition.

Gout and the politics of the body

Gout in the feet is technically known as 'podagra'. There is a lexicon for the condition when it affects other parts of the body, but Roy Porter and George Rousseau note that in the eighteenth century 'gout' became the catch-all term.[12] 'Gout' was used to describe the painful swelling in the foot and leg, which may in reality have been caused by a range of other conditions: historians should be wary of diagnosing illnesses in the past, and our focus here is on the complaint rather than the condition as such. Gout comes from *gutta*, the medieval Latin for 'drop', indicating that ill humours had fallen to the body's extremities, so the condition was primarily associated with the feet, which were thought to be 'the sink of the body'.[13] It was comprehensible within the humoral understanding of the body. Since classical times, physicians believed that bodily health and temperament were governed by the balance of four humours, and the operation of fluids and heat. Illness was caused by an imbalance of the humours, so medical treatment typically consisted of purging in order to restore balance. Over the course of the eighteenth century this was superseded in medical circles by a more mechanistic understanding of anatomy but this, too, emphasized the importance of free circulation, so there were continuities in the ways that gout was understood and treated.

There was no single agreed cause of gout, but much attention was paid to the place of the feet within the fluid economy and the ways in which they were shod. George Nicolson argued that the feet were the most 'important emunctory in the human system', so they needed to perspire freely and be kept warm and dry: 'The connection between the feet and the head, the stomach, the uterus and the urinary passages is such that fits of the gout, suppression of the menses, and pains resembling those of the stone are frequently and almost instantaneously brought on by cold applied to the feet.'[14] It was therefore important to wear stockings made from a material like wool that kept one warm and dry, and to avoid cotton, linen or silk that could become saturated with sweat. Warm and dry weather, too, was thought to be good for the gout. William Cole told Walpole in the hot summer of 1778 that he was enjoying a remission: 'Thank God, this very burning summer, however disagreeable otherwise, has chased the gout, and I have my leathern shoes on, which I never thought I ever should again.'[15] Another of his gouty correspondents, Horace Mann, was also careful in this respect: 'I think I find great benefit by strictly avoiding any damp or cold in my feet, and have for that purpose worn *galoshes* over my shoes all this winter, and would recommend them to you.'[16]

As well as keeping the feet dry and warm, shoes should not be too tight, since this would obstruct free circulation and cause blockages of foetid matter. As we have seen, shoes in the eighteenth-century were constructed on straight lasts and so did not take the shape of the foot; and it was fashionable to wear tight shoes to give the impression of small feet. Podiatric writings were generally critical of this and highlighted the health risks.[17] The following poem takes the perspective of a boy who wears tight breeches and shoes for the first time:

> Our legs must suffer by litigation,
> To keep the blood from circulation:
> And then, our feet, tho' young and tender,
> We to the shoe-maker surrender;
> Who often makes our shoes so straight,
> Our feeble joints they cramp and fret:
> Then, with contrivance most profound,
> Across our insteps we are bound:
> Which is the cause (I make no doubt)
> Why numbers suffer in the gout.[18]

As well as being dangerous in themselves, ill-fitting footwear hindered mobility and caused foot complaints, both of which prevented the wearer from getting exercise. A. F. M. Willich noted that 'such cessations of exercise are extremely detrimental to the health in general, and that they may be registered among the causes disposing to the gout'.[19] Walkers in sensible footwear apparently did not succumb to the condition, unlike those who were conveyed around town in a carriage or a sedan chair.[20]

The causes of gout therefore had a class inflexion. Different types of arthritis apparently affected different classes: Lord Chesterfield noted that 'gout is the distemper of a gentleman; whereas rheumatism is the distemper of the hackney coachman'.[21] Gout related to diet and lifestyle, so was primarily associated with the classes of society who could afford rich food, copious alcohol and a sedentary existence. Satirical prints featuring gout almost exclusively focus on the aristocracy and gentry, and poke fun from the assumed perspective of the commoner. Fat, elderly gentlemen are depicted at heaving tables, consuming large quantities of wine, meat and other expensive dishes, while under the tablecloths their swollen, bandaged legs rest on footstools.[22] The moral critique of their gluttony is often quite pointed: gouty priests count their tithe income while starving parishioners wait outside (Figure 5.3); and justices of the peace barely look up while poor defendants plead their case.[23] Their sin is not just gluttony, since gout was linked to venery: a voluptuary strikes a bargain with a bawd for a girl's virginity;[24] a 'Bad Man' in flannels is confronted by the figure of Death;[25] and some of

Figure 5.3 *Thomas Rowlandson,* The Tithe Pig *(1799). The Metropolitan Museum of Art, New York City: The Elisha Whittelsey Collection, The Elisha Whittelsey Fund, 1959.*

Rowlandson's depictions of gouty men are positively pornographic.[26] In erotic prints, the bulbous gouty limbs are almost attractive, mirroring the shapeliness of women. The message often seems to be that gout was a source of sexual frustration for its male sufferers, who sought an outlet for their desires.[27] Other artists delighted in depicting old men, who were confined to their chair, while behind their backs their servants ran riot or they were cuckolded by their younger wives (Figure 5.4).

While satire was generally judgemental about gout, for many it was almost socially aspirational. One humorous anecdote concerned a lowly ensign on half pay, who was determined to be taken seriously as a gentleman: 'he flannels his leg and hops with a stick, to countenance, with an imaginary gout, the holes in his shoe'. When confronted about his shabby appearance, he retorted, 'I'd have you to know, Sir, that when I'm not afflicted with the gout, I can dress as well as any gentleman in the corps.'[28] Gout was a sign of distinction, a 'gentlemanly disorder'.[29] Because it was believed to be partly hereditary, it was a mark of

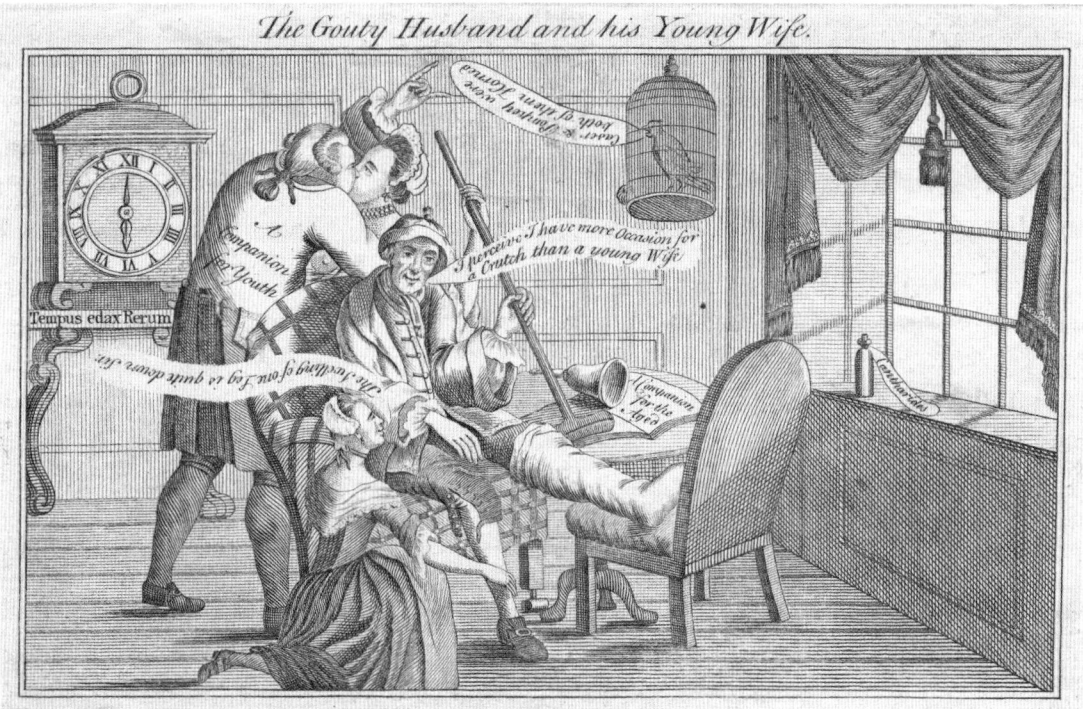

Figure 5.4 Anon., The Gouty Husband and His Young Wife *(1760s). Image courtesy of the Lewis Walpole Library, Yale University.*

good breeding. Some sufferers of gout congratulated themselves on their good fortune, since gout had the reputation of preventing other disorders. Gout helped to balance the humours and so could potentially head off more serious illnesses, not to mention the unwelcome attentions of doctors.[30] Walpole consoled himself that 'the gout certainly carries off other complaints', although David Turner wonders whether this was a coping strategy on his part.[31] Nevertheless, the attitude prevailed that gout was best endured, so assistive objects such as shoes and flannel helped to reduce its pain and inconvenience in the meantime.

All of the representations of gout that we have considered thus far have been of men, since Georgians regarded gout as a masculine complaint. Of the many satirical prints featuring gout, only a handful feature women.[32] It is certainly true that men are more predisposed to gout than women: oestrogen increases the removal of uric acid by the kidneys, so women rarely get gout before the menopause. But some Georgian women did suffer from gout,[33] so their almost complete absence from the cultural record was political rather than biological. Porter and Rousseau argue that disorders were gendered in this period: 'Thus, if a woman's functions were essentially reproductive, it was natural that disease would principally assail her central organ, her womb: hence hysteria. Men, by contrast, were made for action. Their diseases would more likely hit at their mobility: hence gout.'[34] Gout was therefore a disease of masculinity rather than of males. At a time when men's claims to dominate the public sphere were being grounded in their masculine stations and their very bodies,[35] their constant association with gout seems rather deliberate. Men's dress in the eighteenth century rendered gout peculiarly visible. Whereas women could conceal a swollen leg under long skirts, men's legs were constantly on display in breeches and stockings that hugged their form. Even when the breeches ensemble went out of fashion, patrician men replaced it with figure-hugging boots and high-waisted pantaloons. Eighteenth-century ideals of male beauty emphasized the shapely leg, which would enable the polite gentleman to move and dance in a graceful way.[36] A swollen, flannelled leg, terminating in an outsize shoe and forcing a hobbling gait, was therefore a highly visible sign of the disorder.

Besides being associated with public men and the social elite, gout was political in other ways. The body was a common metaphor for the state, and political problems were commonly conceived of in terms of illness within a shared language of the 'constitution'.[37] As with the humoral body, the Polybian constitution was characterized by balance, whereby every branch of the political system was checked by another. This was upset by 'corruption', both in a financial and moral sense: the language of 'Old Corruption' was very pungent, suggesting decay and putrescence. The presence of gout within the political body therefore suggested that it was not functioning as it should. Moreover, classical political theory placed great emphasis upon virtue, since a healthy polity required independent patriots who would be vigilant against any threats to the community. Great empires could be brought low by vice and luxury; and contemporary critics were quick to draw parallels between the fall of the Roman Empire and the precariousness of its British equivalent. Given that gout was a symptom of the gluttony and indolence of the ruling classes, it was a direct example of how luxury was creating a constitutional weakness in both a physical and a national sense.[38] Eighteenth-century Britain witnessed periodic panics about effeminacy, immorality and national weakness – usually in response to the nation's fluctuating fortunes in war – and these concerns focused on the physical bodies of its male citizens.[39]

Gout threatened the independence on which Georgian gentlemen so prided themselves. As well as reducing their mobility and their capacity for public service, it placed them in a dependent relationship with the servants and relatives who cared for them, whom as head of household they were supposed to be governing. Turner notes that Walpole sometimes used overtly political language to describe his condition.[40] As he wrote to Montagu in July 1765: 'Bodily liberty is as dear to me as mental, and I would as soon flatter any other tyrant as the gout, my whiggism extending as much to my health as to my principles.'[41] Walpole was frustrated when gout prevented him from attending parliament and he reports receiving visits from political allies at home, 'when I was so extremely ill and full of pain, that I scarce knew they were there'.[42] It was the lot of gout sufferers that they could only receive visitors; they could not venture out themselves, so much of the political and social life of the time was barred to them.

The most famous literary gout sufferer of the century responded to this lack of mobility by going on an expedition. The Welsh country squire Matt Bramble is the central character of Tobias Smollett's epistolary masterpiece, *The Expedition of Humphry Clinker* (1771). Bramble is a hypochondriac who is plagued by gout and writes about it at length to his regular correspondent, Dr Lewis. Smollett himself was a medic who fretted about his own health and Bramble is often thought to be a version of the author. Bramble is irascible and, as his nephew notes, 'his being tortured by the gout may have soured his temper'.[43] Sufferers were notoriously touchy and, in the holistic understanding of the body, gout disordered the personality as well as the physical constitution. Bramble is restless and unwilling to suffer at home, so he takes his household on the road. They call into resorts such as Bath, Harrogate and Scarborough, in order to take the waters, but none of these improve his health, and he instead comments on the follies that he finds in the spa towns (Figure 5.5).

Bramble is particularly repelled by London, where he perceives only luxury, disorder and illness. The proprietors of the capital's pleasure gardens must be in league with the doctors and the undertakers, he surmises, given how many 'gouts, rheumatisms, catarrhs and consumptions are caught in these nocturnal pastimes'.[44] This is 'Country' politics in a nutshell, where the city is the seat of vice and death, while bracing virtue and liberty is to be found in the countryside. Bramble's symptoms subside the

Figure 5.5 *Charles Grignion I, after Thomas Rowlandson, 'Men Dancing in a Coffee House, an Illustration from Tobias Smollett's* The Expedition of Humphry Clinker' *(1793). The Metropolitan Museum of Art, New York City: The Elisha Whittelsey Collection, The Elisha Whittelsey Fund, 1959.*

further he travels from London, and it is only when he experiences the simple hospitality of Smollett's native Scotland that his physical and mental health really improve:

> I am persuaded that all valetudinarians are too sedentary, too regular, and too cautious – We should sometimes increase the motion of the machine, to *unclog the wheels of life*; and now and then take a plunge amidst the waves of excess, in order to case-harden the constitution. I have even found a change of company as necessary as a change of air, to promote a vigorous circulation of the spirits, which is the very essence and criterion of good health.

Gout was a constitutional disorder of the circulation, so Bramble gets things moving again by travelling around the political body of the nation. Throughout the novel, the gouty Bramble is personified by his shoes. His younger relatives chide him as 'old Square-toes' – alluding to the outdated shoe worn by the old-fashioned – and his constant companion on his travels is his wide gouty shoe.[45]

Gouty shoes

Various treatments for gout were practised in the eighteenth century. Sufferers could take medicines such as Dr James's Powder, or apply poultices to the affected area. Like Bramble, they could take the waters at a spa or bathe in the sea. Most sufferers seem to have tried a combination of treatments, with a regimen of diet and exercise. Gout sufferers were prescribed temperance and a simple diet of milk, porridge and vegetables (which is similar to that currently suggested by the NHS).[46] Clearly podagra impedes locomotive exercise but there are records of patients using dumbbells.[47]

However effective these treatments proved to be, gout would generally return so most patients used assistive objects during its attacks to ease the pain and mitigate its impact. Cushions, footstools and easy chairs provided some relief for the immobile, and other assistive technologies aided mobility. Wealthy sufferers could travel by carriage, some adapted for the purpose.[48] Wheeled chairs were developed known as 'bath chairs', named after the medical resort. Some were small carriages drawn by a pony, whereas others were closer to a modern wheelchair and were pushed by someone else, typically a servant. There is an example of a self-propelled 'gouty chair' in the Victoria and Albert Museum, with a retractable footrest and winding handles for the patient to operate: this would have provided a modicum of independence, but it would only be able to move slowly across short distances.[49] Walking sticks and crutches were commonly used as mobility aids. Crutches became sturdier and more elaborately crafted.[50] In comic literature and satirical prints, they became a weapon with which the irascible gouty patrician could beat the object of his annoyance. Like the outsize shoe and the swollen leg, they were part of the visual repertoire of gout: mid-century caricature was highly emblematic, and William Pitt the Elder (1708–78) is often identified by his crutches.[51] Women used them too: Elizabeth

Seymour Percy, Duchess of Northumberland (1716–76) relied on assistive devices to limit the impact of gout on her travels around Europe. As she reported: 'I got a pair of new crutches, with which I was so charmed, and used so often, that I brought on a fresh fit of pain in my left foot.'[52] It was fashionable for the elite to carry a walking cane in the eighteenth century, but these fell from favour in the nineteenth as they were medicalized and identified with invalidity.

We should also consider footwear as a form of assistive technology. All sufferers of podagra had to contend with what they should wear on their feet. Swelling in their feet meant that they could not wear one or both of their usual shoes, and swelling in the lower leg would make boots impossible too. Percy recorded that she had her foot measured during one attack: 'the ancle was thirteen inches and a half, the instep eleven inches, and at the root of the toes it was ten inches and a half'.[53] Sometimes it would not be possible to wear a shoe at all, but this would hamper mobility and restrict the sufferer to indoors. If he or she wanted to move around or venture out, then there were various footwear options available.

Firstly, the sufferer could wear a gouty shoe. These were constructed along similar lines to conventional shoes, so they would be straight lasted with leather uppers with stiffer leather for the soles. They would, however, be much larger than usual, in order to accommodate the swollen foot and also thick stockings or layers of flannel. Belolan notes that there was no single pattern for such shoes, since they would typically be made on a one-off basis, and every wearer had different requirements.[54] Bespoke footwear was expensive, so this was only a solution for the well-to-do. In subsequent centuries, the mass production of assistive footwear would make them more accessible, but at the cost of standardization. Elizabeth Guffey and Bess Williamson argue that this 'reduced design possibilities for non-standard bodies': 'Modernism had little room for bodies and abilities that existed outside of statistical averages, standardized forms, and other narrowly defined ideals.'[55] It is therefore not the case that the history of disability is one of progress, as eighteenth-century assistive technologies were typically more individualized than those available today.

Gout shoes were distinctive for their size and shape. Sometimes called 'wide shoes', their proportions were different to regular footwear.[56] Fragments of gout boots were recovered from the grave of Abraham Favenc during the excavation of the crypt of Christ Church Spitalfields. The soles are almost half as wide as they are long, which is much wider than a conventional shoe.[57] Wearing such a large shoe would have given the wearer an awkward gait, particularly if they were only afflicted in one foot. Prince Hoare's stage play of 1800, *Indiscretion*, concerns the elderly widower Sir Marmaduke Maxim and his plans to marry again. The younger characters cruelly tease him for his gout, and his shoes and crutches are exploited as comic props. They imagine him approaching a lady 'with all the dignity of a gouty shoe' and challenge him to walk across the room:

> *Max*. That I will directly – plague on the rascal, where has he put my crutches? – oh! there they are. My dear friend, your arm a moment – there, just to get up, because – oh! [*expresses pain, takes his crutches, leans on Burly, rises and walks*]

Bur. How long have you been in that gouty shoe?

Max. Eh! about ten years.

Bur. Say twenty; and you were no youngster when you first were thankful for the gout, as a substitute for a long catalogue of daily infirmities.[58]

The large shoe was visually incongruous, and caricaturists exaggerated this yet further in their depictions of gouty men. William Pitt the Younger (1759–1806) suffered with the gout, like his father. But, whereas caricature in 1760s had relied on symbols like crutches, artists of the 1790s such as James Gillray emphasized facial and bodily features in order to convey meaning about their subjects. Pitt was a drinker – a likely contributor to his gout – so was always caricatured with ruddy cheeks and a pocked nose. He was tall and thin, so caricaturists conveyed his illiberal political tendencies with an emaciated frame. This was further underlined by swollen, bandaged legs and huge gout shoes. Some caricatures of Pitt, such as Isaac Cruikshank's *The Treasury Spectre, or the Head of the Nation in a Queer Situation*, where a skeletal Pitt is plied with alcohol in a bath chair, are quite grotesque (Figure 5.6).

Figure 5.6 *Isaac Cruikshank,* The Treasury Spectre, or the Head of the Nation in a Queer Situation *(1798). Image courtesy of the Lewis Walpole Library, Yale University.*

Gouty shoes may have been inelegant, but they empowered their wearers. This poem celebrates the 'Great Shoe' in the language of liberty:

> Thou wide machine! the cripple's standing prop,
> Thou thing between a splatterdash and a slop!
> For the free born and the free living too,
> Thou mere reverse of Gallia's wooden shoe . . .
> Hail young Gambado! Lo, I venture free
> My worst leg foremost while upheld by thee.
> With haughty airs I measure every stride,
> And throw the crutch disdainfully aside. [59]

If the wooden shoes supposedly worn by the French symbolized oppression, then the leather shoes worn by Englishmen connoted political liberty. For the gout sufferer, the gouty shoe promised individual freedom in a more direct sense, since it emancipated them from the tyranny of gout. Just like the 'gambado' worn by horse riders, the gouty shoe provided protection for the foot and leg, enabling the wearer to stride out as before. Gout shoes were essential when travelling and servants had to remember to pack them.[60] Walpole was in Paris in 1765, and was able to 'limp about enough to amuse my eyes' with the aid of 'a stick and a great shoe'.[61]

Most gout shoes would be made from the same materials as conventional shoes, so the uppers would be black or brown cowhide. These would be sufficiently sturdy and waterproof to be worn outdoors if they were polished regularly, but some sufferers opted for shoes made of softer materials for greater comfort when indoors. Gout shoes could be made of silk and the Spitalfields dig recovered a pair of woollen slippers.[62] George IV famously suffered from gout and wore outsize slippers. Two pairs of these are preserved in the Museum of London, one in silver and one in gold (Figure 5.7). Metallic thread covers the vamps of soft cloth, and they are lined with silk for additional comfort. The soles are leather so they could be worn outside, and the design is elegant, so it is possible that they were used for ceremonial occasions when he had the gout. While not strictly gout shoes, they are an example of how those who could afford bespoke footwear could have it made to their medical requirements.

We can trace the severity of Walpole's condition by what he wears on his feet. In October 1765 he had a bad attack and so was unable to wear shoes, but 'my feet promise themselves the mighty luxury of a cloth shoe in two or three days'.[63] Two weeks later he reports that 'I have not yet had anything but cloth shoes on.' Four months later he reports looking forward to going out to a function in soft leather shoes: 'I have got my cravat and shammy shoes. Adieu!' This cycle would be repeated in future years. In December 1774 he writes: 'No child was ever so delighted to go into breeches, as I was this morning to get on a pair of cloth shoes as big as Jack Harris's.'[64] Given that buckled leather shoes and breeches were a mark of adult masculinity, not being able to wear them was infantilizing, and the ritual of donning them once again was loaded with gendered meaning.

Gout Shoes and Disability 109

Figure 5.7 *Two pairs of slippers owned by George IV, 1820s. Museum of London.*

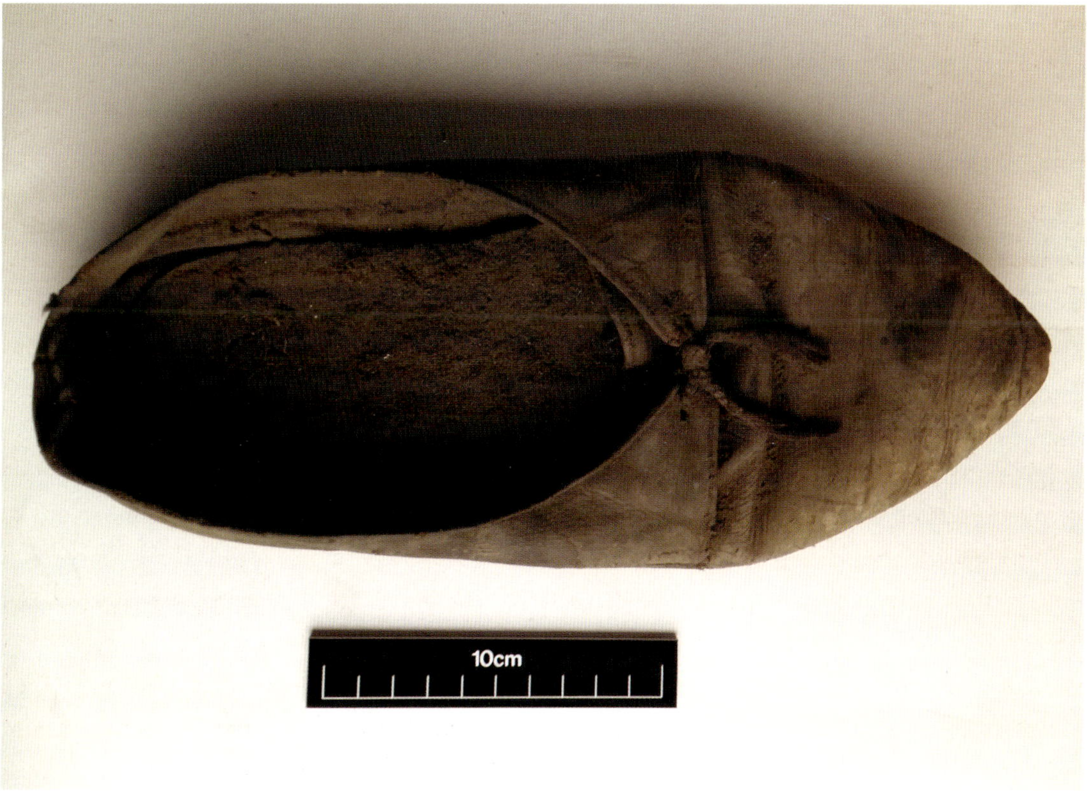

Figure 5.8 *Gout shoe, eighteenth century. © Chatham Historic Dockyard.*

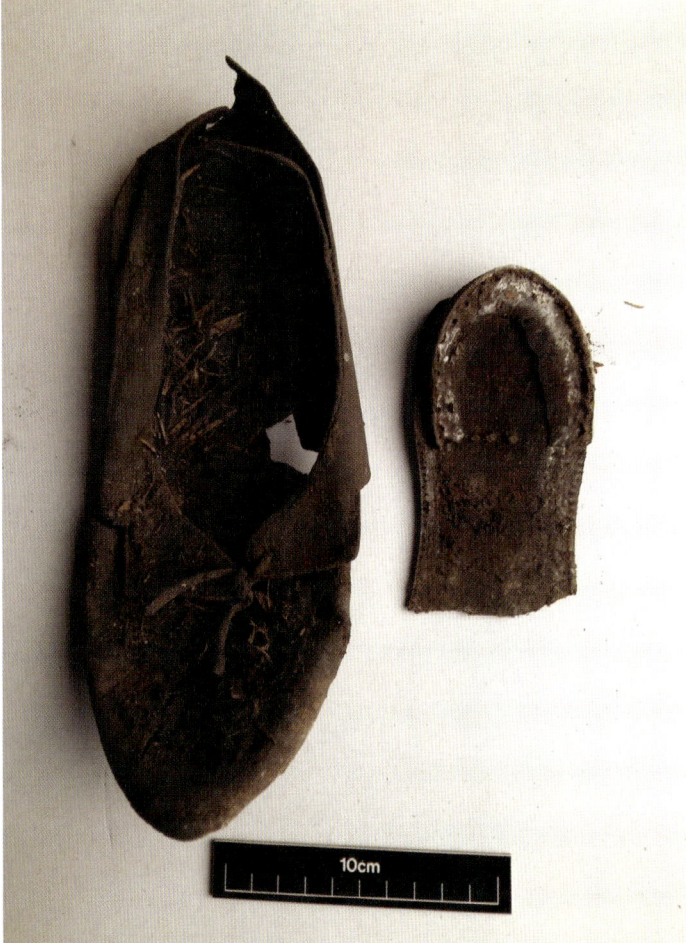

Figure 5.9 *Gout shoe (slit), eighteenth century. © Chatham Historic Dockyard.*

Not everybody would be willing or able to commission a pair of gout shoes. In this period, most gout sufferers improvised.[65] The 'cut shoe' was a common solution, whereby an existing shoe would be cut with long slits to create more room.[66] Given the expense of new shoes, it is likely that this would be done to an old shoe, which would in any case be worn in and more comfortable. Two shoes, which were possibly a pair, were recovered from excavations at Chatham Dockyard (Figures 5.8 and 5.9). Although they are straight lasted and have a pointed toe, they have a very broad construction. They are made from supple leather, and they are fastened by a tie rather than the usual buckle, so they could have been made specifically for a gout sufferer. One of them has slits in the upper (Figure 5.9), which the wearer probably made himself to gain further relief.

Cut shoes with their tell-tale slits often appear in gout caricatures. A popular cartoon that was often reprinted was 'Geoffrey Gambado Esq.' (Figure 5.10). This depicts a horse rider who is unable to enjoy

Figure 5.10 Henry Bunbury, Geoffrey Gambado, Esq. (1786). Image courtesy of the Lewis Walpole Library, Yale University.

his favourite pastime due to the gout. Pictures of riding adorn the walls and his riding boots are hung on the wall, unused. Gout has ironically denied him the one form of exercise he practised that might have kept the condition at bay. His gout is signalled by his slit shoe, his crutch and his wild hair and eyes, suggesting that this is a form of 'flying gout' that has spread to other parts of his body. Porter and Rousseau note that the print dates from a period when gentlemen 'proved their rank by riding', so not being able to do so had implications for masculinity and social status.[67]

Flannel and bootikins

The final type of foot and legwear that we shall consider here are swaddlings and soft boots. These were usually made from flannel, which was manufactured from wool at this time, instead of cotton as it is today. They were a different order of assistive technology to gout shoes, since they were intended to cure gout rather than just facilitate mobility. Binding one's legs in flannel had several benefits. From a cosmetic and practical point of view, layers of flannel could conceal unsightly lumps and absorb any excretions.[68] Their primary purpose was to apply pressure to the limb and induce perspiration, with a view to treating gout and reducing swelling. As a comic poem of the time related:

> And this I hold most highly good
> To smooth and purify the Blood,
> And to help forward Perspiration.
> Hence Flannel came so much in Fashion.
> And by Experience I have found,
> That Flannel Socks all the Year round
> Will help to make the Gouty sound.

Since gout was regarded as a disorder of the humours, sweating purged ill humours from the affected area and rebalanced the body's fluids. Flannel was known to be warm and to absorb liquid, so was ideal for the purpose. This writer, therefore, recommended flannel and rest:

> So lye and sweat till all is o'er,
> Nature will work through ev'ry Pore;
> And th'Humours vanish'd, soon you'll find
> Nothing but Weakness left behind.
> The Joint late stiff you now can move,
> Supple and lithy as a Glove . . .
> And in a few Hours upon that Foot
> Put on a Sock, Stocking, Shoe, or Boot.[69]

At the end of the eighteenth century, physicians commonly recommended flannel as part of a wider regimen to tackle gout. Willich argued that flannel was ideal for the purpose, since it 'is but a slow conductor of *external* heat to the body, and it attracts the more easily *internal* heat, and allows it to evaporate the more readily, as it is possessed of a greater porousness than any other texture'. Furthermore, 'it keeps the vessels of the skin constantly open, makes them perspire freely, and admits but a very small degree of external moisture'. As well as being warm and absorbent, it carried away sweat – which Georgians believed to be acrid and corrosive – unlike materials like cotton that would become saturated. Willich gave this method his wholehearted recommendation: 'By continuing it sufficiently long, and having it frequently changed, the most obstinate gouty and rheumatic complaints have been removed, and many imminent dangers averted by its constant use.'[70] The market for gout remedies was crowded, however, and alternatives were available. An advertisement for 'Holland's New-invented Fleecy Hosiery, For the CURE of the Gout and Rheumatism' promised more warmth and elasticity than flannel.[71]

Some gout sufferers fashioned flannel into a boot (Figures 5.3 and 5.4). Walpole used 'bootikins' to relieve the gout, which was a soft boot of layered flannel covered with oiled silk. He wrote that, 'I have suffered so dreadfully, that I constantly wear them to diminish the stock of gout in my constitution.' His method was as follows: 'You must tie them as tight as you can bear, the flannel next to the flesh; and when you take them off, it should be in bed. Rub your feet with a warm cloth, and put on warm stockings, for fear of catching cold while the pores are open.'[72] Walpole was evangelistic about their benefits to his gouty correspondents, who were not always convinced. Mann thought them 'enormous' and found the heat unbearable, without producing the desired perspiration.[73] Cole was concerned that the bootikins would drive the gout from the leg to the head or the stomach, which would be much more dangerous.[74] This was a common objection in the medical literature. The physician William Smith was concerned that they upset the heat equilibrium of the body and had other harmful effects: 'The boodikin is very improper, and certainly destroys the elasticity of the fibres, inspissates [that is, thickens or congeals] the juices, renders them more acrid, and leaves the affected parts, where it is applied, benumbed.'[75] Walpole swore by them, however, and would not be dissuaded. As he wrote to Mann: 'The bootikins do not cure the gout, but if they defer it, lessen it, shorten it, who would not wear them?'[76]

Walpole was realistic about the extent to which he could heal his gout. Even today, it is a condition that can only be managed rather than cured. His use of bootikins did apparently provide him with some relief and – equally as important – a sense that he was able to do something about the chronic pain that beset him for much of his life. Perhaps their rather infantilizing name made light of the loss of independence that came with the gout. Assistive technologies can therefore add to our understanding of the ways in which people in the past experienced illness and disability, the practical strategies that they employed to manage them, and the ways in which they perceived their ailments and those of others.

In particular, it is relevant to focus on footwear. As well as being a century of gout, it was also a time when walking went from something to be avoided, to an activity that was regarded as fashionable and healthy among the patrician classes. As the urban renaissance transformed the city into somewhere in which one might conceivably want to walk – with paved streets, squares and promenades – shoe design at the end of the century also made walking more comfortable and viable, or at least for men. Heels lowered, leather uppers became more supple, and boots could be worn for walking rather than just riding, as we saw in Chapter 4. Given the increasing normativity of walking, gout was a particularly cruel complaint, with socially exclusionary implications for those who suffered from it. The increasing viciousness of caricature art towards the end of the century only served to highlight how far gout sufferers departed from the social and bodily ideal of the time. The gouty shoe was an awkward article because it represented a compromise between mobility and pain relief. 'Flannel and patience' may have been the medical advice, but many gout sufferers would not have been willing or able to follow it. Material objects, therefore, help historians to look beyond the prescriptions in medical literature, and to engage with how people lived with disability in the past.

Notes

1. George Ramsay, *The Encyclopedia of Anecdotes, Illustrative of Character and Events, From Genuine Sources* (London, 1828), 624.
2. Sally Osborn, 'Gout Gets Even', *History Today* 64, no. 4 (April 2014), 3–4.
3. David Turner, *Disability in Eighteenth-Century England: Imagining Physical Impairment* (Abingdon: Routledge, 2012), 1–3.
4. Ott, 'Disability Things', 119.
5. Roy Porter and G. S. Rousseau, *Gout: The Patrician Malady* (New Haven, CT: Yale University Press, 1998), 254.
6. Elizabeth Seymour Percy, *A Short Tour Made in the Year One Thousand Seven Hundred and Seventy One* (London, 1775), 49.
7. Nicole Belolan, 'The Material Culture of Gout in Early America', in *Making Disability Modern: Design Histories*, ed. Bess Williamson and Elizabeth Guffey (London: Bloomsbury, 2020), 20.
8. Chris Mounsey, 'Variability: Beyond Sameness and Difference', in *The Idea of Disability in the Eighteenth Century*, ed. Chris Mounsey (Lewisburg, PA: Bucknell University Press, 2014), 7.
9. Virgil Nemoianu, 'The Semantics of Bramble's Hypochondria: A Connection Between Illness and Style in the Eighteenth Century', *Clio* 9, no. 1 (1979): 39–51, 41.
10. Turner, *Disability*, 106.
11. Porter and Rousseau, *Gout*, 283. See also Calinda C. Shely, '"The Distemper of a Gentleman": Grotesque Visual and Literary Depictions of Gout in Great Britain, 1744–1826' (PhD thesis, University of New Mexico, Albuquerque, 2016).

12 Porter and Rousseau, *Gout*, 50.

13 William Smith, *A Sure Guide in Sickness and Health, in the Choice of Food, and Use of Medicine* (London, 1776), 168.

14 Anon., *On Clothing* (Manchester, 1797), 16.

15 William Cole to Horace Walpole, 29 August 1778: W. S. Lewis (ed.), *The Yale Edition of Horace Walpole's Correspondence*, 48 vols (New Haven, CT: Yale University Press, 1977), vol. 2, 113.

16 Horace Mann to Horace Walpole, 30 January 1775: Lewis (ed.), *Correspondence*, vol. 10, 79.

17 Anon., *On Clothing*, 18–20.

18 Anon., *The Flower-Piece: A Collection of Miscellany Poems. By Several Hands* (London, 1781), 228.

19 A. F. M. Willich, *Lectures in Diet and Regimen, Being a Systematic Inquiry into the Most Rational Means of Preserving Health and Prolonging Life* (London, 1799), 260.

20 Gay, *Trivia*, 29.

21 Philip Dormer Stanhope, Earl of Chesterfield, *Lord Chesterfield's Letters*, ed. David Roberts (Oxford: Oxford University Press, 1992), 341.

22 James Gillray, 'French Liberty, British Slavery' (1792): British Museum.

23 Carrington Bowles, 'The Secret Discovered, and Dick Brought Before a Country Justice' (1770): British Museum.

24 Jabez Goldar, after John Collet, 'The Sacrifice' (1767): British Museum.

25 T. Chambers, 'The Bad Man at the Hour of Death' (1783): British Museum.

26 Thomas Rowlandson, 'The Concert' (1812): Victoria and Albert Museum.

27 Porter and Rousseau, *Gout*, 248.

28 Philip Dormer Stanhope, *Lord Chesterfield's Witticisms: Or, the Grand Pantheon of Genius, Sentiment and Taste* (London, 1773), 60, 61.

29 Anon., *The Cabinet; or the Selected Beauties of Literature* (Edinburgh, 1825), 394.

30 Belolan, 'Material Culture', 21; Porter and Rousseau, *Gout*, 74.

31 Horace Walpole to William Cole, 25 April 1775: Lewis (ed.), *Correspondence*, vol. 1, 366; Turner, *Disability*, 115.

32 For example, 'The Triumph of Sentiment. The Prospect of Happiness, or a Picture for Dotards' (1800): Lewis Walpole Library, Yale University.

33 One of the most detailed memoirs of a gout sufferer was by Elizabeth Seymour Percy, Duchess of Northumberland: *Short Tour*.

34 Porter and Rousseau, *Gout*, 5.

35 McCormack, *The Independent Man*.

36 Harvey, 'Men of Parts'.

37 George Rousseau, 'Political Gout: Dissolute Patients, Deceitful Physicians, and Other Blue Devils', *Notes and Records of the Royal Society* 63, no. 3 (2009): 277–96.

38 For example, 'The GOUT and other Disorders, cured by a Dream', in *The Twelfth-Day Gift: Or the Grand Exhibition* (London, 1767), 150–3.

39 Turner, *Disability*, 4; McCormack, *Embodying the Militia*, ch. 1.

40 Turner, *Disability*, 110.

41 Horace Walpole to George Montagu, 28 July 1765: Lewis (ed.), *Correspondence*, vol. 10, 164.

42 Horace Walpole to George Montagu, 3 October 1770: Lewis (ed.), *Correspondence*, vol. 10, 320.

43 Tobias Smollett, *The Expedition of Humphry Clinker*, ed. Lewis M. Knapp and Paul-Gabriel Boucé (Oxford: Oxford University Press, 1984), 8.

44 Ibid., 89.

45 Ibid., 339, 50. Emphasis in the original.

46 'Gout': https://www.nhs.uk/conditions/gout/ (24 August 2023) (accessed 7 May 2024).

47 R. Michael James, 'Health Care in the Georgian Household of Sir William and Lady Hannah East', *Historical Research* 82, no. 218 (2009): 694–714 (707).

48 Belolan, 'Material Culture', 19.

49 Gouty chair (*c*. 1800): Victoria and Albert Museum W.103-1978.

50 Porter and Rousseau, *Gout*, 268.

51 For example, Anon., 'The Wheel of Fortune: Or, England in Tears' (1766–67): British Museum.

52 Percy, *Short Tour*, 34.

53 Ibid., 35.

54 Belolan, 'Material Culture', 28.

55 Elizabeth Guffey and Bess Williamson, 'Introduction: Rethinking Design History through Disability, Rethinking Disability through Design', in *Making Disability Modern: Design Histories*, ed. Elizabeth Guffey and Bess Williamson (London: Bloomsbury, 2020), 1, 3.

56 Smollett, *The Expedition of Humphry Clinker*, 28.

57 Theya I. Molleson and Margaret Cox, *The Spitalfields Project: Volume 2: The Middling Sort* (York: Council for British Archaeology, 1993), 199.

58 Prince Hoare, *The Indiscretion: A Comedy* (London, 1800), 21, 41.

59 Christopher Pitt, 'On a Great Shoe being lent to him in a Fit of the Gout by Mr Muston the Grocer', *The European Magazine*, May 1800, 389.

60 An old bachelor's servant 'never forgets his gouty shoe in travelling': Anon., *The Cabinet*, 394.

61 Horace Walpole to George Montagu, 16 October 1765: Lewis (ed.), *Correspondence*, vol. 10, 180.

62 Jez Reeve and Max Adams, *The Spitalfields Project: Volume 1: Across the Styx* (York: Council for British Archaeology, 1993), 112.

63 Horace Walpole to Lady Hervey, 13 October 1765: Lewis (ed.), *Correspondence*, vol. 31, 59.

64 Horace Walpole to Henry Seymour Conway, 28 October 1765, 12 January 1766, 31 December 1774: Lewis (ed.), *Correspondence*, vol. 39, 23, 44, 235. The reference to Jack Harris may concern the pimp who supposedly inspired *Harris's List of Covent Garden Ladies* (London, 1757 to 1795).

65 Belolan, 'Material Culture', 27.

66 David Garrick, *The Clandestine Marriage: A Comedy* (London, 1778), 24.

67 Porter and Rousseau, *Gout*, 277.

68 Belolan, 'Material Culture', 27.

69 William Brownsword, *Laugh and Lye Down; Or, A Pleasant, but sure, Remedy for the Gout, Without Expence or Danger* (London, 1789), 20, 30.

70 Willich, *Lectures*, 230, 240.

71 'By His Majesty's Royal Letters Patent' (Handbill, *c.* 1800).

72 Horace Walpole to William Cole, 25 April 1775: Lewis (ed.), *Correspondence*, vol. 1, 366.

73 Horace Mann to Horace Walpole, 30 January 1775: Lewis (ed.), *Correspondence*, vol. 10, 79.

74 William Cole to Horace Walpole, 30 October 1777: Lewis (ed.), *Correspondence*, vol. 2, 70.

75 Smith, *Sure Guide*, 139.

76 Horace Walpole to Horace Mann, 9 January 1775: Lewis (ed.), *Correspondence*, vol. 24, 70.

6
Dancing feet

MERCUTIO
   Nay, gentle Romeo, we must have you dance.
ROMEO
   Not I, believe me: you have dancing shoes,
   With nimble soles; I have a soul of lead
   So stakes me to the ground I cannot move.[1]

Shoes are central to the dance. In order to move freely, the dancer should either go barefoot or – the next best thing – wear shoes that are light and flexible. Mercutio has 'dancing shoes / With nimble soles', a pun that highlights the contrasting mood of his friend Romeo. As Shakespeare suggests, dancing is both a physical and emotional state, so says a great deal about the relationship between the body and the self. Dancing shoes are material objects with physical properties that are central to their function: although they are a decorative element of formal wear, they have to fulfil certain technical requirements. This chapter will therefore think about dancing shoes from the Georgian period as objects, by examining surviving examples from the time, but will also consider the souls who wore them. Dancing as a social practice is loaded with meaning, and we shall see how the dancing shoe sheds light on gender, self-identity and social relations.

If shoes are central to the dance, then dance is central to our image of the Georgian period. It was part of the social world of the elite, in particular, and no period drama set in the era is complete without a ball. Dances were major social occasions that presented opportunities for sociability, displays of status and supervised mixing between the sexes (Figure 6.1). Their significance for Georgian society goes deeper than that, however. At a time when dancing masters also taught their charges how to walk and comport themselves, dance arguably holds the key to understanding manners and social interactions, and how these were lived in bodily terms. Studying dance as a physical practice therefore sheds light on wider historical issues but, in order to do that, it is necessary to interrogate the physical objects that enable the body to dance.

Figure 6.1 *George Cruikshank,* City Ball at the Mansion House *(1 November 1824). Image courtesy of the Lewis Walpole Library, Yale University.*

As we have seen throughout this book, the shoe has a uniquely close relationship with the body. It supports the whole body and influences the way that it moves; and the body in turn affects the shoe, moulding it to the shape and motions of the foot. These relationships are heightened when additional physical demands are placed on the shoe by activities such as running, climbing, marching or dancing. Specialist footwear enables wearers to undertake these tasks, balancing the requirements for grip, protection or support, against the flexibility offered by going barefoot. Historians of sporting footwear have shown how the development of tennis shoes or football boots involved practical considerations as well as ideological ones.[2] These include the materials used, the nature of the construction and the overall design – which of course also has to meet the requirements of cost, branding and fashion. Indeed, Hilary Davidson argues that dancing apparel should be considered as 'a kind of decorative sporting dress'.[3]

The dancing shoe is therefore an example of an object that has to be studied first-hand in order to be understood. Happily, a number of examples have survived and are accessible in museum collections. I have been able to study these shoes in detail and, by handling them, I have assessed their flexibility, their weight and other physical properties that were essential to their function. In this way, the researcher is able to 're-experience' a past phenomenon, that would otherwise only be accessible at a remove via representations.[4] Of course, it could be re-experienced even better if it was worn while dancing, and re-enactors of historical dance gain a unique insight into this bodily practice by wearing faithful replicas. Clearly this is not possible with fragile originals that have to be examined under museum conditions.

As well as thinking about the dancing shoe in a material way, we shall also explore the symbolic and emotional significance that it had for its wearers. Shoes often say a great deal about their wearer: Maureen Turim argues that shoes 'become a privileged metonymy, one that portrays much about sexuality, desire, class, and culture'.[5] The dancing shoe carries a particular sexual charge, given the fetishization of the foot and the powerful sexual dynamics in dancing (which is, of course, an opportunity for courtship). The female dancing shoe is commonly the subject of fairy tales, such as Cinderella's glass slipper, or the red shoes that punish their wearer by forcing her to dance. They therefore take on magical properties and carry moral judgements about female sexuality.[6] Men's dancing shoes tend not to feature in fairy tales, nor were they a comment on their wearer's sexual morality, but they were, nevertheless, symbolic in very gendered ways. We shall see that they often featured in social satires that sought to highlight their target's departure from true manliness, suggesting his frivolity or addiction to foreign vices.

There is little historical work on dancing shoes. The footwear that women wore when dancing is sometimes mentioned in surveys of women's footwear or dress.[7] This chapter will primarily focus on the shoes that men wore for dancing and formal occasions, which have received even less historical attention. Arguably they are more interesting, because they are more distinct from general wear than women's, particularly in the later Georgian period when male and female footwear styles really diverged. As Colin McDowell notes, 'men's shoes became increasingly suitable for both indoor and outdoor wear and women's shoes remained appropriate only for indoors', highlighting the polarization of their expected social roles.[8] But, while this is true in general terms, the indoor shoes that men wore at the dance were very different to the shoes that they would have worn to get there. The dancing shoe, therefore, has a special significance for late Georgian masculinity.

Dance, masculinity and Georgian society

The ball is evocative of the Georgian age. The movements of the dancers, the style of the clothing and the refinement of the manners are all synonymous with an era that is often characterized by its elegance and poise. Dances were important social occasions and drew attendees from miles around. Besides the great ballrooms of cities like London and Bath, dances were also held on private estates and in civic spaces throughout the land, forming an important fixture in the county's social calendar. They played a particularly important role in the lives of young women, since such events were central to the marriage market. Dances provided an opportunity for respectable mixing between the sexes in a public and chaperoned environment, where suitors could make introductions, and couples could enjoy limited physical contact.

As such, dancing was 'a near universal skill' among respectable Georgians.[9] It was an important part of a young woman's education, along with other 'accomplishments' that would make her marriageable, such as music, needlework and a smattering of polite French.[10] Dancing masters taught girls not only how to dance, but also how to walk, curtsy and comport themselves. Girls' education was frequently criticized for its frivolity, whereas that provided for boys was supposedly more practical and geared towards success in public life. But it is striking that dance played an important part in male curricula too, alongside accomplishments such as horse riding, fencing and public speaking that would prepare them for life as a gentleman. Advertisements for boarding schools boasted of 'the Attendance of good Masters' for dancing.[11] This training continued on the Grand Tour, whereby young gentlemen were sent to the Continent to complete their education and acquire polish. George Herbert, eleventh Earl Pembroke (1759–1827) was sent on tour when he was twenty, and his father wrote to his tutor with a list of his requirements: 'High Dancing for Limbs, & Activity. The best & most active Dancing Master.' A later letter underlined this: 'I can not neither give up my anxiety for your bodily person. Pray stick close at Turin to dancing, fencing, riding, & Tennis.'[12] As with girls, dance for boys was part of a wider regime of corporeal discipline.

This focus on acquiring 'accomplishments' and cultivating the body made sense within Georgian notions of masculinity (Figure 6.2). From the late seventeenth century, promoters of 'politeness' had urged men to lose their rough manners and their propensity towards aggression and, instead, to adopt a common code of refined manners.[13] In this way, men could meet as equals to discuss public questions without coming to blows, and this would supposedly elevate and purify political discourse. One way that men could soften their manners was through conversation with women, so heterosocial events like dances were important to this project. The kind of bodily cultivation that one could acquire from a dancing master was important in a further sense, since politeness involved presenting oneself to best advantage. A man could have all the virtue and genius in the world, but if he expressed himself clumsily then he would never bring this to bear. Politeness was therefore not a superficial front but was rather a means of synchronizing one's inner and outer virtues. The intended effect was manners that were 'easy' and 'natural'; in practice they were very studied, of course, but they were not supposed to look that way.

As the century wore on, many Georgians became sceptical of polite manners. Because anybody with a modicum of time and money could acquire the trappings of politeness, critics complained that it was difficult to tell who was a gentleman and who was not:

> The clown in rug or duffel can, at a moment's be furnished with a complete suit of lace or embroidery from *Monmouth-Street*; his long lank greasy hair may be exchanged in *Middle Row* for a smart bag or jemmy scratch; and his clouted shoes, with the rough hobnails in the heel and sole clumping at every step, may be transformed into a pair of dancing pumps at the *Yorkshire* Warehouse, or the *Old Crispin* in *Cranbourn Alley*.[14]

Figure 6.2 *Kellom Tomlinson,* Passacaille *from* The Art of Dancing *(London, 1735). Alamy stock photo.*

For critics like this, exchanging the traditional markers of status for exterior refinements had made society dangerously fluid. Worse still, it suggested that politeness might be superficial after all, concealing a lack of real merit and, when taken to excess, might slide into effeminacy. Might the foreign manners that men picked up on the Grand Tour, or learned from fashionably continental dancing masters, be corrupting true English virtue? 'Patriots' argued that the ruling classes were addicted to foreign manners and luxuries, and that this was undermining their manliness and public spirit.[15] They argued that the people's true interests would be supported by men of sincerity and independence, qualities that were essential to the balanced constitution that protected the Englishman's liberties.[16] Foreign material goods were anathema to this indigenous model of masculinity: one satire lambasted 'dancing-pumps, made of the skins of frogs, originally designed for Monsieur *le Dauphin*'.[17]

Such criticism did not, however, diminish the appeal of dancing, nor the need for elite men to refine their bodies and manners. Men recognized the effect of dancing on their overall appearance, their 'mien'. Anthropologists of dance have noted that the way people walk in a given society relates closely to the style of their dances, and that both of these are influenced by what they wear on their feet. As Paul Spencer notes, this can have implications for social power: 'the element of manneristic display, typified by the exquisite nuances of the minuet, emphasized the exclusiveness of the privileged ranks threatened by an aspiring middle class'.[18] Dance styles embody a society's way of life, and the dancing body is peculiarly expressive as a mode of communication.[19] A review of a dance manual in 1824 noted that dance 'has often been called the poetry of motion', and, given the popularity of dance at the time, 'the poetry of the present moment is, therefore, the poetry of the feet'.[20] Men were conscious of the need to make a good impression at the ball. Captain Gronow noted an incident at Almack's, in which an elderly gentleman attempted a particularly tricky step with a younger partner and 'unluckily fell heavily on the floor'. When another gentleman mocked him for this, it was taken as a slight upon his honour that resulted in a challenge to duel.[21]

One masculine sphere in which dance was particularly prized was the military. Dances were an important part of regimental life, emphasizing the physical prowess, fine appearance and heterosexual gallantry of the soldier. When the militia comes to town in *Pride and Prejudice*, the Bennett sisters are excited about the prospect of socializing with eligible young men.[22] Dances were also used to entice potential recruits with the prospect of glamour, sexual adventure and fine uniforms. John Cowell recalls that this was among his pleasanter tasks when he was an officer in the Guards:

> Hail, sweet recruiting service! pleasing toil,
> Ball-room campaigns, tea-parties, dice, Hoyle:
> Ye days when dancing was my only duty,
> Envied by cits, caress'd by every beauty,
> Dreaded by mothers, trembling at each glance
> Shot at by their daughters going down the dance.
> Ah! how tormenting memory sad reviews
> Those happy hours when in silk hose, thin shoes,
> And sprightly scarlet, much the tailor's pride,
> I loung'd and flatter'd at the fair one's side![23]

The 'thin shoes' that he wore to dances contrasted with the heavy boots that he would otherwise have worn, so were synonymous with the occasion.

As well as being important for military sociability, dance was thought to have a more utilitarian function. Dance cultivated the body in much the same way as military drill.[24] Manuals for dance and drill were remarkably similar, codifying the minutiae of bodily movement in text and image. In the era of the musket, soldiers spent hours practising complex loading operations, and marching around the parade ground in the geometric formations that were required for concentrated volley fire. This type of warfare required a body that was elongated and supple, and which could move in unison with other bodies, so dance had calisthenic and coordinating functions. Histories such as John Weaver's *An Essay Towards an History of Dancing* (1712) noted its warlike origins, particularly in ancient Greece and Rome where it was used to prepare young men's bodies for war. Modern military theorists revered the Classics, and often argued that these lessons similarly applied in the present day.[25] Dance often featured in the curricula of military academies. At Lewis Lochée's Royal Military Academy in Chelsea, students were instructed in the 'exercise of the body in dancing, fencing, riding and the manual exercise during the day; and in the evening in sports for the improvement of agility and strength'.[26] Most officers in this period did not receive any formal training, but the accomplishments of an officer were essentially those of a gentleman, so dance would have been an expected part of their education.

Dance was therefore important for exercise and bodily cultivation. Weaver argued that dance 'regulates the Carriage; invigorates the active Motion of the Limbs; fashions the Body with a just and graceful Position, and enlivens and unbends the Mind.'[27] Medical writers agreed that this type of exercise was useful for these reasons. One treatise argued that foot complaints were thus particularly serious, since a lack of locomotion or exercise 'must soon impede the due development of every other faculty, whether bodily or mental!' It continued that it was important to pay attention to the health of the feet, since the body placed considerable strain on them, particularly when walking or dancing: 'Thus it happens that we alternately throw the whole weight of the body upon the toes, especially the great toe of each foot; but more particularly in dancing as the whole frame is placed upon the tip-toe which resists, for a long time, its continual pressure.'[28] The dances of the time often involved bouncing on the balls of the feet. This placed great stresses upon the foot's delicate bone structure, which is designed to absorb shock and maintain balance. In order to facilitate this, dancing shoes needed to have supple uppers and soles. It also strained the legs and ankles, which similarly had to absorb the impact and spring back. Given that balls went on into the early hours, dancing was physically exhausting and placed great demands on the body, so dancers required strong legs. Legs were important to Georgian notions of male beauty, and dancing showed off the calves and thighs.[29] The Earl of Bute was a famously good dancer with famously good legs, and his full-length portrait by Joshua Reynolds displays them to best effect. His robes of state part to reveal shapely legs in figure-hugging silk stockings and breeches, atop a fine pair of white leather shoes with dazzling buckles (Figure 6.3).

Not everybody enjoyed this level of physical perfection and many Georgians suffered physical ailments that would have prevented them from dancing. As we saw in the previous chapter, Horace

Figure 6.3 *Joshua Reynolds,* John Stuart, 3rd Earl of Bute *(1758). Alamy stock photo.*

Walpole suffered from gout in his feet, like many men of his class. But he was also fond of dancing and was determined that gout should not stop him. As he wrote to Lady Ossory in July 1781:

> Poor human nature, what a contradiction 'tis! today it is all rheumatism and morality, and sits with a death's head before it: tomorrow it is dancing! – oh! my Lady, my Lady, what will you say, when the next thing you hear of me after my last letter, is, that I have danced three country-dances with a whole set forty years younger than myself!

He then added this qualification:

> Danced – I do not absolutely say, *danced* – but I swam down three dances very gracefully with the air that was so much in fashion after the battle of Audenarde, and that was still taught when I was fifteen, and that I remember General Churchill practising before a glass in a gouty shoe.[30]

Elsewhere he writes about dancing in his '*big shoes*'.[31] As we saw in the previous chapter, the gout shoe is another example of footwear that is designed for a particular purpose, in this case to accommodate and protect the swollen foot. Gout shoes are large and inelegant articles, which would have been incongruous at a dance. They helped Walpole to move, but sufferers like him would not have moved very gracefully with a painful foot condition and big, heavy shoes. Gout shoes were quite different to the dancing shoe which, as we shall now see, was designed to fulfil very different requirements.

Dancing shoes

The shoes that men and women wore to dances in the Georgian period should be considered as part of a wider ensemble of formal dress. Women would wear the latest fashions to the ball, and would go to great lengths to present themselves to best advantage. In *Northanger Abbey*, Catherine Morland is subjected to 'three or four days' of shopping and preparation before she attends her first ball in Bath.[32] Fashions changed over the course of the century. The structured dresses, stays, petticoats and heeled shoes of the mid-eighteenth century would presumably have been quite challenging to dance in. Women's dress shoes up to this period had a high heel of carved wood: as a poem of 1753 noted, 'Mount on French heels when you go to a ball, / 'Tis the fashion to totter and show you can fall.'[33] Heels lowered towards the end of the century, until women were effectively wearing flats. Sometimes called 'Grecian sandals', these were similar to today's ballet pumps, and were either slip-ons with no fastening, or were tied to the leg with ribbon. These were very insubstantial and were only really suitable for wearing indoors, but were ideal for dancing: indeed, McDowell relates the popularity of dance at this time to the fashion for flats.[34] The classicism of Regency dress for women involved lighter fabrics and looser-cut clothing, and Davidson notes that the ballroom was one place where this was an advantage.[35]

No such advantage was enjoyed by men, who continued to wear heavy, tailored fabrics to dances throughout this period. Dances were notoriously hot, since many people were packed into a room that was lit by candles, and men would have sweltered their way through hours of dancing in thick woollen coats. Men's clothing styles altered over the eighteenth century – coats shortened, the trouser leg lengthened and fabrics became less colourful – but the basic model remained the three-piece suit, which was the established uniform of the patrician male. Men's clothing was essentially outdoor wear, which meant that it was practical for wearing both indoors and out, embodying men's ability to bestride the public and private spheres. Although it had its downsides for vigorous indoor activity, in some ways it suited the dance styles of the time. The tailored jackets and waistcoats suited the fact that the upper body was not supposed to move a great deal, and poise had to be maintained at all times. The bottom half had much more flexibility, since dances were all about the legs and feet. Silk stockings and dancing shoes lengthened the appearance of the leg; breeches allowed a full bend at the knee and those made from knitted silk provided further elastication.[36] Trousers and pantaloons paired with boots came into fashion at the end of the eighteenth century; these were less flexible, but stockings and breeches remained the favoured wear for formal occasions and for dances.

As a dancing manual put it, 'no gentleman should dance in their boots'.[37] Indeed, venues maintained a strict dress code in order to enforce this. In 1806, Margate Assembly Rooms had the following rule: 'That on ball-nights no ladies be admitted into the great room in habits, nor gentlemen in swords, boots, or pantaloons; military gentlemen excepted.'[38] Not all venues were so accommodating to the military, and even the Duke of Wellington was once famously turned away from Almack's for wearing trousers.[39] The military itself was punctilious about dress, and military men would continue to wear the formal ensemble to dances even after pantaloons became the norm for their uniforms. We can see this in the standing orders of the garrison at Gibraltar in 1803, which only permitted officers to wear shoes and stockings when attending a ball:

> The Shoes to be worn with Buckles of the same coloured metal as the buttons of the Coat; & no other Waistcoat or Breeches, but Kerseymere, (& *these with Regimental Buttons*) are to be worn; nor *any* deviation allowed from the other established Rules for Dress, such as wearing Nankeen, or Linen, small Cloths, Neck Cloths, Stocks, or Shoes *with strings*, small Swords, &c.[40]

Dress historians have written about the close relationship between military uniforms and male fashions, and the red coat of the army or the blue of the navy was essentially in the style of the patrician coat of the day. A military coat was a marker of a gentleman – something that lowly officers from humbler backgrounds used to their social advantage – so military men would wear their uniforms at both military and civilian occasions: indeed, if a man wore a red coat to a ball then his masculine social qualifications were assured.

The shoes that men wore for dancing changed over the course of the eighteenth century, in a similar way to women's. For much of the century, men danced in the shoes that they wore for formal indoor occasions: as Margo DeMello notes, dancers 'wore fashionable shoes of the time rather than special dance shoes'.[41] These were not necessarily the black shoes that men would wear outdoors, and could be made from soft imported leather in bright colours, or be covered in pattered fabric. At the beginning of the century, these could have quite high heels: an example from 1710 has heels of around two inches (Figure 2.4). The fashion for high-heeled dancing shoes was mocked in *The Tatler*:

ADVERTISEMENT.

A Stage-Coach sets out exactly at Six from Nando's *Coffee-House to Mr.* Tiptoe's *Dancing-School, and returns at Eleven every Evening, for* 16 d.

N. B. *Dancing Shoes not exceeding Four Inches Height in the Heel, and Periwigs not exceeding Three Foot in Length, are carried in the Coach-Box* gratis.[42]

A few years later, heels had lowered to around an inch.[43] Whereas women's heels were carved from wood and could be quite shapely, men's were constructed of stacked leather, but they could be covered with a coloured panel so they looked similar. Some elite men followed Louis XIV's fashion for red heels,[44] which enjoyed revivals throughout the century, as we can see in Bute's portrait of 1758 or the 'macaroni' craze of the 1770s.

It was from the 1790s that the shoes men wore for dancing really diverged from everyday wear. At a time when men were increasingly adopting boots for general wear, the dress shoes that they would have danced in were quite different; it is at this point that we can talk about a distinctive 'dancing shoe' for men. Men wore a sleek pump for dancing, with soft black leather uppers, thin soles and heels of only a few millimetres (Figure 6.4). These were of a similar shape to women's shoes, when footwear fashions were otherwise very different for men and women. This raises the question of how dancing as an activity – and the dancer as a man – would have been gendered at the time. But we shall see that men's dancing shoes remained distinctive from women's in several key respects, and this did little to undermine the manliness of dancing.

These shoes were not suitable for wearing outdoors, in a period when even paved streets could be muddy and uneven. One commentator in 1811 noted the dilemma of what to do when invited to a dance at a house near one's own: should you walk there in your dancing shoes?

> Alas! all your *tiptoe* caution avails you not; for within ten paces of your place of destination, your unwary feet light on a mischievous loose stone, vulgarly called a *beau-trap*, which most plentifully bespatters with mud your dancing pumps and white silk stockings. In this delectable situation, your preferable alternative is to return, change your dress, order a coach, and set out again, cursing your folly at not having taken the resolution to ride at first.

This results in a late arrival at the ball, meaning that you miss the first few dances with your favourite partner, to whom you are 'obliged to make a thousand apologies for your apparent rudeness and

Figure 6.4 *Man's black leather, buckle latchet shoe, 1820s. Image courtesy of Northampton Museum and Art Gallery.*

neglect'.⁴⁵ It was common for dancers to travel to the ball in outdoor shoes and change when they got there, carrying their dancing shoes in a bag or in their pockets.⁴⁶ Invitations to balls encouraged guests to bring their dancing shoes with them, suggesting that they were carried rather than worn.⁴⁷ Whereas women had the option of overshoes or pattens – which protected delicate footwear by raising it above the muddy street – men did not tend to wear them, perhaps because they could not conceal these unsightly metal and wood contraptions under skirts. They were therefore more likely to change their footwear. In Thomas Otway's stage comedy, *Friendship in Fashion*, the foppish Caper berates his servant for forgetting to bring them: 'Rascal, Dog, Fool; when did you even know me to go abroad without my Dancing-shoes?' He added, 'I would no more dance in a pair of shoes that we commonly wear, than I would ride a Race in a pair of Gambado's.'⁴⁸

Embodied objects

The rest of this chapter will focus on the dancing pump that men wore from the 1790s onwards. As we have seen, they are a true 'dancing shoe', in contrast to the indoor shoes worn by previous generations of dancers, which were very different in terms of their appearance, their physical properties and the experience of wearing them. In particular, we shall think about the dancing pump as a material object that had a close relationship with the dancing body that it shod.

Most dancing pumps were made of leather. The uppers were typically thin, supple leather, rather than the thick cowhide from which outdoor shoes and boots were usually made. This allowed the foot to flex and, in particular, to bend at the toe, which was so important for Georgian dance styles. An example in Northampton Museum dates from the 1820s and contains a label revealing the maker as Doggett and Taylor, from Berkeley Square in London (Figure 2.6). It is therefore a high-end example, which we can see from the fine stitching and materials. The leather uppers are notably supple, as are the kid leather lining and insole, which would have provided additional comfort when dancing. The sole is made from tougher leather than the upper, as was usually the case, but it is nevertheless thin and flexible, with only a slight rise to the heel. This would allow the foot to bend, having a minimal impact on the natural movement of the naked foot, and would allow the foot to feel the ground: perfect for an even wooden dancefloor, but offering little protection for rough surfaces. This is a worn example, with evidence of movement at the toe and wear to the sole and insole, so has likely been used for dancing. Given the likely socio-economic status of its owner, he had probably stopped wearing it when it looked tatty, rather than because it had worn out.

Like many such shoes, the uppers are shiny black leather. Patent leather dominated men's footwear fashions from the 1790s onwards. Nowadays, patent leather is covered in plastics, but in the 1790s manufacturers started to treat tanned leather with black dye, boiled linseed oil and varnish.[49] This was intended to improve waterproofing, but also gave the leather a high shine, which became hugely fashionable. Shiny black shoes or boots were key to the classical male fashions of the Regency, where dark colours were nevertheless presented with immaculate tailoring and attention to detail, showing off the masculine body to best effect. Importantly, they were also known to be expensive to buy and maintain, so patent leather shoes were an example of conspicuous consumption. Using early nineteenth-century techniques, it was difficult to apply patent without making the leather stiff, which would make them unsuitable for dancing, so it could not be done cheaply. The uppers had then to be regularly blacked in order to preserve their waterproofing and suppleness, and to retain their colour and shine. This dirty and dangerous job – for the ingredients were often poisonous – fell to servants and bootblacks, so the immaculate shine of elite footwear was maintained by the working classes.[50]

Occasionally, men's dancing shoes were made from other materials. This example from the 1840s has uppers of soft fabric on thin leather soles (Figure 6.5). The material is possibly cotton, which has been machine woven into a tight weave, producing a fabric that is very supple. The colour is now dark brown but it may originally have been black, so could have been worn with the formal evening ensemble. The cream-coloured linings are also fabric, possibly linen, although there is a section at the heel of soft buckskin for additional comfort. It was much more common for women's shoes to be made from materials other than leather, such as silk or wool. These also came in a wide variety of colours, to

Figure 6.5 *Man's black, woven textile pump, 1840s. Image courtesy of the Alfred Gillett Trust.*

match their outfits; Austen records owning shoes in green, pink and white. These shoes were very insubstantial and were very much for indoor occasions. In 1811 Lady Bessborough wrote with shock that Lady Lansdowne, 'with her three daughters following her, wrapt in thin lace veils, blue silk shoes, and bare-headed, not only braved the wind and rain, but the sharp stones and muddy streets of Southampton, and the astonished gaze of the passengers'.[51] Although the shape of men's dancing shoes was similar to women's in the early nineteenth century, their colours and materials were visibly different – and, crucially, men had more suitable footwear options for other activities.

Dancing shoes could have a range of fastenings. If they were sufficiently well fitted, then they might not need fastenings at all: before the availability of elastic, this probably meant that the shoe had been expensively made to measure. Most dancing pumps had either laces or a buckle. As we saw in Chapter 1, buckles had been the standard fastening for shoes from about the 1690s, until they rapidly fell from fashion in the 1790s.[52] In the era of the French Revolution, buckled shoes came to be associated with the excesses of the aristocracy, along with the stockings-and-breeches ensemble, which was replaced with the wartime fashion for boots and trousers. Although they ceased to be part of general male wear, buckles were retained for formal occasions, along with the traditional ensemble, and continued to be worn at court and for balls. By the early nineteenth century, buckles were fairly small, so did not present an impediment to dancing like the enormous examples of the 1770s and 1780s. The jewel-encrusted 'Artois' buckles of this period were large and heavy, so would have been awkward for dancing, as we saw in Chapter 1.[53] These expensive articles were also vulnerable to loss or damage:

Lord Bellamont's diamond buckles 'very seldom lasted him above two or three minuets, from a certain elasticity in the muscle of his foot at a certain passage in his performance, which bent, if not broke them almost of course'.[54] While they could be impractical, buckles were visually important, and provided men with an opportunity to decorate their otherwise plain shoes. At a candlelit dance, the jewels in buckles reflected the light, drawing attention to the movements of the feet. Buckled shoes could therefore highlight a man's skill as a dancer and the contours of his body, as well as his wealth.

Dancing shoes were much less substantial than those that men generally wore, so wore out more quickly. Although they would only be worn for certain occasions, and only indoors, the nature of Georgian dances put great strains upon footwear. Surviving examples often show wear to the soles and uppers, and it is likely that they were thrown out when shabby or broken, so heavily worn examples have not survived. At the same time, wearers would probably want to wear them in before taking them to a dance, or they could be uncomfortable. Ballet dancers today spend hours wearing in their pumps, which they then wear out after only a few hours of performing. As Gerri Reaves notes: 'Through force and sweat, the dancer accelerates the disintegration that results in the shoe's absorption by the dancer's body, its being owned by the foot. As the shoe's glue dissolves, its surfaces fray, and its inner cotton lining tears, it becomes the dancer's skin, an encasement that hides the individuality of the foot.'[55] Given how quickly they wore out, consumers often bought multiple pairs at a time. When Prince Frederick was living in Hanover, he struggled to obtain fashionable articles, so often wrote to his brother George to request them: 'order Blaymer a dozen pair of accoutreman leather soaled dancing pumps and two pair of half boots of the shining leather; all this is besides the usual complement which I ordered to be sent quarterly before I quitted England'.[56] The consumption of the royal family could, of course, be extravagant, but it is likely that other wealthy men did this too. Women were certainly known to buy several pairs of pumps at once, since theirs wore out even more quickly.

The wear that is visible in surviving examples of dancing shoes is a record of the dancer's body. As with all worn shoes, this provides a unique primary source about their wearer. Stretching and wear reveal the shape of the wearer's foot and show where the weight of the body has been exerted. As a record of bodily movement, it sheds light on the nature of dance in this period: heavy wear to the sole in the area of the forefoot shows how dancers were required to bounce on the ball of the foot, and how much pressure this exerted on their feet. Worn shoes also contain other bodily traces. Stains in the lining reveal where the wearer has sweated, which is to be expected when performing a vigorous activity in heavy clothes in a warm room (Figure 6.6). Georgians were preoccupied with perspiration, since it was a way for the humoral body to purge and stay healthy: they were therefore concerned about anything that obstructed perspiration, or that retained unhealthy matter close to the body. We have seen that medical treatises on foot health put a great deal of emphasis on the materials used for socks and stockings:

Figure 6.6 *Man's brown leather shoe, 1830s.* © 2024 Bata Shoe Museum, Toronto, Canada.

Persons who have a great tendency to perspire in their feet, and who increase this exhalation by much walking or dancing, will no doubt be sensible of the contaminated parts of their cotton, thread, or silk stockings, which, instead of removing the exhaled matter, actually absorb it; bring it in contact with the skin; preserve it in a state of heat favourable to putrefaction; and check all further perspiration.[57]

This writer does not therefore recommend wearing silk stockings to a ball, favouring materials such as wool that carry the moisture away, but it is unlikely that fashionable gentlemen would have followed such advice.

As we have seen throughout this book, shoes had an effect on the body, as well as the other way around. The chapter has shown how dancing shoes had specific physical properties that enabled the dancer to move in the way that was required by the dances of the time. The light and supple construction of the dancing shoe means that less of the naked foot's natural flexibility is compromised, in contrast with an outdoor shoe that is intended to be protective and hardwearing. On the other hand, these shoes could be constraining as well as enabling. Until the 1790s, most shoes were straight lasted, and some later examples were too (Figure 6.7). The shape of this sole is symmetrical, and it is also very narrow with a pointed toe. Happily for the wearer, the soft uppers would have accommodated the

Figure 6.7 *Man's black leather tie shoe, c. 1830. Image courtesy of Northampton Museum and Art Gallery.*

shape of the foot, but they would have been very tight. Even shoes that are lasted to the left or right appear strikingly narrow. It was fashionable to have the appearance of small feet, so it is likely that many dancers suffered in ill-fitting footwear. Chapter 2 showed how treatises on chiropody from this period bemoaned the design of footwear and highlighted that it was the cause of medical complaints such as corns and bunions.[58]

The dancing shoe, therefore, has the potential to tell us a great deal about Georgian society. As a physical object, it sheds light on the nature of dance, in terms of how the body was supposed to move and how it was supposed to look. It highlights the strains that dancing placed upon the body and provides a historical record of a body's movements, ailments and excretions. The dancing shoe is a very good example of a shoe that was designed for a particular purpose and, therefore, the shoe itself provides a valuable insight into that activity. It also gave men of the polite classes an opportunity to show off their bodies and their physical accomplishments, in tight-fitting footwear that drew attention to the contours of their feet and legs. This highlighted their elite masculinity, in contrast to working men who were shod in bulkier and clumsier utilitarian footwear, which did not enable them to move with the grace of a public man. If dance was central to fashionable society in the early nineteenth century, then the shoes that Georgians wore to those dances provide us with a fascinating way into their world.

Notes

1 Act 1, scene 4, ll. 13–16: William Shakespeare, *Romeo and Juliet* (London: Bloomsbury, 2017), 51–2.

2 Elizabeth Semmelhack, 'From Lawn Tennis to Eugenics: A History of Women and Sneakers', *Costume* 53, no. 1 (2019): 92–109; Jean Williams, 'Given the Boot: Reading the Ambiguities of British and Continental Football Boot Design', *Sport in History* 35, no. 1 (2015): 81–107.

3 Davidson, *Dress in the Age of Jane Austen*, 200.

4 Fairhurst, 'Eighteenth-Century Women's Shoes', 21.

5 Maureen Turim, 'High Angles on Shoes: Cinema, Gender and Footwear', in *Footnotes: On Shoes*, ed. Shari Benstock and Suzanne Ferriss (New Brunswick, NJ: Rutgers University Press, 2001), 58.

6 Davidson, 'Holding the Sole'.

7 Fairhurst, 'Eighteenth-Century Women's Shoes', 22–5; DeMello, *Feet and Footwear*, 27.

8 Colin McDowell, *Shoes: Fashion and Fancy* (London: Thames & Hudson, 1989), 32.

9 Davidson, *Dress in the Age of Jane Austen*, 199.

10 Anthony Fletcher, 'Polite Accomplishments', *History Today* 58, no. 4 (April 2008): 439.

11 *Gazetteer and New Daily Advertiser*, 16 May 1764.

12 Lord Herbert (ed.), *Pembroke Papers (1734–1780): Letters and Diaries of Henry, Tenth Earl of Pembroke and His Circle* (London, 1939), 53, 187.

13 Klein, 'Politeness and the Interpretation of the British Eighteenth Century', 874–5.

14 *The Connoisseur. By Mr Town*, 77 (17 July 1755), 458.

15 Carter, 'An "Effeminate" or "Efficient" Nation?', 436–40.

16 McCormack, *The Independent Man*.

17 *The Literary Magazine: Or Universal Review, for the Year MDCCLVII* (London, 1757), 393.

18 Paul Spencer (ed.), *Society and the Dance: The Social Anthropology of Process and Performance* (Cambridge: Cambridge University Press, 1985), 24.

19 Ted Polhemus, 'Dance, Gender and Culture', in *The Routledge Dance Studies Reader*, ed. Alexandra Carter (London: Routledge, 1993), 171–9.

20 *The Westminster Review* (January 1824), 213–14.

21 Gronow, *Reminiscences*, 73.

22 Jane Austen, *Pride and Prejudice*, ed. James Kinsley (1813; Oxford: Oxford University Press, 2019), 22.

23 John Stepney Cowell, *Leaves from the Diary of an Officer of the Guards* (London, 1854), 194.

24 McCormack, 'Dance and Drill'.

25 Robert Donkin, *Military Collections and Remarks* (New York, 1777); John Clarke, *Military Institutions of Vegetius* (London, 1767).

26 Lewis Lochée, *An Essay on Military Education* (London, 1773), 75. The 'manual exercise' was musket drill. See also J. E. Screen, 'The "Royal Military Academy" of Lewis Lochée', *Journal for the Society of Army Historical Research* 70, no. 283 (1992): 143–56.

27 John Weaver, *An Essay Towards an History of Dancing, in Which the Whole Art and its Various Excellencies are in Some Measure Explain'd* (London, 1712), 17.

28 Anon., *Art of Preserving the Feet*, xii, 191.

29 Harvey, 'Men of Parts'.

30 Horace Walpole to Lady Ossory, 25 July 1781: Lewis (ed.), *Correspondence*, vol. 33, 282–3. The 'battle of Audenarde' is likely the Battle of Oudenarde, 11 July 1708, which was fought (and won) by Charles Churchill, Duke of Marlborough.

31 Horace Walpole to George Montagu, 1 September 1760: Lewis (ed.), *Correspondence*, vol. 9, 293.

32 Jane Austen, *Northanger Abbey*, ed. by Marilyn Butler (1817; London: Penguin, 1995), 19.

33 Quoted in Swann, *Shoes*, 30.

34 McDowell, *Shoes*, 34.

35 Davidson, *Dress in the Age of Jane Austen*, 200.

36 Ibid.

37 Anon., *Country-Dancing Made Plain and Easy to Every Capacity* (London, 1764), 71.

38 Feltham, *A Guide to the Watering and Sea-Bathing Places*, 33, 356, 295.

39 Gronow, *Reminiscences*, 72.

40 Trench-Gascoigne, 'Extracts from the Standing Orders in the Garrison of Gibraltar (1803) (Continued)', *Journal for the Society for Army Historical Research* 2, no. 9 (1923): 127–8.

41 DeMello, *Feet and Footwear*, 89.

42 *The Tatler* 181 (May 1710), 329.

43 Swann, *Shoes*, 26.

44 Semmelhack, *Standing Tall*, 38.

45 'A Couple of Miseries', *European Magazine, and London Review* (London, 1811), 327.

46 Davidson, *Dress in the Age of Jane Austen*, 199; Mr Pratt (Samuel Jackson), *Family Secrets, Literary and Domestic* (Cork, 1800), 291.

47 *The Critical Review, Or, Annals of Literature* (November, 1811), 297.

48 Thomas Otway, *The Works of Thomas Otway, In Two Volumes* (London, 1718), 236–7. Gambados were heavy riding boots.

49 DeMello, *Feet and Footwear*, 234.

50 David, *Fashion Victims*, 116–19.

51 Jane Austen, *Jane Austen's Letters*, ed. Deirdre Le Faye (Oxford: Oxford University Press, 1995), 34, 51, 160, 543.

52 McCormack, 'So Manly and Ornamental'.

53 Hughes and Hughes, *Georgian Shoe Buckles*, 4.

54 George Hardinge to Horace Walpole, 13 April 1775: Lewis (ed.), *Correspondence*, vol. 35, 577.

55 Gerri Reaves, 'The Slip in the Ballet Slipper: Illusion and the Naked Foot', in *Footnotes: On Shoes*, ed. Shari Benstock and Suzanne Ferriss (New Brunswick, NJ: Rutgers University Press, 2001), 259.

56 Frederick to George, 24 March 1781: A. Aspinall (ed.), *The Correspondence of George Prince of Wales, 1770–1812*, vol. 1 (London: Cassell, 1963), 53–4.

57 Willich, *Lectures*, 242.

58 Anon., *Art of Preserving the Feet*.

7

The soldier's shoe

Writing at the time of the First World War, the army captain and physician Cecil Webb-Johnson argued that more attention needed to be paid to soldiers' footwear. This was of course highly relevant to the conditions of the Western Front, but to make his point he drew upon authorities from an earlier period:

> Napoleon said he made war with legs as well as arms. Marshal Niel thought good shoes as important for his infantry as good mounts for his cavalry. Saxe said that military tactics depended upon the feet of his soldiers. Wellington, when asked the most important part of a soldier's equipment, replied, 'firstly, a pair of good shoes; secondly, a second pair of good shoes; and thirdly, a pair of half soles'.[1]

Commanders recognized that providing suitable footwear for soldiers was therefore an important factor in military efficiency and, ultimately, operational success. Armies faced a significant logistical challenge in procuring a sufficient quantity of adequate footwear, in a range of sizes to fit a wide variety of feet and in delivering it to where it was needed. In practice, they sometimes failed to achieve this, with serious consequences for their campaigns.

Of course, it also had serious consequences for soldiers themselves. During the Napoleonic Wars, the provision of footwear was a common cause of complaint among the men. In the Peninsular campaign, in particular, soldiers marched huge distances while supply lines became very stretched, and soldiers frequently complained about the state of their footwear and the pain in their feet. John Cooper served with the 7th Royal Fusiliers, and his memoirs record blisters, cold feet and broken shoes. On 16 March 1811 he commenced a forced march 'over hilly stony roads . . . I hobbled on with the column, but I suffered dreadfully from hunger, thirst, little shoes, and blistered feet'.[2] The British Army's passage through Spain was marked in red, with blood from the feet of its soldiers.[3]

The study of military footwear is therefore important in both a strategic sense and in terms of the common soldier's experience: it should be central both to operational military history and to the social history of war, and is an example of how the two fields should be inseparable. To date, however, neither field has devoted much attention to footwear. Shoe history has more to say here. Alison Matthews David has shown how the material culture of shoes can provide important insights for the histories of social class and empire. She particularly focuses on the history of medicine, since military medicine in the era of the First World War became particularly preoccupied with foot health and shoe design, as we have seen.[4] In this chapter we shall apply these perspectives to an earlier period, showing how these were important concerns for armies in the eighteenth and nineteenth centuries.

Studying material culture in this area is a challenge due to the lack of surviving examples. Whereas Chapter 4 included many examples of military boots, these tended to belong to officers and – as we have seen throughout this book – the shoes that are preserved in museum collections are generally those worn by the elite. Finer examples were more likely to be kept, and the wealthy owned several pairs of shoes and so were less likely to wear them to destruction. Common soldiers, on the other hand, really put their footwear to the test and, in common with other plebeian wearers, wore their shoes until they could no longer be repaired, and had to be discarded. Huge numbers of shoes were produced for common soldiers over the course of the long eighteenth century, but hardly any have survived, and I have not been able to locate any that were available to handle.

This chapter therefore relies mostly on written forms of evidence. Alongside treatises from military and medical writers, and documents relating to military production and supply, it utilizes life writings in order to get an insight into soldiers' perspectives on their feet and footwear. Wearing shoes is a quotidian phenomenon that rarely gets written about but, in the conditions of war, the importance of footwear is such that it is commented upon much more frequently than in civilian writings. There are numerous memoirs written by common soldiers from the Napoleonic Wars. Whereas the perspective of the ordinary soldier would not previously have been deemed worthy of publication, his experience of the extremities of war was of great interest to the Romantic generation, and there was a huge market for these memoirs after Waterloo.[5] The genre does tend to emphasize suffering, so common soldiers mostly discuss their bad experiences of shoes, which may not be entirely representative. The rich detail here can nevertheless help us to understand the experience of shoe wearing in this period.

Military footwear

Soldiers are synonymous with their feet and what they wear on them. Infantrymen were 'foot soldiers' who served in 'regiments of foot' or 'marching regiments'. We still talk about 'boot camp' and 'boots on the ground'. This speaks to the importance of feet and footwear to the business of soldiering, particularly in the period before motorized transport. Some military writers recognized this, and emphasized footwear provision and foot care in their prescriptions for a well-run regiment. Robert Jackson wrote in 1804 that 'the feet are an essential part of the soldier's body' and that shoes, 'while they are sufficiently strong to endure the march', should also be 'sufficiently easy, so as not to confine the necessary play of the foot or injure parts by their pressure'.[6] As with all footwear, that worn by soldiers had to balance competing requirements. On the one hand, shoes had to be hardwearing and protective; on the other, sufficiently comfortable and flexible so as not unduly to impede locomotion. As military shoes, they had also to look presentable and uniform, even when subjected to the most extreme conditions.

The style of military footwear changed over the course of the Georgian period. Until the later eighteenth century, common soldiers wore shoes that would be similar to the black leather shoes worn by civilians of their social class. As such, they would be straight lasted with two straps that would be fastened by a buckle. In contrast with civilian buckle fashions, soldiers' buckles would have a plain metal ring (Figure 7.1). Shoes were sourced from a large number of manufacturers but were fairly uniform, as they worked to a standard pattern issued by the Clothing Board,[7] and we see specifications for the shoes in military orders and manuals. Orders issued to the troops in Flanders in 1745 stated that 'good marching shoes' should have 'a broad round toe, high quarters, and the buckle in the right

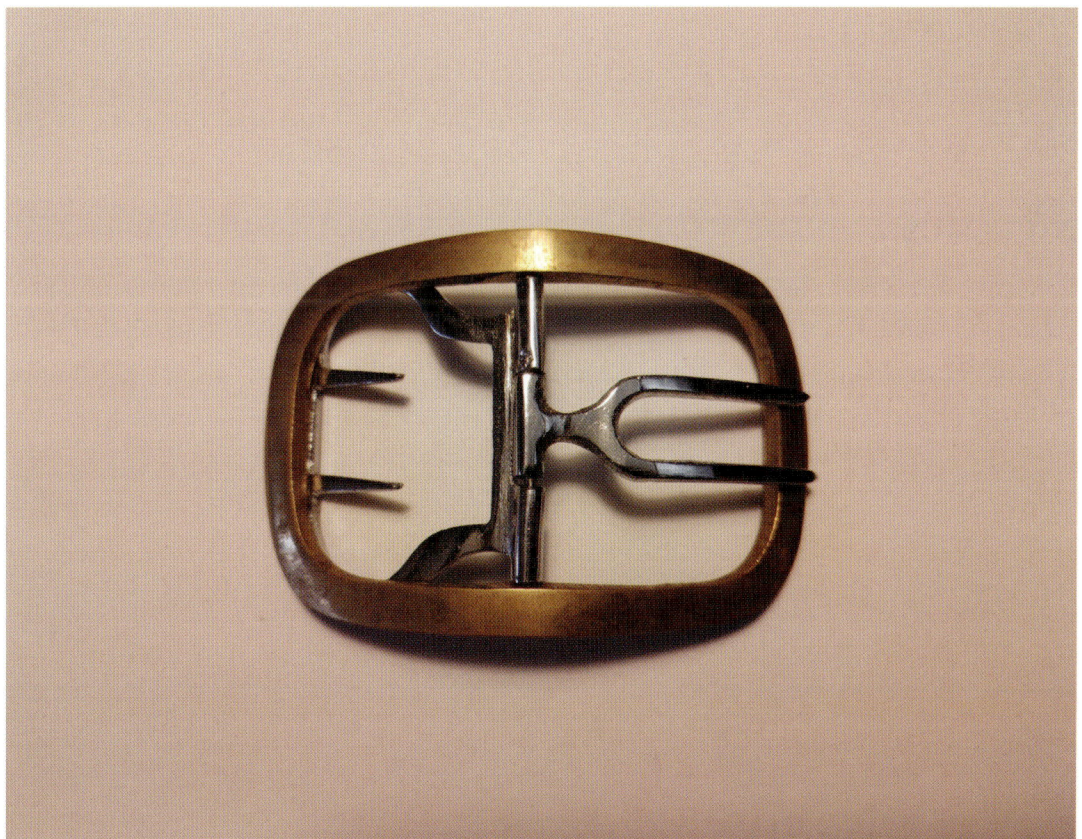

Figure 7.1 *Replica of a military shoe buckle from the late eighteenth century. Author's collection.*

place, not like the rope dancers'.[8] That was a dig at unmanly and un-English fashions, but was also a practical point since a buckle worn close to the toe would provide a less secure fastening than one higher up the foot. Bennett Cuthbertson's manual of 1768 stated that 'the toes should be round and flat; the straps large enough to fill the buckle; and the quarters high, tight and short'.[9] These shoes would therefore be broad and practical, with plenty of room at the front for the toes: this was important in shoes that were straight lasted, as narrow shoes would not accommodate the shape of the foot. A high-quartered shoe would come up close to the ankle, so would almost be a half-boot.

The standing orders of the 37th Foot in 1775 similarly stated, 'that they be sufficiently high quartered, that the buckle may never come out, from under the gaiter'.[10] Army shoes were worn in conjunction with gaiters that covered the ankle and the lower leg (Figure 7.2). These were made from linen but could be blacked with the same polish used on the shoes, so at first sight could look like boots: real boots were for officers, whereas privates wore this cheaper alternative. Military manuals emphasized their practical purpose. Jackson notes that 'it prevents sand and dust penetrating to the feet' and 'it keeps the shoe fast, embracing the ancle, in such manner, as to foster warmth, and give useful support to the parts which require such assistance'.[11] They therefore apparently had many of the advantages of boots, and further enhanced 'the good appearance of the leg'.[12] Manuals emphasized that they should be smooth and close fitting, and that they should cover the buckle to give an even appearance. Soldiers themselves were more sceptical about gaiters and suggested that they were mostly for show. Cooper complained that they were 'tight of course', like much of the uniform, and should he reach to the ground 'it would have been fatal to some article of his set-off. Nothing could be contrived worse for real service.'[13]

Another way that the military attempted to enhance their footwear was through the addition of hobnails and metal plates. Most of the wear to shoes is to the sole, so the addition of metal studs to the sole and a horseshoe-shaped plate to the heel made the shoes last longer (Figure 7.3). This was important on a long campaign and also helped to drive down costs. Hobnails also had the advantage of providing grip on muddy surfaces, in a similar way to studs on modern football boots, but they also made the boots heavy, noisy and slippery on hard surfaces. There was a class dimension to this: officers, needless to say, did not wear them; whereas the common men were shod with iron, just like the horses.[14]

As we approach the Napoleonic Wars, the buckle shoe of the eighteenth century was replaced by the laced half-boot. Changes in military uniforms related to wider changes in men's fashion and, indeed, helped to drive them. As we have seen, from the 1790s buckles went out of fashion, and the stockings-and-breeches ensemble was replaced by pantaloons or trousers. With the exception of the men of the Highland regiments, who continued to wear buckled shoes (Figure 7.4), soldiers wore laced ankle boots, referred to as 'half-boots' or indeed 'shoes'.[15] The 1800 dress regulation for the Royal Staff Corps prescribed that NCOs, privates and drummers should wear 'Half Boots, which are to come

Figure 7.2 *Sir William Young, sketch of a Grenadier Private, Royal Buckinghamshire Militia (King's Own) (1793). Buckinghamshire Military Museum Trust.*

Figure 7.3 *Charles Hamilton Smith,* Soldiers of the 1st Regiment of Foot Guards in Marching Order, 1812 *(1812–15). S. P. Lohia Collection.*

Figure 7.4 *Franz Joseph Manskirch,* Anecdote of the bravery of the Scotch piper of the 71st Highland Regiment, at the Battle of Vimiero *(1819). Alamy stock photo.*

up sufficiently high above the Ankle to prevent an Opening from appearing between them and the Pantaloons'.[16] When William Wheeler of the 51st Light Infantry arrived in Portugal in 1811, he was issued with 'two pair stockings and two pair boots, one pair soles and heels': by then, trousers had superseded pantaloons, and were worn over the boot.[17] These boots were very basic articles, similar to the brogans worn by working people, and the quality was variable.

The issues with quality control related to the way that footwear was produced for the military. Footwear provision is a good example of pre-industrial mass production, since shoemaking mechanized late in relation to industries such as textiles. As we saw in Chapter 1, machinery was not widely introduced until the 1850s and even then many shoemaking processes relied upon traditional manual skills. Shoe factories were relatively small scale, so military contractors would subcontract a number of them in order to fulfil a large order. Since the shoes were ready-made in bulk rather than bespoke, they were manufactured and delivered in a range of sizes: the origins of standard sizing that we have today.

Northampton would become the centre of the shoemaking industry in Britain, and the large concentration of boot and shoe manufacturers in the town was partly driven by demand from the military. The number of shoemakers increased during the American War of Independence, as the town fulfilled orders for the army and navy, and the trade also spread to neighbouring towns such as Kettering and Daventry.[18] Shoemaking increased again during the Revolutionary and Napoleonic Wars, and the new canal network enabled boots and shoes to be shipped around the country: in 1804 a depot was constructed at nearby Weedon where orders were inspected and stockpiled. In theory, if a consignment was found to be substandard in quality, or deviating from the standard pattern, then it would be rejected and the contractor fined. But, in practice, the inspection system 'was lax in its operation and ineffective as a safeguard against corruption'.[19] The contracting system lent itself to reducing costs and skimming profits. Unscrupulous contractors cut corners or filled the soles with clay to make them appear sturdier than they really were: 'This, while in dry weather produced extreme heat to the foot, in wet weather dissolved and left the soldier in a most distressed condition.'[20]

When the bedraggled barefoot troops returned from the Peninsula, one observer at Portsmouth docks was deeply troubled by what he saw. The engineer and inventor, Marc Isambard Brunel (father of Isambard Kingdom) resolved to come up with a better method for manufacturing footwear for the troops. He devised a mechanized process, whereby thick leather soles and uppers were clamped together and riveted in place. Rather than the skilled craftsmen who were usually employed in bootmaking, the machinery was so simple that it could be operated by the unskilled; and he further displayed his philanthropy by employing disabled veterans. His factory in Battersea produced strong boots in nine sizes, and visitors to the factory were impressed with what they saw. In 1812, the Foreign Secretary, Lord Castlereagh was persuaded to make large orders for the army, and production increased to 400 pairs per day.[21] These boots were widely worn in the latter stages of the Napoleonic Wars, but the loss of orders at the end of hostilities spelt the end of Brunel's factory. Nor were the boots as good as advertised: in practice they were 'inferior and rigid' and the metal rivets pierced the soles, so they offered little comfort to the common soldier.[22]

The Napoleonic Wars came to a conclusion at the Battle of Waterloo on 18 June 1815. Famously, the Prussians, commanded by Field Marshal von Blücher, arrived just in time after unexpectedly completing a long march across muddy ground. The boots that enabled them to do this came to be known as 'Blücher boots', and the name is appropriate since their commander took a great interest in soldiers' footwear and had designed them some years before. British Army boots thereafter followed this model, and were later renamed 'Derbys'. A pair of boots dating from the Crimean War was discovered under a floor at Weedon Barracks and are now on display in Northampton Museum (Figure 7.5). It is notable that these very rare survivals were found under a floor, where they either

Figure 7.5 *Pair of army boots, 1850s. Image courtesy of Northampton Museum and Art Gallery.*

ended up by accident or as an example of 'concealed shoes' to ward off evil spirits: in the normal course of things, they would have been worn until they wore out.[23] They nevertheless have been heavily worn, with extensive wear to the soles, despite a large number of hobnails, and the uppers are misshapen. They are very simple articles, and the upper is constructed from two thick pieces of leather, comprising the vamp and the quarters. While sturdy, it makes few concessions to comfort, being unlined and inflexible. The sole is thick and unyielding and the toe rises at the front, to compensate for lack of flexibility when walking. This contrasts with the flexible flat sole on a gentleman's boot from this period, which would enable a more natural walk. The 'toe-spring' forced an ungainly marching gait, which later medical writers complained was unhealthy and a waste of energy. Alison Matthews David judges that boots like these 'proved woefully inadequate for soldiers on campaign', with a legacy of injury and military inefficiency.[24]

The soldier's experience of shoes

While the military went to great lengths and expense to provide soldiers with footwear, we have seen that the reality of wearing military shoes was another matter entirely. Footwear was one of a soldiers' most important pieces of equipment, and his relationship with his shoes was involved and complex. Shoes are highly individual articles since they mould to the body of the wearer, and civilians usually 'own' their shoes in a financial sense. This was also true of officers, who received a grant from central government with which they were expected to purchase their equipment, such as the bespoke boots we saw in Chapter 4. This was not the case for private soldiers, however, since their relationship with their clothing was more indirect and subject to the authority of others. John Styles's concept of 'involuntary consumption' is again relevant here: he applies it to servants to explain their relationship with their livery, but soldiers have much in common with this group (indeed, military uniforms have their origins in livery).[25]

Soldiers did not choose their shoes or directly purchase them. Instead, shoes were provided for them by the regiment, and the cost of providing and replacing items of clothing was paid for by stoppages to their pay. The following 'list of necessaries, to be provided for the Foot Soldier out of his pay' was issued in 1792:

	£	s.	d.
One pair of black gaiters, per year	0	4	0
Two pair of shoes, per year, at 6s. per pair	0	12	0
Soleing, and heelpiecing, per year	0	4	0
One pair of stockings, or two pair of socks	0	1	6
Three shoe brushes, per year, at 5d. per brush	0	1	3
Black ball, per year	0	2	0

Around of a third of the total list of items that the soldier was responsible for concerned the purchase and maintenance of his footwear.[26] Should he go on furlough, he was responsible for paying for any wear to his shoes. As far as the military was concerned, soldiers were responsible for their shoes but did not own them, whereas soldiers did not necessarily see it that way. Soldiers sometimes sold their shoes, suggesting that they thought they were theirs to sell. Cuthbertson judged that this was from 'irregularity . . . and their unconquerable desire for drink' and urged officers to mark the shoes to stop them doing this.[27] The military authorities were clear that selling kit was against the regulations, and soldiers who sold their shoes received harsh punishments.[28] A pair of shoes might be granted as a reward, such as those given to soldiers who fought at Waterloo, but soldiers were prone to see perks as customary rights.[29]

Shoes were provided to the regiment in bulk and in a range of sizes. They would then be assigned to soldiers according to size. Cuthbertson suggested that this process should be supervised: 'Officers commanding companies ought not to permit a pair of shoes to be delivered to a man, until they have been examined … else every Soldier will certainly indulge his own particular taste, in the fashion of his shoes, without considering any other advantage.'[30] Strikingly, footwear writers from the First World War articulated the same concerns,[31] but it is unlikely that vanity was the main obstacle to shoes being a good fit. Whereas officers' footwear was bespoke, a soldier would be fortunate indeed if the 'standard' sizes in which shoes were manufactured actually fitted his foot, and it is fair to assume that in many cases they did not. Since military shoes up to the 1840s were straight lasted, they would not fit the shape of the foot to begin with, and had to be broken in. Military shoes tended to be broad, and wide at the toes in particular, so could be worn on either foot, but would be much more comfortable once a shoe had moulded to a particular foot. As we have seen, soldiers were ordered to swap their lefts and rights, to stop them wearing unevenly and to make them last longer, but it is questionable how many actually did this.[32]

Soldiers were responsible for maintaining their shoes. Shoes had to be regularly blacked, using 'black ball' manufactured from beeswax, mutton tallow and lamp or bone black. Manuals contain recipes for making this, or soldiers were expected to purchase it as part of their 'necessaries'.[33] We have seen that applying polish was a practical task, to preserve the leather and contribute to waterproofing, but the military also fetishized shoe maintenance as an aspect of discipline. It had a moral and governmental dimension as well as occupying time when they might otherwise be idle. Soldiers spent hours polishing their shoes to a high shine, that they might appear to best advantage at parade, even though shoes would quickly be dirtied again through use.

Shoes had also to be repaired. We have seen that spare soles and heels were issued as part of a soldier's kit, which along with spare shoes and other shoe-care equipment contributed to the weight of his pack. These would enable repairs to be made, to eke out his shoes for as long as possible: this was particularly important on campaign when replacements might not be available. Jackson mused that 'every soldier ought to be so far a taylor or cobbler, as to be able to repair, in a becoming and useful manner, the ordinary damages which happen to his clothing or his shoes', and the ability to perform tasks such as sewing was certainly expected of soldiers.[34] But cobbling was a specialized occupation, and certain soldiers in the regiment who possessed these skills would be expected to take responsibility for all but the most basic repairs. It helped that most soldiers would have had a former trade: this was certainly true of the militia, but regular soldiering, too, was typically a phase rather than a lifelong occupation.[35] Due to fluctuations in the shoemaking industry, there were often cobblers in the ranks.

One such was Benjamin Harris, who served with the 95th Rifles and later published one of the most celebrated memoirs of the Napoleonic Wars. He had formerly been a shoemaker so, on joining the regiment, he was assigned that responsibility. One disadvantage was the weight of the extra equipment that he had to carry around:

I marched under a weight sufficient to impede the free motions of a donkey; for besides my well-filled kit, there was my greatcoat rolled on its top, my blanket and camp kettle, my haversack, stuffed full of leather for repairing the men's shoes, together with a hammer and other tools (the lapstone I look the liberty of flinging to the devil) . . .

Without his heavy lapstone – a last which sat on the lap, instead of on a bench – he could not carry out major repairs, so, when on campaign, he tended to take over a local shoemaker's shop to work in. Harris often recorded working long into the night repairing shoes, in addition to his other duties. His contribution was certainly valued, however; during one action his commanding officer removed him from a dangerous post, laughing 'what shall we do . . . without our head shoemaker to repair our shoes?' And Harris was also remunerated on top of his basic pay for his services, enabling him to save a tidy sum for when he left the army.[36]

Soldiers only tended to write about shoes in their memoirs when they were having a negative experience of them, but the frequency of such comments suggests that the experience of wearing shoes on campaign was not a happy one. Memoirs of the Peninsular War often record long marches with broken shoes or none at all. On the retreat to Corunna (La Coruña), Harris recalls that 'the shoes and boots of our party were now mostly either destroyed or useless to us, from foul roads and long miles'. Even the regimental shoemaker found himself marching without shoes, and his feet became 'a mass of bleeding sores'.[37] Wheeler too recalled that 'shoes failed and many were barefoot'; and Cooper concurs: 'During our long marches we became ragged, shirtless, stockingless, and shoeless. In 1809 all the stockings I had were in my shoes, and the sole of one of my shoes was many a mile behind me. I have known more than 100 of the men of our regiment without shoes at one time.'[38] In the winter months, marching with inadequate shoes must have been particularly grim. George Simmons recalled of the winter of 1812, 'most of us walking barefooted, my shoes having no bottoms, as well as my friends'; my legs and feet much frostbitten; could hardly crawl'.[39]

Under these circumstances, soldiers would try to get footwear from wherever they could. During the battle of Vimeiro on 21 August 1808, Harris came upon the body of a dead British officer, whose belongings had already been plundered. It occurred to him that 'perhaps the officer's shoes might serve me, my own being considerably the worse for wear, so . . . pulled one of his shoes off, and knelt down on one knee to try it on. It was not much better than my own; however, I determined on the exchange'.[40] After the battle of Foz de Arouce on 15 March 1811, Simmons and his comrades plundered what they could from the French dead, acquiring 'shoes and shirts of better quality than our own'.[41] (It is notable that British soldiers commonly compared their own shoes unfavourably with those of other nations, which contrasts with civilian attitudes.) The enemy would also plunder footwear: Wheeler had his boots and stockings taken from him when he was taken prisoner.[42] Soldiers would also improvise, making sandals from the hide of bullocks that had been slaughtered for food, and these proved to be very comfortable and suited to the climate. When a consignment of French shoes was captured at Madrid, officers struggled to 'induce the men to quit the easy, well-fitting, and pliant sandal, for the hard and cumbrous leather shoe'.[43]

Military commanders recognized the importance of good footwear for their men. In addition to any paternalistic concern, it was a vital element of operational success, in terms of mobility, morale and fitness for active service. For these reasons, the fiscal-military state took its duty of care towards the men very seriously, as Erica Charters has argued.[44] The Duke of Wellington was famously interested in footwear: while he was indifferent to the appearance of his troops, he was deeply concerned about practicalities and the effect that it was having on his campaigns. His correspondence from the Peninsula frequently returned to the state of his men's footwear. He reported in May 1809 that 'the troops have no shoes to their feet' and that this was delaying his march, although he added that the French did not have any either. Later that month he issued a general order specifying how the 6,000 pairs of shoes that had arrived were to be distributed among the regiments.[45] He frequently wrote to the government and the War Office to demand more shoes. As he wrote to the Secretary of War in October 1810:

> As it is possible that the army may be obliged to make marches during the winter, on which there will be a great consumption of shoes, I take the liberty of recommending to your Lordship to order to Lisbon without loss of time 100,000 pairs of soldiers' shoes of the best quality, and that orders should be given to continue the manufacture of them.

In March 1811 he requested 150,000 shoes 'of the largest size' since the current shoes were of 'bad quality' and 'in general too small': 'as the soldiers pay for the shoes they receive, it is but just that they should be of the best quality for their purpose, and should fit them'.[46]

The system of supply improved over the course of the war – likely a result, in part, of Wellington's constant petitioning – and there were fewer complaints of shortages in later years.[47] Indeed, at the war's end, manufacturers were saddled with large quantities of unbought stock. As John Brewer has argued, Britain's success in war in the long eighteenth century owed much to its financial muscle and administrative efficiency.[48] Historians often focus on the fiscal-military state's ability to build ships and manufacture munitions, but not enough attention has been placed on the importance of footwear manufacturing to a state's ability to project its power across the globe. Britain's successes and failures on this score during the Napoleonic Wars have to form part of historians' assessment of its military performance.

Shoes and the soldier's body

This chapter opened with writings about military footwear from the period of the First World War. Indeed, there was a plethora of military writings about foot health and footwear in the early twentieth century. Even before soldiers experienced the wet and muddy conditions of the trenches in Flanders, the British military was concerned about the feet of its men, in line with wider anxieties about the physical fitness of recruits.[49] There was widespread interest in the new science of eugenics at the end of the nineteenth century, and anxieties about the fitness of the race. This came to a head during the South African War of 1899–1902, when the British state struggled to recruit enough fit men to serve in the army, and prompted calls for social reform. If Britain was to maintain its status as an imperial power, the state needed to take a more interventionist approach to the health and social conditions of the working classes. Alison Matthews David argues that, in this period, 'physiologists and doctors begin to treat the body as a machine' and sought to maximize efficiency and minimize fatigue in soldiers' bodies. This led to a transformation in infantry boots, which were 'designed with solidity, hygiene and ergonomics in mind'.[50]

As we saw in Chapter 2, however, medical science had taken a close interest in feet and footwear for a century or more. Chiropody was establishing itself as a science and was taking aim at the design of contemporary shoes, blaming them for a range of conditions including bunions, corns and flatfoot. While ostensibly scientific, much of the language was moralistic, criticizing the vanity and luxury of contemporary lifestyles. As Peter McNeil and Giorgio Riello argue, footwear was at the centre of a long-standing debate about morality and bodily health.[51] Military writings were supposedly practical and scientific, but their discussions of soldiers' foot health were hardly neutral from a moral point of view, so should be considered as part of this wider discourse. Edward Cutbush, for example, considered dress and footwear in his 1808 treatise, and balanced health against smartness. Legwear should be loose enough to prevent 'tight ligatures' but not so loose as to give the soldier 'a *slovenly* appearance'. When it came to footwear:

> The shoes which are generally supplied for the use of soldiers are not sufficiently strong and *well made*; the soles are like a sponge in wet weather, and during the dry would separate from the upper leather in a march of one hundred miles; consequently the soldiers' feet will be cut by marching over rough roads and be rendered unfit perhaps for duty by the inflammation excited.[52]

Such writings were unanimous in their criticism of the current design of military shoes. A chiropody treatise from 1818 compared them unfavourably with those of the ancients: 'the broad expanded foot of a Roman soldier, resting solely on a sandal … must have had great advantages over the chafed foot of an Englishman cramped up in a contract shoe, which perhaps falls in pieces before his day's march is half over'. Venerating the ancients was a common theme in political writings, but the author also preferred the sandals 'of our Sepoys in India' to the regulation army boot. As we have seen, medical writers paid close attention to the materials used in stockings and socks, preferring wool for its ability to stay dry and draw moisture from the feet. This treatise noted that soldiers 'always found it most convenient to wear woollen ones on a march', having formerly been forced to attend parade in cotton

The Soldier's Shoe 153

Figure 7.6 *Thomas Rowlandson,* Measuring Substitutes for the Army of Reserve *(1815). The Metropolitan Museum of Art, New York City: The Elisha Whittelsey Collection, The Elisha Whittelsey Fund, 1959.*

or silk stockings.⁵³ The physician Donald Monro concurred, adding that the men should be provided with an extra pair of stockings, as 'it would be of great use to the service'.⁵⁴

When soldiers were recruited, they were subject to a medical examination to ensure that they were fit for service (Figure 7.6). The health of their legs and feet was particularly important, given the amount of marching that they were expected to do, and the heavy loads that they were required to carry. Jackson provides a comprehensive checklist of the qualities that an army surgeon should be on the lookout for. Legs should possess 'a firm calf and a sinewy ankle', which not coincidentally was also the epitome of male beauty at the time. Toes 'must not croud upon one another, nor rise up in the middle, so as to favour the production of corns'. Toenails must not 'penetrate the flesh'. Flatfoot was a common reason for soldiers being rejected for service, because if a foot does not have an arch, then it cannot absorb shock or move efficiently. It produces an awkward gait and reduces one's ability to walk long distances, so would have been incompatible with soldiering at this time. Jackson also recommended that soldiers receive regular foot examinations from their officers, but whether officers actually put this prescription into practice is doubtful.⁵⁵

Finally, soldiers themselves were urged to pay attention to their health and cleanliness. Jackson suggested that, on a long march, soldiers should be given an hour's rest in the middle to care for their feet: 'the shoes, socks and pantaloons taken off, the feet, legs and thighs washed, or well bathed with cold water'. Or if there was not a source of water, 'they may be rubbed with a wet towel and exposed to the cool air. This process restores vigour to the limbs, as effectually as a repose of several hours'.⁵⁶ Monro appreciated the challenges that soldiers faced in keeping clean. When on campaign, they slept in damp tents or on the ground, in all weathers, with little time for personal hygiene; fixed encampments had the dangers of 'putrid effluvia' of dead animals and privies, along with 'corrupted stagnating water'; and soldiers had to serve in unfamiliar climates, with extremes of hot and cold.⁵⁷ All of these were threats to the health of the humoral body, but the ultimate responsibility lay with the men themselves. Charters notes that the military medicine in this period sought to avoid 'disorder', 'meaning both disease as disorder within an individual, and also the lack of discipline in a camp directly related to an outbreak of disease'.⁵⁸ Foot health was a moral and disciplinary concern, as well as a medical one.

Footwear was therefore a very serious matter in the Georgian military. It was of great concern to military commanders and medics but, whereas the British state spent vast sums on military footwear and got better at providing the numbers of shoes that were required, the quality of the shoes themselves left much to be desired. This had a huge impact on the soldiers, and historians should pay attention to this important aspect of their life experience. Ultimately, it was in the interests of privates and generals alike that adequate footwear should be provided, so this is an example of the fiscal-military state taking an interest in the well-being of its servicemen. Military medicine in the era of the First World War may have focused on the feet of the soldier and the ways in which they were shod, but many of the same concerns preoccupied military men in the preceding two centuries.

Coda: the sailor's shoe

This chapter has focused on common soldiers, but shoes were, of course, important to personnel in other branches of the services. As far as the navy is concerned, there are fewer written sources about footwear. Sailors' shoes do not appear to have preoccupied chiropodists or other medical writers: Cutbush's *Observations on the Means of Preserving the Health of Soldiers and Sailors* (1808) had little to say about sailors and nothing about their footwear. Orders for shoes appear in official sources, such as letters to the Admiralty,[59] but they appear much less frequently in personal sources than they do in the army. For the common soldier, who was marching miles every day, they were a vital piece of equipment and loomed large in his experience, but this appears not to have been the case for sailors. There are fewer memoirs for ratings than there are for privates, and shoes are mentioned but rarely in personal correspondence.[60]

On the other hand, there is more material evidence. The Historic Dockyard at Chatham holds finds from the wreck of HMS *Invincible*, which sank in the Solent in 1758. It was rediscovered in 1979 and subsequently excavated. These excavations turned up a huge quantity of articles from the mid-eighteenth century, which give an unprecedented insight into everyday life on board ship. Happily, the haul included many shoes. These ranged from small fragments of leather and accessories like metal buckles, to complete shoes. One might expect leather items that had been under the sea for over two centuries to be in poor condition, and some were indeed heavily decayed, but others were in remarkably good condition and look little different to shoes from the period that had been carefully

Figure 7.7 *Rating's shoe, 1750s. © Chatham Historic Dockyard Trust.*

stored. This is partly a fluke of the conditions in which they were buried, but is also, of course, a credit to the archaeologists, conservators and curators who have preserved them.

One of the best-preserved shoes is a man's shoe that would be about a UK size four today (Figure 7.7). It is straight lasted, but evidence of wear suggests it was consistently worn on the right. It would have been fastened by a buckle, which is now missing, but its piercings are still visible on the two straps. The construction is sturdy rather than fine, as this is utilitarian rather than fashionable footwear. It is therefore likely that it was worn by a rating. By eighteenth-century standards, the shoe looks comfortable and practical. It is square at the toe and is fairly broad with a low heel. The leather uppers seem fairly supple, and the sole is relatively thin, so they would have been pleasant to wear and would not have impeded movement (Figure 7.8). They were not intended to be heavy and hardwearing like army shoes, but rather to provide grip on wet decks and rigging ropes.

The naval sailor was a prominent figure in Georgian popular culture. The 'wooden walls' of the navy defended the nation and its liberties, and its heroic sailors had 'hearts of oak'. Again, we see the symbolic importance of the oak tree, the bark and acorns of which were used to tan the hides of the bulls who grazed under its shade, providing leather for the shoes of the armed forces. 'Jolly Jack Tar' often appeared on the stage, or on material and visual culture, and was a highly stereotyped figure that was instantly recognizable, with his distinctive dress and swarthy appearance. Joanne Begiato has shown how his brawny frame was an appealing embodied model of working-class masculinity.[61] The usual image of Jolly Jack Tar is that he went barefoot, in keeping with his rugged and exotic persona (Figure 7.9). The rating Jack Crawford became a popular hero after the Battle of Camperdown. During the battle, the mast of the flagship was hit, which caused the admiral's standard to fall, signifying surrender. But

Figure 7.8 *Rating's shoe, 1750s. © Chatham Historic Dockyard Trust.*

Figure 7.9 *Daniel Orme,* John [Jack] Crawford. *Alamy stock photo.*

Crawford grabbed the flag and climbed the mast under heavy fire, fixing it in place with a marlin spike. Crawford's bravery is celebrated in numerous prints, where he is invariably depicted barefoot.

The image of the barefoot sailor is likely a romantic myth, however. The argument goes that bare feet grip better when climbing the rigging but, in reality, soaking feet would be ripped to shreds on coarse rope.[62] Sailors, therefore, wore supple shoes like the example from HMS *Invincible*, which would have enabled them to grip while also protecting their feet. They also wore shoes at other times on board ship, and certainly for going ashore. The material culture evidence can therefore help us to get beyond the stereotype and to reconstruct an aspect of the sailor's bodily experience. The shoe from the shipwreck is typical of historic plebeian shoes, in that it only survived for an unusual reason, and is able to give us an insight into an aspect of people's everyday lives for which there are few other types of evidence.

Notes

1. Cecil Webb-Johnson, *The Soldier's Manual of Foot Care and Foot Wear* (London: Dryden Pub. Co., 1916), iv.
2. John Cooper, *Fusilier Cooper: Experiences in the 7th (Royal) Fusiliers during the Peninsular Campaign of the Napoleonic Wars and the American Campaign to New Orleans* (Milton Keynes: Leonaur, 2007), 51.
3. Ian Fletcher, *Napoleonic Wars: Wellington's Army* (London: Brassey's, 1996), 60.
4. David, 'War and Wellingtons'.
5. Neil Ramsey, *The Military Memoir and Romantic Literary Culture, 1780–1835* (Farnham: Ashgate, 2011).
6. Robert Jackson, *A Systematic View of the Formation, Discipline, and Economy of Armies* (London, 1804), 305.
7. Anon., *Collection of Orders, Regulations, and Instructions for the Army, published by Order of the Secretary of War* (London, 1807), 465.
8. Percy Sumner, 'Orderly Books at Windsor, 1742 to 1745', *Journal of the Society of Army Historical Research* 28, no. 113 (1950): 54–8 (57).
9. Cuthbertson, *System for the Compleat Interior Management*, 98.
10. Strachan, *British Military Uniforms*, 226.
11. Jackson, *Systematic View*, 248.
12. Cuthbertson, *System for the Compleat Interior Management*, 98.
13. Cooper, *Fusilier Cooper*, 132.
14. David, 'War and Wellingtons', 124.
15. Noted by Oman, *Wellington's Army*, 294.
16. W. J. Carman, 'Infantry Clothing Regulations, 1802', *Journal of the Society for Army Historical Research* 19 (1940): 200–35 (228).

17 Liddell Hart (ed.), *The Letters of Private Wheeler 1809–1828*, 55.

18 Hatley, 'Shoemakers in Northamptonshire', 4.

19 Church, 'Gotch & Sons, Kettering', 486.

20 Richard Beamish, *Memoir of the Life of Sir Marc Isambard Brunel* (London: Longman, Green, Longman & Roberts, 1862), 129–30.

21 Paul Clements, *Marc Isambard Brunel* (Chichester: Phillimore & Co., 2006), 52–3.

22 Swann, *Shoes*, 32.

23 Ceri Houlbrook and Rebecca Shawcross, 'Revealing the Ritually Concealed: Custodians, Creators and the Concealed Shoe', *Material Religion* 14, no. 2 (2018): 163–82.

24 David, 'War and Wellingtons', 124.

25 Styles, *The Dress of the People*.

26 Strachan, *British Military Uniforms*, 197–8.

27 Cuthbertson, *System for the Complete Interior Management*, 169, 104.

28 Liddell Hart (ed.), *Letters of Private Wheeler*, 70.

29 John Gurwood (ed.), *The Dispatches of Field Marshall the Duke of Wellington*, 12 vols (Cambridge: Cambridge University Press, 2010), vol. 7, 393; vol. 8, 270.

30 Cuthbertson, *System for the Complete Interior Management*, 98.

31 Webb-Johnson, *Soldier's Manual*, 13.

32 Cuthbertson, *System for the Complete Interior Management*, 135.

33 Strahan, *British Military Uniforms*, 111.

34 Jackson, *Systematic View*, 158.

35 Kevin Linch and Matthew McCormack, 'Defining Soldiers: Britain's Military, c. 1740–1815', *War in History* 20, no. 2 (2013): 144–59.

36 Christopher Hibbert (ed.), *The Recollections of Rifleman Harris: As Told to Henry Curling* (Moreton-in-Marsh: Windrush Press, 1996), 13, 25–6, 117.

37 Ibid., 85, 99.

38 Liddell Hart (ed.), *Letters of Private Wheeler*, 102; Cooper, *Fusilier Cooper*, 129.

39 George Simmons, *A British Rifle Man: The Journals and Correspondence of Major George Simmons, Rifle Brigade during the Peninsular War and the Campaign of Waterloo*, ed. Willoughby Verner (London: A. & C. Black, 1899), 265.

40 Hibbert (ed.), *The Recollections of Rifleman Harris*, 38.

41 Simmons, *British Rifle Man*, 145–6.

42 Liddell Hart (ed.), *Letters of Private Wheeler*, 62.

43 John Stepney Cowell of the Coldstream Guards, quoted in Fletcher, *Napoleonic Wars*, 63.

44 Erica Charters, 'The Caring Fiscal-Military State during the Seven Years War, 1756–63', *The Historical Journal* 52, no. 4 (2009), 921–41.

45 Gurwood (ed.), *Dispatches*, vol. 3, 241, 257, 263.

46 Ibid., vol. 4, 348, 716.

47 Keith Bartlett, 'The Development of the British Army during the Wars with France, 1793–1815' (PhD thesis, University of Durham, 1997), 212.

48 John Brewer, *The Sinews of Power: War, Money and the English State, 1688–1783* (London: Unwin Hyman, 1989).

49 Henry Holden, *Flat-Foot or Splay-Foot (Valgus)* (London: Holden Brothers, 1905); Melville, *Military Hygiene and Sanitation*.

50 David, 'War and Wellingtons', 126.

51 McNeill and Riello, 'Art and Science of Walking'.

52 Edward Cutbush, *Observations on the Means of Preserving the Health of Soldiers and Sailors* (Philadelphia, 1808), 10–11.

53 Anon., *Art of Preserving the Feet*, 195, 214.

54 Donald Monro, *Observations on the Means of Preserving the Health of Soldiers* (London, 1780), 8.

55 Jackson, *Systematic View*, 31, 305.

56 Jackson, *Systematic View*, 307–8.

57 Monro, *Observations*, 2-3.

58 Charters, 'Caring Fiscal-Military State', 927.

59 For example, Reginald Fenwich to the Navy Board, 10 April 1740: The National Archives ADM 106/919/136.

60 Only one letter (by a midshipman) mentions shoes in Helen Watt and Anne Hawkins (eds), *Letters of Seamen in the Wars with France, 1793–1815* (Woodbridge: Boydell, 2016), 208.

61 Begiato, *Manliness in Britain*, 123.

62 Matthew Brenckle, 'Slip Shod: The Truth About Early Navy Shoes' (7 February 2014): https://ussconstitutionmuseum.org/2014/02/07/slip-shod-truth-about-early-navy-shoes/ (accessed 8 May 2024).

Conclusion
Wearing Georgian shoes

This book has explored eighteenth-century shoes and their relationship with their wearers. In particular, it has focused on the historical experience of wearing shoes, in terms of social roles and the body. To a large extent, these are questions that cannot be answered with reference to the historian's conventional written sources. As we have seen, wearing shoes was a quotidian experience that was rarely written down, and printed sources about shoes were dominated by moral polemics about fashion and consumption that had a clear political agenda. In most cases, our primary sources for eighteenth-century shoes are the shoes themselves. By assessing their style, their physical properties and signs of damage and wear, we find out about the objects themselves, the person who wore them, and the importance that they had in terms of the wearer's position in society and his or her physical practice. Indeed, studying physical objects allows the historian to critique the representations in written sources from the time.

On the other hand, studying objects in museums has its limitations. Museums always have to balance access with preservation, and there are instances where the latter consideration has to take priority. Historic shoes are fragile objects that have to be handled with great care. While many shoes in museum collections are in excellent shape and have been preserved in optimum conditions, others are heavily worn or decayed, and archaeological finds are often very fragile indeed. Historic leather is vulnerable to oil, moisture and salt from the fingers, so researchers are usually required to wear latex or cotton gloves when handling them. Over time, leather deteriorates and becomes brittle, so any assessment of its physical properties (such as its suppleness or flexibility) has to bear in mind how it has changed in the intervening period. While shoes are very eloquent historical sources, there are therefore practical restrictions that affect what you can say about them.

Shoes are worn objects, and in order to assess what they are like to wear, one should ideally put them on. Fundamentally, this book is about the relationship between the shoe and the body, so shoes need to be assessed in conjunction with a body rather than separately. It is also about the experience of wear, and it is only possible to assess issues such as comfort, posture, walking gait, the grip of the sole by actually wearing them. Clearly this is not possible with fragile, irreplaceable objects – quite apart from the fact that eighteenth-century shoes are much smaller than those made for modern feet. The controversy around the celebrity Kim Kardashian wearing a dress to the Met Gala that had belonged to Marilyn Monroe – and whether she damaged it in the process – highlighted the ethical issues around wearing historic clothing.[1]

While it is not possible to wear shoes from the eighteenth century, it is possible to wear replicas. These can be constructed according to contemporary patterns and using contemporary methods, and can be handled and worn with none of the restrictions associated with originals. Sarah Bendall argues that wearing reconstructed garments 'allows for the testing of hypotheses that would otherwise be impossible', so it is 'a powerful research tool'.[2] This book therefore concludes with an experiment in making and wearing. I commissioned a pair of shoes to an eighteenth-century pattern and wore them for an extended period while documenting the process. This enabled me to ask questions about wearing eighteenth-century shoes that I have not been able to answer by assessing museum artefacts or other primary source types. What are eighteenth-century shoes like to wear? How do they affect mobility, walking gait and posture? And what effect does my body have upon them, in terms of changes to the shoes themselves and ultimately wearing them out?

Methodologies of making and wearing

Wearing an object is an unusual research method for a historian, although we shall see that it is less unusual in other fields. The study of material culture by historians at the end of the twentieth century was a departure from their traditional focus on texts and other representations. In exploring the researcher's physical, experiential and emotional reaction to source material, it took a significant step away from the supposed objectivity of Rankean empiricism, where the historian was the detached observer of the primary source. Even after the linguistic and cultural turns – which emphasized the subjectivity of both researcher and source material – this sense of the separation of the historian from the source still lingers in the profession. There are even elements of it in the history of material culture itself, since the object is still distinct from the researcher, even if the effect of the object on the researcher is taken into account. Practical considerations such as accessing museums, preservation practices and handling restrictions further emphasize the distance between the researcher and the object.

Wearing an object serves to reduce this distance, or even break it down entirely. If the researcher is the one doing the wearing, then they themselves become the research subject, so it is necessary to engage with research methodologies that embrace this. Auto-ethnography involves the researcher researching themselves, effectively doing an anthropological study where they are problematizing their own everyday behaviour rather than that of others. It involves writing about themselves, so the author is brought to the fore and ceases to be 'silent' like they are in typical academic writing: Sally Denshire argues that it falls 'somewhere between anthropology and literary studies'.[3] This writing is typically very personal and can be an uncomfortable thing to do, so is akin to therapy.[4] It is certainly very different to the invisible, omniscient author typical of historical writing, and its narratives are less tidy. The present study involved the author as research subject and did use some auto-ethnographical methods, such as a research diary. Because the research involved a live subject (myself), it required approval from a university ethics committee, which is unusual for historical work. This also involved a risk assessment to ascertain whether I would be harmed by the exercise and to put mitigations in place to reduce this. (The risks involved were fairly low-level, such as slips, blisters or discomfort.) On the other hand, the project was not strictly an auto-ethnography, since I was not doing critical work on myself and was focusing more narrowly on the physical experience of wearing shoes.

Related fields, therefore, have more to offer here. This project involves the relationship between subject and object, and phenomenology explores this in terms of how we experience the world through perception and bodily sensation. Maurice Merleau-Ponty argues that 'the relations between the subject and world are not strictly bilateral', emphasizing that thinking and perception are bound up together. Indeed, he uses the example of wearing a shoe to demonstrate this:

> Because I know that the light strikes my eye, that contact is made with the skin, that my shoe hurts my foot, I distribute through my body perceptions which really belong to my soul, and past perception into the thing perceived ... If I consider them from the inside, I find one single, unlocalized knowledge, one single indivisible soul, and there is no such difference between thinking and perceiving as there is between seeing and hearing.[5]

Fields such as dance studies have thought about corporeal experience in this holistic way, trying to understand the somatic knowledge that we produce about our bodies. When we work with objects, and in particular when we wear them, we create types of embodied knowledge that are not captured by other approaches. For example, Sally Dean asks how does 'the weight, texture, form, movement' of costume affect our bodies, as a 'direct and tactile experience'?[6]

In practice, disciplines that are close to history do this already. Hilary Davidson notes that archaeology is 'inherently embodied', since things are 'excavated by people with their bodies ... while considering the relationship of their bodies to the space of excavation'. The process of making and wearing can be approached as an exercise in experimental archaeology, whereby objects are reconstructed according to strict guidelines and then used to test hypotheses in a scientific manner: Davidson calls it 'experimental history' when not used in an archaeological context.[7] The practice of historical re-enactment can also provide these insights. Historians were long dismissive of re-enactment, and they would still take issue with re-enactors' preoccupation with 'authenticity' and their conviction that it is possible to recreate historical events, collapsing the distance between the past and the present.[8] But, more recently, the 'affective turn' in history has emphasized questions such as sympathy and individual experience, prompting historians to take the practice of re-enactment more seriously.[9] Historical re-enactors are hugely knowledgeable about past material artefacts, both in terms of getting the details 'right' and in respect of insights that they have gained from actually using them in recreated historical situations – knowledge that they are very generous about sharing.[10]

Making and wearing are becoming increasingly common as approaches to the history of dress. Davidson argues that this makes the 'implicit' knowledge of the dressmaker – which is often embodied and learned through practice – explicit.[11] Bendall reconstructed a farthingale, a structuring undergarment worn under sixteenth-century dresses for which there are no surviving examples: the process of making it provided knowledge of lost artisan cultures and techniques.[12] Ellen Sampson explored wearing shoes as an artist and as a shoemaker in her book *Worn* (2020). Sampson sought to explore the embodied experience of wear and, in particular, the way that the body becomes 'entangled' with the object. She made pairs of shoes to her own design and then wore them, capturing the experience auto-ethnographically via a reflective diary and Polaroid photographs. In particular, she was interested in the process of wearing out, so made a pair of shoes from cloth that would wear out quickly. Our relationship with our shoes develops through wear and, indeed, wearing is itself a kind of 'making' as the shoe changes and takes on the form of the body. Sampson adds that there is 'an unacknowledged violence in wearing' since 'we destroy our clothes': in order to wear shoes in, we have to wear them out.[13] This happens to shoes more than any other garment, due to the forces imposed by the body, so making and wearing is a particularly fruitful approach here.

Making

To conduct this study I commissioned a pair of replica eighteenth-century shoes. The shoemaker Andy Burke, from Bridgend in south Wales, was recommended to me by contacts among the military re-enactment community, for the high quality and historical accuracy of his work. As well as making and repairing footwear for re-enactors, he also makes historical shoes to order for film and theatre productions. I approached Andy and explained the nature of my project: he was keen to participate in it, as he is himself a re-enactor and has a keen interest in the history of footwear. The pair I ordered from his catalogue were hand-sewn 'soldier's shoes'.[14] These are manufactured from a pattern taken from François de Garsault's *L'Art du cordonnier* (1767), so were typical of the types of shoes worn by European common soldiers and plebeian men in the later eighteenth century.[15] They are basic, unlined shoes with a broad squared toe: they would therefore have been functional rather than fashionable. Andy scaled the pattern up to modern sizes; I drew around my feet on a piece of paper and measured their circumference with a tape measure, and he confirmed that these were a modern UK size twelve with a slightly wider midfoot.[16] As Davidson notes, replica costume has to be adapted to modern bodies.[17] Insofar as they were made to order and were the correct size for the foot, the project departed from the eighteenth-century common soldier's experience, since soldiers' shoes would have been provided in bulk and the common soldier would have been fortunate indeed if they were a good fit.

Unlike some practitioners of making and wearing, I am not myself a skilled maker, so the shoes were made by the shoemaker. I spent a day at his workshop, where I observed him completing most of the processes for making the upper and sole for one of the shoes (Figure 8.1). This enabled me to observe the making process and to ask questions while it was happening. I was also able to try out some of the processes myself under his tutelage, such as cutting, stitching and marking holes. This gave me a practical, embodied experience of the shoemaking process. Bendall notes that sources from the time

Figure 8.1 *Andy Burke in his workshop.*

tacitly assume that makers had these skills, so they were not written about; they are therefore only revealed through practice.[18] It was telling that my fingers lacked the practised skill and strength to carry out the processes with the required speed and dexterity, and they also lacked callouses (apart from those I have from playing the guitar) to protect them against the pricks of the needle and awl. Making the holes around the edge of the sole with an awl is physically demanding work, placing repetitive strain on the elbow in particular, which is a potential source of long-term injury. Stitching is intricate work that strains the eye, even by modern artificial light, so would be even more straining by candlelight.

The shoes were made by hand, mostly using materials, techniques and tools that would have been familiar in the eighteenth century. Andy uses some modern tools, such as a metal needle, but he did demonstrate how stitching would have been done with a boar's bristle. The leather is vegetable tanned, which is stiffer than leather tanned using modern methods such as chrome tanning. While it is not identical to the leather used in the eighteenth century, it is close enough for our purposes: experiments in reconstruction often use the equivalent modern materials.[19] Because it comes from the hide of an animal, it varies in its properties across a piece, so he assesses it for stiffness before clicking (cutting out the pieces) to ensure that the correct parts of the shoe have appropriate qualities. Clicking is a hugely skilled process, and the high cost of leather is such that shoemakers have to maximize the number of pieces that they can cut from a sheet (Figure 8.2). It requires physical strength and a very sharp knife, which is sharpened regularly with a strop: if it is not sharp, it places additional strain on the shoemaker's body.

The construction of the shoe is simple by modern standards. They are straight lasted, so both shoes are made up on identical wooden lasts. Because my instep is slightly wider than the standard last, the last was built up with scraps of leather to provide extra room. The vamp is made from a single piece, which is hand sewn to two quarters with linen thread. There is no lining, but a heel quarter of softer leather is attached with a whipping stitch. The shoes are unlined, but the leather is 'rough out' so the smooth side is within (Figure 8.3). This was typical of plebeian shoes, whereas elite shoes would have the smooth side out and a soft lining. Because the smooth side is on the inside, it does not rub the foot, and because the uppers are only made from four large pieces of leather, there are no exposed seams. Having the rough texture on the outside gives them an appearance of suede to begin with but, with the application of black dye and polish, it gradually becomes smoother. It is a matt finish, so soldiers who were required to buff their shoes to a high shine had a lot of work to do. The soles are made from thick hard leather, which is attached to the uppers with a leather welt. The heel is constructed from offcuts of sole leather, to keep waste and costs down. It is glued together in a stack of twenty millimetres, which is then shaped and attached to the sole with glue and nails.

After my day in the workshop, the construction of the shoes took a few more days, and they were posted to me when they were finished. Before I could start wearing them, I had to fix the buckles. The

Figure 8.2 *Clicking the soles.*

shoes were constructed without fastenings, as they would have been at the time, and the quarters had two long straps that needed fixing together with a buckle (Figure 8.4). Andy supplied a pair of buckles – of a plain brass style similar to that worn by soldiers (Figure 7.1) – and instructions for how to attach them.[20] This is a tricky process for the uninitiated, but presumably eighteenth-century wearers would do this to numerous pairs over their lifetime so would become adept at it. As Joanne Entwistle writes, 'getting dressed is an ongoing practice, requiring knowledge, techniques and skills'.[21] It is easier to have somebody else do it for you, so a servant would probably have performed the task for the wealthy. It requires you to pierce the leather in just the right places, allowing for the length of the prong so that they are in the correct position when pulled tight (Figure 8.5). The prongs on the buckle are fairly sharp, but you need a sharp tool to make the holes. These holes are of course permanent, so it is important to get it right. This personalizes the shoes to the wearer's size, and also designates whether the shoe is a left or a right since the straps are pulled outwards to tighten. Changing the buckle, swapping

Figure 8.3 *Uppers of rough-out leather.*

lefts and rights, adjusting the size, or changing the owner would therefore require a new set of holes. Shoes in museum collections with multiple holes indicate that this has been done. Once the buckles are in place, they are easy to fasten and unfasten – quicker than tying laces – and they hold the shoes in place securely.

The shoes were now ready to wear, but they had to be maintained. Black leather shoes in the eighteenth century were maintained with 'black ball'. As we saw in Chapter 7, black ball was an essential part of the soldier's kit. It is possible to make this yourself but the process is notoriously smelly, and it can be purchased ready-made from re-enactment suppliers. This is rubbed on the leather and then buffed with a stiff brush (Figure 8.6). Applying black ball regularly helps to keep the leather supple and waterproof, so is a practical task of shoe maintenance as well as improving their appearance. I periodically applied black ball to the shoes, and the 'rough out' finish became smoother and shinier as the polish built up.

Figure 8.4 *Completed shoes without buckles.*

Figure 8.5 *Fixing the buckles.*

Figure 8.6 *Applying black ball.*

Wearing

I wore the shoes for a total of forty days. These days were non-consecutive, between July and November 2022. This took in the hottest summer on record and a wet autumn, so they were exposed to a range of weather conditions. On a given day I would typically wear them for eight hours, the minimum being five and the maximum ten. In a sense I should have worn them with stockings and breeches, but I deliberately paired them with modern cotton socks and everyday clothes as I wanted to wear them as everyday shoes. I did not want to draw attention to them unduly, but rather wanted to assess how they would perform as regular footwear. If we can get through a day without thinking about our shoes, then they are arguably doing their job properly: it is usually when they cause discomfort or impede movement that it occurs to us that we have them on. Bendall notes that 'historians must be cautious of trying to recover sensory experiences of wearing': eighteenth-century bodies would be conditioned to wearing such shoes and mine is not.[22] Nevertheless, I reflected on what the shoes were like to wear in a handwritten diary, where I recorded my experiences of wear on each given day. I took daily photographs of the shoes, which I posted on social media.[23] I also took more detailed photos at the beginning, middle and end of the process to document how the shoes were changing as a result of my wearing them.

The shoes were initially uncomfortable to wear. Straight-lasted shoes are not pre-formed to the shape of the foot and take time to mould to the correct form. On the shoemaker's advice, I soaked the leather before putting them on, which helped to stretch the leather to my feet, and once it dried it retained that shape. My wearing diary for day two noted that they were 'starting to take the form of the foot – L/R shape visible in uppers' and by day six they fitted 'like a glove'.[24] So, whereas eighteenth-century shoes are not initially in the shape of the foot, they are designed to mould to it with wear and so become more individual than modern shoes. Thereafter they were comfortable. Because of the smooth-in leather and lack of exposed seams, I did not get any blisters from wearing them. The heel quarter is soft and accommodating, unlike modern shoes that typically have a rigid plastic quarter, and the lack of a rubber sole also removes a potential hard surface for rubbing. (Indeed, one day during the process I wore modern formal shoes instead, because I was attending a function in the evening, and got a blister within a few hours.) The downside of wearing them in comparison to wearing trainers is that they are relatively stiff and the hard soles provide no shock absorption, so after a long day when I did a lot of walking my feet did ache slightly.[25] The broad toe meant that there was room for my feet and the effect of wearing straight-lasted shoes was less pronounced than I had assumed it would be. It did slightly force the big toes inwards, providing occasional discomfort to my left foot, in particular. We saw in Chapter 2 how Georgian chiropodists were concerned that this shoe shape could exacerbate *hallux valgus* (bunions). Having worn straight-lasted shoes, it is easy to see why, and a more fashionable pointed pair of shoes would have been much less comfortable for this reason.

Walking in these shoes was a different experience to modern shoes. Because of the heel and the lack of grip on the soles, I walked differently to the way I would in rubber-soled shoes. I adopted a toe-first gait, placing the shoes more deliberately on the ground than I normally would. On day seven I went for a rural walk in the shoes with my son, and he mentioned that I was walking differently, so the shoes visibly affected my whole gait. Sampson notes that walking 'holds a particular place in our culture; not only are our movements learned, but they are socially and culturally specific'. We walk in different ways in different situations, and how we walk is key to how we present ourselves in society. Our shoes are part of our self-presentation, and materially affect how our bodies move. 'Shoes alter the way we walk and in doing so change our experience of the spaces we occupy.'[26] They also affect how we see ourselves, and in this respect the project did take an auto-ethnographic turn. Whereas many studies of material culture emphasize the emotional power of objects, I tended to regard the shoes as a research instrument and was not as emotionally involved with them as I might be with a pair of my own shoes. On the other hand, I was self-conscious about wearing unusual footwear and was aware that other people were looking at me. This was, of course, an anachronistic reflection, since, presumably, people in the eighteenth-century would not have found them unusual, but it was noticeable how it was the buckle in particular that drew attention to them.[27] If the buckle was covered with a wider trouser hem, then they were visually indistinguishable from modern formal shoes. This does highlight the visual importance of the buckle, and the way that it draws attention to the feet and their motions.

I used the shoes for everyday wear, so wore them in my usual indoor and outdoor locales. Around the house and on campus, they were notably comfortable to wear on carpet, since it provided some cushioning and the leather soles were able to glide without slipping. They would therefore have been comfortable to wear on fabric surfaces in a well-to-do eighteenth-century house, although it was notable how much dirt the leather soles picked up on wet days in comparison with rubber soles, and they quickly transferred dirt to textile surfaces, so on such days I tended to change out of them at the door. The uppers were waterproof so my feet stayed dry but, as with all leather shoes, the soles become saturated on wet days so they need to dry out. As well as on carpet, the shoes were also quiet and comfortable to wear on wooden and linoleum indoor surfaces, but hard surfaces were a different matter. The shoes were notably noisy on stone and tile, which in turn made me more conscious of wearing them and drew attention to them. The noise that our shoes make is an important part of the sensory experience of wearing them, and the history of shoes can therefore be productively approached via the history of the senses. Different walking surfaces and architectural acoustics have a significant effect, so the sound that shoes make is dependent on our environment and becomes part of our experience of it. The sounds of walking should therefore be part of our understanding of Georgian soundscapes: the clean paved streets and ordered built environment of the urban renaissance would have sounded very different to other locales. These soundscapes also change through the year, since it was notable that fallen leaves dampened the sound of my tread, and also provided some welcome cushioning to the hard soles.

Another respect in which the history of the senses is relevant here is smell.[28] The smell of feet and footwear is occasionally mentioned in eighteenth-century sources. In *The Expedition of Humphry Clinker*, Matt Bramble complains of the '*compound of villainous smells*' at Bath's Assembly Rooms, including 'sour flatulencies, rank armpits, sweating feet, running sores and issues, plasters, ointments, and embrocations'.[29] Medical and podiatric treatises often focused on the smells issuing from socks: as we have seen, they were concerned about materials such as cotton that apparently became saturated and putrid.[30] I have not yet found any complaints about smelly shoes, which is not to say that this was not an issue for Georgians. But the shoes that I wore did not have an unpleasant sweaty smell, despite

Figure 8.7 *James Gillray,* Very slippy weather *(10 February 1808). Alamy stock photo.*

wearing them on some very hot days; instead they smelled of leather and polish. Modern shoes such as trainers often become malodorous because they contain inorganic materials such as plastics that do not allow the foot to breathe, and foam or fabric that absorbs bodily moisture. These shoes, by contrast, were made entirely from organic materials that allow the foot to breathe.

As well as wearing them on typical modern surfaces, I sought out surfaces that would have been familiar to Georgian pedestrians. On day thirteen I happened to be in Richmond in Yorkshire, so wore the shoes on the flagstones and cobblestones of its Georgian town centre. The centre of Richmond is hilly and the cobblestones are highly polished with centuries of wear, so the shoes were notably slippery on these surfaces. I therefore had to walk quite gingerly to avoid falling over, and it would have been even worse if it had been wet or icy. Georgian caricatures of people slipping on cobblestones are therefore comprehensible (Figure 8.7). I also sought out unfinished surfaces such as grass, dirt and mud. The shoes provided noticeably less grip than the modern walking boots that I would typically have worn on these surfaces and, again, I had to adjust my walking style to avoid slipping. The addition of hobnails would have helped here, so it is understandable why soldiers typically wore them as they would largely have been walking on unfinished rural surfaces – but they would likely have been slippery if they were stationed in a town. Although I could have had hobnails fitted to these shoes, I did not opt for them as I knew that I would often wear them indoors, where they would damage a wooden or textile floor.

Although the shoes were straight lasted, I wore them consistently on the same feet. As we saw in Chapter 7, instruction manuals for eighteenth-century officers suggested that the men should 'not always wear their Shoes on the same feet, but that they change them day about, to prevent them runing crooked'.[31] This would prevent uneven wear to the soles and so would make them last longer. Economy is, of course, a priority in the military, but the experience of wearing straight-lasted shoes suggests that it is unlikely that these prescriptions were put into practice. Once the uppers form to the shape of one foot it is very uncomfortable to wear them on the other: I tried to do this and could barely get them on. I also did not want to create additional holes for the buckles, as the fitting is specific to left and right. If soldiers were going to wear the shoes for long periods and march long distances, it was vital that they be as comfortable as possible, so it is unlikely that these orders were actually made or obeyed.

Over a matter of days, the shoes took the form of the foot. After ten days of wear, I took detailed photographs and the outlines of the absent body were already visible in the uppers and sole (Figure 8.8). By the end of the process, these were even more pronounced (Figure 8.9). The uppers mould to the asymmetrical arch of the midfoot, and creasing is visible at the toes, providing evidence of movement and an outline of their contours. The sole too has a distinctive pattern of wear, highlighting where the foot comes into contact with the ground (Figure 8.10), and my footprint is visible in the insole, including individual toes. The wearer is therefore captured in the garment. As Peter Stallybrass writes of cloth, its magic is that 'it receives us: receives our smells, our sweat, our shape even'.[32] In the

Figure 8.8 *Uppers showing the shape of the foot after ten days' wear.*

Figure 8.9 *Uppers showing the shape of the foot after forty days' wear.*

Figure 8.10 *Outline of the foot visible on the sole after forty days' wear.*

language of sewing, wrinkles are 'memory', so they record part of ourselves. Sophie Woodward adds that the material changes to garments that occur through wear 'enact relations between people and encode memories, as the material and the social are entangled and co-constituted'.[33]

The wear to the heel and sole is particularly revealing as it records the nature of my walking gait. Wear therefore concerns the motion of the whole body as well as the shape of the foot itself. As a historical source, it reveals more than a snapshot of a particular moment in time, but rather captures dynamic activity over the whole life of the object. The soles at the toe were initially flat to the ground, but over time they curled upwards and wore unevenly, with additional wear to the edge by the big toe. Wear to the heel was even more pronounced: the heel is the part of the shoe that endures the most wear, so was the most common part of the shoe to be replaced. At the rear of the heel, wear to the outside edge was around ten millimetres, as opposed to around a millimetre on the inside edge (Figure 8.11). This suggests that my feet slightly point outwards when I walk and that pressure is exerted diagonally, from the outside at the back to the inside at the front. At the end of the wearing process, I consulted a

Figure 8.11 *Wear to the heel after forty days.*

podiatrist at my university, who noted that this is a common arrangement for walking. Any departure from this wear pattern in historic shoes would therefore suggest an abnormality in the walking gait. The podiatrist also confirmed that my feet had not been harmed by the process of wearing the shoes, but that the inward pressure on the great toes could have exacerbated a case of *hallux valgus* if it was already congenital.[34]

Conclusion

I drew many lessons from this exercise, which informed the approach that I have taken to the history of shoes in the rest of the book. Fundamentally, the experience of wearing Georgian shoes was distinct from the modern shoes that I was accustomed to wearing. They impacted my body and its motion, affecting the way that I stood and walked. They were different in sensory terms, providing a particular olfactory and acoustic experience, as well as a distinctive look and feel. The processes of fixing, fastening and unfastening the buckles would have been familiar to eighteenth-century wearers, but was a new haptic experience for me. Wearing these shoes therefore created distinctive embodied knowledge, which helped me to historicize the corporeal and sensory experience of wearing shoes, in ways that would not have occurred to me had I not worn them. When studying the history of footwear, it is vital to bear these considerations in mind, since these fundamentally embodied objects need to be understood within a bodily and experiential frame of reference. Work on material culture can be rather disembodied, or even un-material, so this approach is a useful corrective to that.

Wearing eighteenth-century shoes highlights that they were more individual than modern shoes. We saw in Chapter 5 that assistive technologies for conditions such as gout were more individualized in the eighteenth century than they are today. Modernity standardizes bodies, and even assistive objects for non-standard bodies have to be mass produced to standard patterns. But, even if the shoes were not made to order, or made to measure, they became individualized through the process of wear. Eighteenth-century shoes were not constructed in the form of the foot but were designed to adapt to the wearer's body in a unique way. Two pairs of shoes made to the same pattern and size by the same shoemaker would be unique to start off with, as they were handmade, but they would quickly become very different once their wearers started to wear them. Wearers would customize their shoes by adding decorative buckles or adapting the fabric of the shoe itself, perhaps making a cut to a boot top to make it easier to get on, or a slit to the upper to accommodate the swelling of gout. And the practices of buying second-hand, cobbling and repurposing footwear meant that a shoe might change its appearance and function over the course of its life.

The adaptability of eighteenth-century footwear highlights that it was designed to be repaired. The life of a pair of shoes could be considerably extended by replacing the soles and heels, and by repairing damage or wear to the uppers. Today's mass-produced shoes cannot generally be repaired, so have a shorter lifespan and are less sustainable. Georgian shoes were made from entirely organic materials, so are a far more sustainable proposition. Shoes today are often made from synthetic materials – such as 'vegan leather' made from petrochemicals – that are very polluting to produce and do not easily biodegrade. Even today's leather shoes are more polluting, since they are tanned with substances such as chromium. In the twenty-first century, shoes are unusually cheap from a historical point of view, mostly being mass produced in the global south where labour costs and environmental protections are low. Consumers in the global north think nothing of owning multiple pairs and often have a throwaway attitude towards them. Shoes are therefore part of the story of globalized capitalism and the impact that it has had on our environment. The process of commissioning a pair of handmade shoes highlighted the real time and costs (both for materials and skilled labour) associated with producing them. It is therefore comprehensible how shoes in the eighteenth-century were such a substantial investment, and why most people might only own one or two pairs.

Georgians, therefore, had a different relationship with their shoes to that which we have today. We have seen that it was common for the wealthy to purchase bespoke shoes and therefore to have a relationship with the producer, with whom they would have a dialogue about their requirements: this dialogue presupposed specialist knowledge about the way that shoes were constructed. Shoes could be constructed to fit their bodies, especially if their shoemaker or bootmaker were using personalized lasts. To a certain extent, this was mirrored in the production process for my own shoes, even though they were to a humbler design. Most Georgians acquired their shoes ready-made, which is much more like the modern experience of shoe shopping. Before the arrival of standard sizing, it was more of a lottery whether they would fit (and, given that shoes today are increasingly bought online, rather than tried on in a store with a knowledgeable assistant, the element of luck is possibly returning). Also, as we have seen, it was much more common to acquire shoes second-hand, which had already formed to the body of their previous owner, further reducing the likelihood of a good fit.

We have seen how different types of shoe could be worn for particular activities. Those who could afford multiple pairs might own footwear for riding, for dancing, for walking in mud, or for special occasions. Because shoes enable us to perform some activities – while preventing us from doing others – they relate very closely to the roles that their wearers have in society. For this reason, they have historically been deeply ideological objects, and this was certainly true in the Georgian era. This book has argued that it was particularly the case in terms of gender. Shoes for men and women diverged in style and function over the course of the eighteenth century, signalling their suitability for different social roles. Historians have long argued that this period witnessed the emergence of 'separate spheres' or 'two sexes' and was therefore a pivotal one in the establishment of modern gender relations. These narratives have been substantially critiqued in recent years, not least on the grounds of poor fit with actual everyday experience. But it is still necessary to understand the process by which masculinity and femininity developed in this period, and thinking about material objects – and particularly ones that had such a direct impact upon bodies and behaviour – is a way to ground these prescriptions in historical practice.

Finally, wearing shoes like those I had made for me highlights the close and reciprocal relationship that we have with our footwear. Chapter 2 explored how both the body impacts the shoe and the shoe impacts the body. This means that historic shoes constitute a record of the wearer's body, providing a record of how that body moved, and allowing us to infer the impact that the shoe itself had on the movements of the body. Even after only forty days, it was possible to see a record of my body and its movements, and this experience has helped me to gauge the extent of wear on shoes that I examined in museum collections. Having created a primary source about myself, it gave me insights into the ways that shoes were primary sources about historic bodies. No other garment captures the body in the way that shoes do. As Sampson notes, shoes are 'records of lived experience'.[35] They are uniquely powerful primary sources that tell us things that other sources do not, or tell us about things for which there is no other evidence. They are entangled with our bodies and our daily experiences, and inform how we see ourselves and how others see us. Shoes are part of who we are and who we used to be.

Notes

1. Catherine Shoard, 'Kim Kardashian Accused of Doing "Permanent Damage" to Marilyn Monroe's Dress', *The Guardian*, 14 June 2022: https://www.theguardian.com/film/2022/jun/14/kim-kardashian-accused-of-doing-permanent-damage-to-marilyn-monroe-dress (accessed 7 December 2022).

2. Sarah Bendall, 'The Case of the "French Vardinggale": A Methodological Approach to Reconstructing and Understanding Ephemeral Garments', *Fashion Theory* 23, no. 3 (2019): 363–99 (364).

3. Sally Denshire, 'On Auto-ethnography', *Current Sociology Review* 62, no. 6 (2014): 831–50 (831).

4. Sherick A. Hughes and Julie Pennington, *Autoethnography: Process, Product, and Possibility for Critical Social Research* (London: Sage, 2017), 5.

5. Maurice Merleau-Ponty, *Phenomenology of Perception*, trans. C. Smith (1962; London: Routledge, 1998), ix, 213.

6. Sally Dean, 'Where Is the Body in the Costume Design Process?', *Studies in Costume and Performance* 1, no. 1 (2016): 97–111 (98).

7. Davidson, 'The Embodied Turn', 338.

8. Stephen Gapps, 'Mobile Monuments: A View of Historical Re-enactment and Authenticity from Inside the Costume Cupboard of History', *Rethinking History* 13, no. 3 (2009): 395–409.

9. Vanessa Agnew, 'History's Affective Turn: Historical Re-enactment and Its Work in the Present', *Rethinking History* 11, no. 3 (2007): 299–312; Iain McCalman and Paul Pickering (eds), *Historical Re-enactment: From Realism to the Affective Turn* (Houndmills: Palgrave, 2010).

10. I should particularly like to thank Gemma Bagshaw, Rory Butcher, Rob Griffith, Bethan Jenkins and Andy Smith.

11. Davidson, 'The Embodied Turn', 331.

12. Bendall, 'Case of the "French Vardinggale"', 366. See also Serena Dyer, *Material Lives: Women Makers and Consumer Culture in the 18th Century* (London: Bloomsbury, 2021).

13. Sampson, *Worn*, 228.

14. See: https://www.andyburke.co.uk/c18th.htm (accessed 9 December 2022).

15. D. A. Saguto (ed. and trans.), *M. de Garsault's Art of the Shoemaker* (Williamsburg, VA: Colonial Williamsburg Foundation, 2009).

16. The equivalent of EU size 47 or US size 13.

17. Davidson, 'The Embodied Turn', 344.

18. Bendall, 'Case of the "French Vardinggale"', 379.

19. Ibid., 378.

20. There are also instructional videos on YouTube: for example, American Duchess, 'How to Fit 18th Century Buckles', https://www.youtube.com/watch?v=yP-eTBMfrqo (accessed 9 December 2022).

21. Entwistle, *The Fashioned Body*, 7.

22. Bendall, 'Case of the "French Vardinggale"', 386. See also: Pat Poppy, 'Fancy Dress? Costume for Re-enactment', *Costume* 31, no. 1 (1997): 100–4.

23. I posted these on my Twitter account: @historymatt, using the hashtag #georgianshoes.

24. Wearing diary for 2 August 2022 and 9 August 2022.

25. Wearing diary for day forty, 15 November 2022.

26. Sampson, *Worn*, 103, 110.

27. 'Buckles draw attention to the feet!': wearing diary for day four, 4 August 2022.

28. On the history of smell, see William Tullett, *Smell in Eighteenth-Century England: A Social Sense* (Oxford: Oxford University Press, 2019).

29. Smollett, *The Expedition of Humphry Clinker*, 66.

30. Anon., *Art of Preserving the Feet*, 16.

31. Cuthbertson, *System for the Compleat Interior Management*, 135.

32. Peter Stallybrass, 'Worn Worlds: Clothes, Mourning and the Life of Things', *Yale Review* 81, no. 2 (1993): 35–50 (36).

33. Sophie Woodward, 'Object Interviews, Material Imaginings and "Unsettling" Methods: Interdisciplinary Approaches to Understanding Materials and Material Culture', *Qualitative Research* 16, no. 4 (2015): 359–74 (360).

34. I am grateful to Manju Mital from Podiatry at the University of Northampton.

35. Sampson, *Worn*, 139.

Select bibliography

Primary sources

Museum collections and archives

Objects and unpublished sources were consulted at the following institutions:

Alfred Gillett Trust, Street, Somerset.
Bata Shoe Museum, Toronto.
British Museum, London.
Castle Museum, York.
Chatham Historic Dockyard.
Fashion Museum, Bath.
Lewis Walpole Library, Connecticut.
Museum of Leathercraft, Northampton.
Museum of London.
National Army Museum, Stevenage.
National Museum of Scotland, Edinburgh.
National War Museum, Edinburgh.
Northampton Museum and Art Gallery.
Royal Archives, Windsor.
Platt Fields Gallery, Manchester.
The National Archives, Kew.
The Shoe Museum, Street, Somerset.
Trowbridge Museum.
Victoria and Albert Museum, London.

Newspapers and periodicals

The Connoisseur.
The Christian Reformer: Or, Unitarian Magazine.
The Critical Review: Or, Annals of Literature.
The European Magazine.
The European Magazine, and London Review.
The Gazetteer and New Daily Advertiser.
Literary and Fashionable Magazine.

The Literary Magazine: Or Universal Review.
London Magazine and Review.
The Tatler.
The Westminster Review.

Printed primary sources

Anon. *The Art of Preserving the Feet; Or, Practical Instructions for the Prevention and Cure of Corns, Bunnions, Callosities, Chilblains, &c.* London, 1818.
Anon. *The Cabinet; or the Selected Beauties of Literature*. Edinburgh, 1825.
Anon. *Collection of Orders, Regulations, and Instructions for the Army, published by Order of the Secretary of War*. London, 1807.
Anon. *Country-Dancing Made Plain and Easy to Every Capacity*. London, 1764.
Anon. *The Flower-Piece: A Collection of Miscellany Poems. By Several Hands*. London, 1781.
Anon. *On Clothing*. Manchester, 1797.
Anon. *The Secret History of an Old Shoe*. London, 1734.
Anon. *The Twelfth-Day Gift: Or the Grand Exhibition*. London, 1767.
Aspinall, A., ed. *The Correspondence of George Prince of Wales, 1770–1812*. 4 vols. London: Cassell, 1963–67.
Austen, Jane. *Northanger Abbey*. 1817. London: Penguin, 1995.
Austen, Jane. *Pride and Prejudice*. 1813. Oxford: Oxford University Press, 2019.
Austen, Jane. *Jane Austen's Letters*, edited by Deirdre Le Faye. Oxford: Oxford University Press, 1995.
Beamish, Richard. *Memoir of the Life of Sir Marc Isambard Brunel*. London: Longman, Green, Longman & Roberts, 1862.
Boswell, James. *Boswell's London Journal, 1762–1763*, edited by Frederick Pottle. New Haven, CT: Yale University Press, 1950.
Brownsword, William. *Laugh and Lye Down; Or, A Pleasant, but sure, Remedy for the Gout, Without Expence or Danger*. London, 1789.
Buchan, W. *Buchan's Domestic Medicine Modernized; Or, A Treatise on the Prevention and Cure of Diseases by Regimen and Simple Medicine*. London, 1809.
Burke, Edmund. *Reflections on the Revolution in France*. 1790. Oxford: Oxford University Press, 1993.
Clarke, John. *Military Institutions of Vegetius*. London, 1767.
Cooper, John. *Fusilier Cooper: Experiences in the 7th (Royal) Fusiliers during the Peninsular Campaign of the Napoleonic Wars and the American Campaign to New Orleans*. Milton Keynes: Leonaur, 2007.
Cooper, Samuel. *Practice of Surgery: Being an Elementary Work for Students and a Concise Book of Reference for Practitioners*. Hanover, NH, 1815.
Cowell, John Stepney. *Leaves from the Diary of an Officer of the Guards*. London, 1854.
Cowper, William. *The Letters and Prose Writings of William Cowper: Volume 1*, Adelphi *and Letters 1750–1781*, edited by James King and Charles Ryskamp. Oxford: Clarendon Press, 1979.
Cruikshank, George. *The Spirit of English Wit, or Post-Chaise Companion*. London, 1813.
Cutbush, Edward. *Observations on the Means of Preserving the Health of Soldiers and Sailors*. Philadelphia, 1808.
Cuthbertson, Bennett. *A System for the Complete Interior Management and Oeconomy of a Battalion of Infantry*. Dublin, 1768.
Donkin, Robert. *Military Collections and Remarks*. New York City, 1777.
Durlacher, Lewis. *A Concise Treatise on Corns, Bunions and the Disorders of Nails*. London, 1845.
Feltham, John. *A Guide to the Watering and Sea-Bathing Places*. London, 1806.
Ford, James, ed. *A Medical Student at St Thomas's Hospital, 1801–1802: The Weekes Family Letters*. London: Wellcome, 1987.

Garrick, David. *The Clandestine Marriage: A Comedy*. London, 1778.
Gay, John. *Trivia: Or the Art of Walking the Streets of London*. London, 1716.
Gregory, James, trans. *The Catechism of Health: Selected and Translated from the German of Dr Faust*. Edinburgh, 1797.
Gronow, Rees Howell. *Captain Gronow: His Reminiscences of Victorian and Regency Life 1810–60*, edited by Christopher Hibbert. London: Kyle Cathie, 1991.
Gurwood, John, ed. *The Dispatches of Field Marshall the Duke of Wellington*. 12 vols. Cambridge: Cambridge University Press, 2010.
Hall, Joseph Sparkes. *The Book of the Feet: A History of Boots and Shoes, with Illustrations*. New York City, 1847.
Herbert, Lord, ed. *Pembroke Papers (1734–1780): Letters and Diaries of Henry, Tenth Earl of Pembroke and His Circle*. London, 1939.
Hibbert, Christopher, (ed.), *The Recollections of Rifleman Harris: As Told to Henry Curling* (Moreton-in-Marsh: Windrush Press, 1996).
Hoare, Prince. *The Indiscretion: A Comedy*. London, 1800.
Hodgson, E. *The Trial of Kenith McKenzie*. London, 1784.
Holden, Henry. *Flat-Foot or Splay-Foot (Valgus)*. London: Holden Brothers, 1905.
Jackson, Robert. *A Systematic View of the Formation, Discipline, and Economy of Armies*. London, 1804.
Johnson, Samuel. *A Dictionary of the English Language*. 2 vols. London, 1792.
Lewis, W. S., ed. *The Yale Edition of Horace Walpole's Correspondence*. 48 vols. New Haven, CT: Yale University Press, 1977.
Liddell Hart, B. H., ed. *The Letters of Private Wheeler 1809–1828*. Moreton-in-Marsh: Windrush Press, 1998.
Lochée, Lewis. *An Essay on Military Education*. London, 1773.
Locke, John. *Some Thoughts Concerning Education*. London, 1693.
Low, D. *Chiropodologia, Or, A Scientific Enquiry into the Causes of Corns, Warts, Onions and Other Painful or Offensive Cutaneous Excrescences*. London, 1785.
Mayhew, Henry. *The Unknown Mayhew: Selections from the Morning Chronicle, 1849–1850*, edited by E. P. Thompson and Eileen Yeo. London: Merlin, 1971.
Melville, Charles Henderson. *Military Hygiene and Sanitation*. London: E. Arnold, 1912.
Monro, Donald. *Observations on the Means of Preserving the Health of Soldiers*. London, 1780.
Nisbet, William. *A Practical Treatise on Diet, and on the Most Salutary and Agreeable Means of Supporting Life and Health, by Ailment and Regimen*. London, 1801.
Otway, Thomas. *The Works of Thomas Otway, In Two Volumes*. London, 1718.
Pembroke, H. H. *Military Equitation: Or, A Method of Breaking Horses, and Teaching Soldiers to Ride. Designed for the Use of the Army*. London, 1813.
Percy, Elizabeth Seymour. *A Short Tour Made in the Year One Thousand Seven Hundred and Seventy One*. London, 1775.
Ramsay, George. *The Encyclopedia of Anecdotes, Illustrative of Character and Events, From Genuine Sources*. London, 1828.
Saguto, D. A., ed. and trans. *M. de Garsault's Art of the Shoemaker* (François Alexandre Pierre de Garsault, *L'Art du cordonnier* [1767]). Williamsburg, VA: Colonial Williamsburg Foundation, 2009.
Simmonds, George. *A British Rifle Man: The Journals and Correspondence of Major George Simmons, Rifle Brigade, during the Peninsular War and the Campaign of Waterloo*, edited by Willoughby Verner. London: A. & C. Black, 1899.
Smith, William. *A Sure Guide in Sickness and Health, in the Choice of Food, and Use of Medicine*. London, 1776.
Smollett, Tobias. *The Expedition of Humphry Clinker*. 1771. Oxford: Oxford University Press, 1984.
Stanhope, Philip Dormer, Earl of Chesterfield. *Lord Chesterfield's Letters*, edited by David Roberts. Oxford: Oxford University Press, 1992.

Stanhope, Philip Dormer. *Lord Chesterfield's Witticisms: Or, the Grand Pantheon of Genius, Sentiment and* Taste. London, 1773.

Strachan, Hew. *British Military Uniforms 1768–1796: The Dress of the British Army from Official Sources*. London: Arms & Armour Press, 1975.

Struve, Christian August. *A Familiar Treatise on the Education of Children, during the First Period of their Lives*. London, 1802.

Swaysland, Edward. *Boot and Shoe Design and Manufacture*. Northampton, 1905.

Swift, Jonathan. *Gulliver's Travels*. 1726. Oxford: Oxford University Press, 1971.

Trench-Gascoigne, F. R. T. 'Extracts from the Standing Orders in the Garrison of Gibraltar'. *Journal of the Society for Army Historical Research* 2, no. 8 (1923): 86–9.

Trench-Gascoigne, F. R. T. 'Extracts from the Standing Orders in the Garrison of Gibraltar (1803) (Continued)'. *Journal for the Society for Army Historical Research* 2, no. 9 (1923): 124–9.

Underwood, Michael. *A Treatise on the Diseases of Children with Directions for the Management of Infants*. 3 vols. London, 1805.

Vaughan, Walter. *An Essay, Philosophical and Medical, Concerning Modern Clothing*. London, 1792.

Weaver, John. *An Essay Towards an History of Dancing, in Which the Whole Art and its Various Excellencies are in Some Measure Explain'd*. London, 1712.

Willich, A. F. M. *Lectures in Diet and Regimen, Being a Systematic Inquiry into the Most Rational Means of Preserving Health and Prolonging Life*. London, 1799.

Wollstonecraft, Mary. *A Vindication of the Rights of Woman*. 1792. Oxford: Oxford University Press, 2008.

Secondary sources

Alexander, Kimberly. 'Shoes and the City: Shoes and Their Sphere of Influence in Early America, 1740–1789'. In *The Routledge History Handbook of Gender and the Urban Experience*, edited by Deborah Simonton, 296–308. London: Routledge, 2017.

Alexander, Kimberly. *Treasures Afoot: Shoe Stories from the Georgian Era*. Baltimore, MD: Johns Hopkins University Press, 2018.

Anderson, Vivi Lena. 'Old Shoes in a New Perspective – Fashioning Archaeology'. *Fashion Practice* 9, no. 2 (2017): 168–82.

Begiato, Joanne. *Manliness in Britain, 1760–1900: Bodies, Emotion, and Material Culture*. Manchester: Manchester University Press, 2020.

Belolan, Nicole. 'The Material Culture of Gout in Early America'. In *Making Disability Modern: Design Histories*, edited by Bess Williamson and Elizabeth Guffey, 19–42. London: Bloomsbury, 2020.

Bendall, Sarah. 'The Case of the "French Vardinggale": A Methodological Approach to Reconstructing and Understanding Ephemeral Garments'. *Fashion Theory* 23, no. 3 (2019): 363–99.

Benstock, Shari, and Suzanne Ferriss, eds. *Footnotes: On Shoes*. New Brunswick, NJ: Rutgers University Press, 2001.

Bide, Bethan. 'Signs of Wear: Encountering Memory in the Worn Materiality of a Museum Fashion Collection'. *Fashion Theory* 21, no. 4 (2017): 449–76.

Bondi, Federico, and Giovanni Mariacher. *If the Shoe Fits*, translated by Jane Chisholm. Venice: Cavallino, 1979.

Brant, C., and S. Whyman, eds. *Walking the Streets of Eighteenth-Century London: John Gay's* Trivia *(1716)*. Oxford: Oxford University Press, 2007.

Breward, Christopher. *The Culture of Fashion: A New History of Fashionable Dress*. Manchester: Manchester University Press, 1995.

Breward, Christopher. 'Fashioning Masculinity: Men's Footwear and Modernity'. In *Shoes: A History from Sandals to Sneakers*, edited by Giorgio Riello and Peter McNeil, 206–23. Oxford: Berg, 2006.
Brewer, John. *The Sinews of Power: War, Money and the English State, 1688–1783*. London: Unwin Hyman, 1989.
Brooke, Iris. *A History of English Footwear*. London: St Giles, 1945.
Carter, Philip. 'An "Effeminate" or "Efficient" Nation? Masculinity and Eighteenth-Century Social Documentary'. *Textual Practice* 11, no. 3 (1997): 429–44.
Carter, Philip. *Men and the Emergence of Polite Society: Britain, 1660–1800*. London: Longman, 2001.
Charters, Erica. 'The Caring Fiscal-Military State during the Seven Years War, 1756–63'. *The Historical Journal* 52, no. 4 (2009): 921–41.
Charters, Erica. *Disease, War and the Imperial State: The Welfare of the British Armed Forces during the Seven Years' War*. Chicago: Chicago University Press, 2014.
Clements, Paul. *Marc Isambard Brunel*. Chichester: Phillimore & Co., 2006.
David, Alison Matthews. *Fashion Victims: The Dangers of Dress Past and Present*. London: Bloomsbury, 2015.
David, Alison Matthews. 'War and Wellingtons: Military Footwear in the Age of Empire'. In *Shoes: A History from Sandals to Sneakers*, edited by Giorgio Riello and Peter McNeil (eds), 116–37. Oxford: Berg, 2006.
Davidson, Hilary. *Dress in the Age of Jane Austen: Regency Fashion*. New Haven, CT: Yale University Press, 2019.
Davidson, Hilary. 'The Embodied Turn: Making and Remaking Dress as an Academic Practice'. *Fashion Theory* 23, no. 3 (2019): 329–62.
Davidson, Hilary. 'Holding the Sole: Shoes, Emotions, and the Supernatural'. In *Feeling Things: Objects and Emotions Through History*, edited by Stephanie Downes, Sally Holloway and Sarah Randles, 72–93. Oxford: Oxford University Press, 2018.
Dean, Sally. 'Where Is the Body in the Costume Design Process?' *Studies in Costume and Performance* 1, no. 1 (2016): 97–111.
DeMello, Margo. *Feet and Footwear: A Cultural Encyclopedia*. Santa Barbara, CA: Greenwood Press, 2009.
Denshire, Sally. 'On Auto-ethnography'. *Current Sociology Review* 62, no. 6 (2014): 831–50.
Earle, Rebecca. '"Two Pairs of Silk Satin Shoes!!" Race, Clothing and Identity in the Americas (17th–19th Centuries)'. *History Workshop Journal* 52 (2001): 175–95.
Entwhistle, Joanne. *The Fashioned Body: Fashion, Dress and Modern Social Theory*. Cambridge: Polity Press, 2000.
Fairhurst, Alison. 'Eighteenth-Century Women's Shoes: A Valuable Historical Resource'. *Costume* 53, no. 1 (2010): 20–42.
Finn, Margot. 'Men's Things: Masculine Possession in the Consumer Revolution'. *Social History* 25, no. 2 (2000): 133–55.
Flügel, J. C. *The Psychology of Clothes*. London: Institute of Psycho-Analysis and Hogarth Press, 1930.
Forth, Christopher. *Masculinity in the Modern West: Gender, Civilization and the Body*. Basingstoke: Palgrave Macmillan, 2008.
Harvey, J. *Men in Black*. London: Reaktion, 1995.
Harvey, Karen, ed. *Material Culture: A Student's Guide to Approaching Alternative Sources*. London: Routledge, 2009.
Harvey, Karen. 'Men of Parts: Masculine Embodiment and the Male Leg in Eighteenth-Century England'. *Journal of British Studies* 54, no. 4 (2015): 797–821.
Hatley, Victor. 'Shoemakers in Northamptonshire, 1762–1911: A Statistical Survey'. *Northampton Historical Series* 6 (1971): 1–13.
Hobsbawm, Eric, and Joan Scott. 'Political Shoemakers'. *Past & Present* 89, no. 1 (1980): 86–114.
Hollander, Anne. *Seeing Through Clothes*. Berkeley: University of California Press, 1993.
Hood, Adrienne. 'Material Culture: The Object'. In *History Beyond the Text: A Student's Guide to Approaching Alternative Sources*, edited by Sarah Barber and Corinna Peniston-Bird, 176–98. London: Routledge, 2009.
Houlbrook, Ceri. 'Ritual, Recycling and Recontextualization: Putting the Concealed Shoe in Context'. *Cambridge Archaeological Journal* 23, no. 1 (2013): 99–112.

Houlbrook, Ceri, and Rebecca Shawcross. 'Revealing the Ritually Concealed: Custodians, Creators and the Concealed Shoe'. *Material Religion* 14, no. 2 (2018): 163–82.

Kerfoot, Alicia. 'Declining Buckles and Movable Shoes in Frances Burney's *Cecilia*'. *The Burney Journal* 11 (2011): 55–79.

Kerfoot, Alicia. 'Virtuous Footwear: Pamela's Shoe Heel and Cinderella's "Little Glass Slipper"'. *Eighteenth-Century Fiction* 31, no. 2 (2019): 343–71.

Klein, Lawrence. 'Politeness and the Interpretation of the British Eighteenth Century'. *The Historical Journal* 45, no. 4 (2002): 869–98.

Kuchta, David. *The Three-Piece Suit and Modern Masculinity: England, 1550–1850*. Berkeley: University of California Press, 2002.

Langford, Paul. 'Politics and Manners from Sir Robert Walpole to Sir Robert Peel'. *Proceedings of the British Academy* 94 (1997): 103–25.

Laqueur, Thomas. *Making Sex: Body and Gender from the Greeks to Freud*. Cambridge, MA: Harvard University Press, 1990.

Lemire, Beverly. 'Consumerism in Preindustrial and Early Industrial England: The Trade in Secondhand Clothes'. *Journal of British Studies* 27, no. 1 (1988): 1–24.

Lemire, Beverly. 'A Question of Trousers: Seafarers, Masculinity and Empire in the Shaping of British Male Dress, *c.* 1600–1800'. *Cultural and Social History* 13, no. 1 (2016): 1–22.

Mays, S. A. 'Paleopathological Study of Hallux Valgus'. *American Journal of Physical Anthropology* 126, no. 2 (2005): 126–39.

McCormack, Matthew. 'Dance and Drill: Polite Accomplishments and Military Masculinities in Georgian Britain'. *Cultural and Social History* 8, no. 3 (2011): 315–30.

McCormack, Matthew. *Embodying the Militia in Georgian England*. Oxford: Oxford University Press, 2015.

McCormack, Matthew. *The Independent Man: Citizenship and Gender Politics in Georgian England*. Manchester: Manchester University Press, 2005.

McCormack, Matthew. 'So Manly and Ornamental: Shoe Buckles and Britain's Eighteenth Century'. *The English Historical Review* 138, no. 592 (2023): 474–96.

McCormack, Matthew. 'Tall Histories: Height and Georgian Masculinities'. *Transactions of the Royal Historical Society* 6, no. 26 (2016): 79–101.

McDowell, Colin. *Shoes: Fashion and Fancy*. London: Thames & Hudson, 1989.

McKendrick, Neil, John Brewer and J. H. Plumb. *The Birth of a Consumer Society: The Commercialisation of Eighteenth-Century England*. Bloomington: Indiana University Press, 1982.

McNeil, Peter, and Giorgio Riello. 'The Art and Science of Walking: Gender, Space and the Fashionable Body in the Long Eighteenth Century'. *Fashion Theory* 9, no. 2 (2005): 175–204.

Merleau-Ponty, Maurice. *Phenomenology of Perception*. 1962. London: Routledge, 1998.

Myerly, Scott Hughes. *British Military Spectacle: From the Napoleonic Wars Through the Crimea*. Cambridge, MA: Harvard University Press, 1996.

Navickas, Katrina. '"That Sash Will Hang You": Political Clothing and Adornment in England, 1780–1840'. *Journal of British Studies* 49, no. 3 (2010): 540–65.

Oman, C. *Wellington's Army, 1809–1814*. London: E. Arnold, 1913.

Ott, Katherine. 'Disability Things: Material Culture and American Disability History, 1700–2010'. In *Disability Histories*, edited by Susan Burch and Michael Rembis, 119–45. Urbana: University of Illinois Press, 2014.

Persson, Helen, ed. *Shoes: Pleasure and Pain*. London: Victoria and Albert Museum, 2015.

Porter, Roy, and G. S. Rousseau. *Gout: The Patrician Malady*. New Haven, CT: Yale University Press, 1998.

Pratt, Lucy, and Linda Woolley. *Shoes*. London: V&A Publications, 2000.

Ribeiro, Aileen. *Dress in Eighteenth-Century Europe, 1715–1789*. London: Holmes & Meier, 1985.

Riello, Giorgio. '*La Chaussure à la Mode*: Product Innovation and Marketing Strategies in Parisian and London Boot and Shoemaking in the Early Nineteenth Century'. *Textile History* 34, no. 2 (2003): 107–33.

Riello, Giorgio. *A Foot in the Past: Consumers, Producers and Footwear in the Long Eighteenth Century*. Oxford: Oxford University Press, 2006.
Riello, Giorgio, and Peter McNeil. 'Footprints from History'. *History Today* 57, no. 3 (2007): 30–6.
Riello, Giorgio, and Peter McNeil, eds. *Shoes: A History from Sandals to Sneakers*. Oxford: Berg, 2006.
Rublack, Ulinka. 'Matter in the Material Renaissance'. *Past and Present* 219, no. 1 (2013): 41–85.
Sampson, Ellen. *Worn: Footwear, Attachment and the Affects of Wear*. London: Bloomsbury, 2020.
Semmelhack, Elizabeth. *Shoes: The Meaning of Style*. London: Reaktion, 2017.
Semmelhack, Elizabeth. *Standing Tall: The Curious History of Men in Heels*. Toronto: Bata Shoe Museum, 2016.
Shawcross, Rebecca. *Shoes: An Illustrated History*. London: Bloomsbury, 2014.
Siena, Kevin. *Rotten Bodies: Class and Contagion in Eighteenth-Century Britain*. New Haven, CT: Yale University Press, 2019.
Stallybrass, Peter. 'Worn Worlds: Clothes, Mourning and the Life of Things'. *Yale Review* 81, no. 2 (1993): 35–50.
Steele, Valerie. *Shoes: A Lexicon of Style*. London: Scriptum, 1998.
Styles, John. *The Dress of the People: Everyday Fashion in Eighteenth-Century England*. New Haven, CT: Yale University Press, 2007.
Swallow, A. W. 'Interpretation of Wear Marks Seen in Footwear'. *Museum Assistants' Group Transactions* 12 (1973): 28–32.
Swann, June. *Shoes*. London: Batsford, 1982.
Swann, June. 'Shoes Concealed in Buildings'. *Costume* 30 (1996): 56–69.
Thornton, J. H. 'Left – Right – Left'. *Journal of the British Boot and Shoe Institution* 7, no. 4 (1959): 164–70.
Tosh, John. 'Gentlemanly Politeness and Manly Simplicity in Victorian England'. *Transactions of the Royal Historical Society* 12 (2002): 455–72.
Tosh, John. *A Man's Place: Masculinity and the Middle-Class Home in Victorian England*. New Haven, CT: Yale University Press, 1999.
Tullett, William. *Smell in Eighteenth-Century England: A Social Sense*. Oxford: Oxford University Press, 2019.
Turner, David. *Disability in Eighteenth-Century England: Imagining Physical Impairment*. Abingdon: Routledge, 2012.
Vickery, Amanda. *Behind Closed Doors: At Home in Georgian England*. New Haven, CT: Yale University Press, 2009.
Vickery, Amanda. 'Golden Age to Separate Spheres? A Review of the Categories and Chronology of English Women's History'. *The Historical Journal* 36, no. 2 (1993): 383–414.
Walsh, Claire. 'Shops, Shopping and the Art of Decision Making in Eighteenth-Century England'. In *Gender, Taste and Material Culture in Britain and North America 1700–1830*, edited by John Styles and Amanda Vickery, 151–77. New Haven, CT: Yale University Press, 2007.
Webb-Johnson, Cecil. *The Soldier's Manual of Foot Care and Foot Wear*. London: Dryden Pub. Co., 1916.
Wilcox, Turner. *The Mode in Footwear: From Antiquity to the Present Day*. London: Charles Scribner's Sons, 1948.
Wilson, Eunice. *A History of Shoe Fashions*. London: Pitman, 1969.
Woodward, Sophie. 'Object Interviews, Material Imaginings and "Unsettling" Methods: Interdisciplinary Approaches to Understanding Materials and Material Culture'. *Qualitative Research* 16, no. 4 (2015): 359–74.

Index

Alexander, Kimberly 6, 60
America 3, 6, 60, 85
archaeology 7, 10, 36, 156
Austen, Jane 124, 127, 132
auto-ethnography 10, 162–3, 172

Bath 74, 104, 121, 127
Begiato, Joanne 156
Bell, Sir Charles 39
Belolan, Nicole 97, 106
Bendall, Sarah 162, 164–5, 171
Burke, Andy 164
blacking 81–2, 131, 149, 168
blisters 42, 49, 171
body 1, 4, 8, 14, 35–54, 47, 97
    bodily materials 2, 42
    cultivation 5, 122, 125
    humoral 42–3, 99, 102
    history of 7
    weight of 2, 97
Bonaparte, Napoleon 139
boots 9, 21, 26, 29, 47, 61, 69–70, 73–94
    Blücher 68, 146
    brogan 68
    Derby 30, 146
    Hessian 74, 86
    jackboot 81–3
    postilion 76
    top-boots 73, 84
    Wellington 37–9, 46, 69–70, 74, 84–90
Boswell, James 46
breeches 23, 42, 100, 103, 108, 125, 128
Breward, Christopher 86
Brummell, George Bryan 'Beau' 83, 87
Brunel, Marc Isambard 146
buckles 3, 14, 22–5, 29, 68, 73, 110, 125, 132–3, 141–2, 156, 166–8

bunions (*hallux valgus*) 7, 49, 171, 177
Burke, Edmund 60
Bute, John Stuart 3rd Earl of 81, 125, 129

caricature 81, 84, 90, 97–9, 105–7, 114, 174
Charles II 63
Charters, Erica 151, 154
Chartism 56
Chesterfield, Philip Stanhope 4th Earl of 100
children 47, 59
chiropody 36, 42, 46, 49, 136, 152
    see also podiatry
citizenship 55, 58, 80
class 9, 22, 27, 32, 48–9, 55, 59, 66–9, 80, 90–1, 95, 131
clogs 41, 63–6
cobblers 17, 58, 149
Cole, William 99, 103
concealed shoes 3, 39, 147
consumption 13, 19–22, 51, 55, 76
Cooper, John 139, 142
cordwainers *see* shoemakers
corns 35, 42, 49, 80
cotton 42–3, 131
Cowper, William 3
Crawford, Jack 156–8
Cruikshank, Isaac 107
Cutbush, Edward 152, 155

dance 9, 25, 47, 60, 88, 119–138
David, Alison Matthews 80, 140, 147, 152
Davidson, Hilary, 3, 5, 120, 127, 163–5
DeMello, Margo 48, 67, 129
deportment 13, 27–8
disability 7, 9, 46, 95–117
Durlacher, Lewis 36, 45–6, 49
Dutch Republic 63

Earle, Rebecca 68
emotions 3, 5, 14, 29, 36, 74, 162, 172
Enlightenment 6, 45, 58

Fairhurst, Alison 42
fashion 5, 49
fashion studies 5, 7
Faust, Bernard 45, 47
feet 37, 39–40, 42, 45, 96
    shape 1, 48–9
fencing 47, 122
Finn, Margot 21, 76
First World War 43, 139–40, 149, 151–4
flannel 112–14
Flügel, J. C. 79
football 40, 120, 142
Forth, Christopher 51
France 63, 79
French Revolution 56, 132
gaiters 76, 142

Garsault, François de 164
Gay, John 35, 41, 46, 59, 63
gender 6, 14, 35, 43, 59, 84, 90
George IV 23, 108, 133
Gibraltar 74, 128
Gillray, James 63, 96, 107
Glorious Revolution (1688) 79
gout 9, 95–117, 127, 178
Grand Tour 60, 122–3
Gronow, Rees Howell 124

Hall, Joseph Sparkes 43, 48, 69
Harris, Benjamin 149–50
Harvey, Karen 68, 80, 84
heels 7, 14, 26–7, 29, 46, 58, 68, 79, 83, 129, 166, 176
height 27
history 5, 35
hobnails 68, 122, 142, 174
Hoby, George 73, 75, 79, 86, 90
Hogarth, William 60
horse riding 9, 26, 46–7, 73–6, 83, 90, 110–12, 122
Houlbrook, Ceri 3

industrial revolution 19

Jackson, Robert 140, 142, 149, 154
Johnson, Samuel 76

Kardashian, Kim 162
Kuchta, David 27, 79

laces 29, 132, 143, 168
Laqueur, Thomas 28, 43
leather 1, 4, 15–17, 29, 35, 41–2, 59–60, 161
    patent 131
Lemire, Beverly 22
linen 15, 17, 43, 99, 142, 166
London 104–5, 121
Louis XIV 27, 61, 129
Low, D. 46–7
luxury 51, 55, 58–9, 103, 123

macaronis 60–3, 129
McNeil, Peter 1, 36, 45, 61, 68, 73, 80, 152
Mann, Horace 99, 113
masculinity 6, 9, 13, 43, 51, 55, 58–9, 69, 74–94, 122, 179
material culture 5, 7, 10, 36, 74, 162
Mayhew, Henry 58
medicine 1, 28, 36, 42–5, 80, 95–7, 114, 154
Merleau-Ponty, Maurice 163
militia 7, 9, 149
Monro, Donald 154
museums 2–4, 8, 10, 36–7, 161
    Historic Dockyard Chatham 155
    Metropolitan Museum of Art 3
    Museum of Leathercraft 47, 67
    Museum of London 108
    National Army Museum 74
    Northampton Museum 37, 66, 74, 131, 146
    Trowbridge Museum 97
    Victoria and Albert Museum 105

national identity 9, 13, 32, 56, 60, 69
nerves 43
Nicolson, George 99
Nisbet, William 1, 41, 43
North, Frederick Lord 95
Northampton 18, 22, 146
Northumberland, Duchess of (Elizabeth Seymour Percy) 106

Ott, Katherine 96

pain 1, 9, 42–3, 74, 95, 99, 105, 113, 139
pattens 8, 15, 130
Pembroke, George Herbert 11th Earl 122

Pitt the Elder, William 105
Pitt the Younger, William 107
plastic 1, 41
podiatry 43, 80, 177
   see also chiropody
polish 42, 168
   see also blacking
politeness 5, 9, 19, 22, 27, 29, 47, 60, 122
politics 5, 9, 55–72, 103
Porter, Roy 99, 102, 112
Portugal 145
proverbs 3

race 49, 59, 68, 90, 152
re-enactment 10, 121, 163
Reform Act (1832) 65
representation 7, 14, 161–2
Richmond 174
Riberio, Aileen 28, 60
Richardson, Samuel 2
Riello, Giorgio 1, 36, 45, 61, 68, 73–4, 80, 84, 152
Rossi, William A. 26
Rousseau, George 99, 102, 112
rubber 1, 41

sailors 155–8
Sampson, Ellen 164, 170
second-hand 2, 13, 22, 67, 178–9
senses 8, 21, 66, 172, 177–8
   see also smell, sound
sensibility 19, 43, 58
   see also nerves
servants 22, 42, 76, 83, 101, 103, 167
sexuality 1, 76, 121
Shakespeare, William 14, 119
shoemakers 17–19, 56–8
shoemaking 17–19, 145–6, 164–8
   bespoke 21, 39, 47, 74–5, 86, 90, 106, 179
   factories 19
   lasts 8, 48, 90, 166, 179
   ready-made 21–2
   stages of the process 17, 165–6
   workshops 19
shoe styles
   common shoe 14
   mule 73
   Oxford 30
   trainers 171, 174

Siena, Kevin 42
silk 2, 15, 29, 108, 129, 131, 135
Simmons, George 150
sizing 10, 22, 146
skin 42, 60
smell 42, 172–4
Smollett, Tobias 103–5
socks 42, 133, 148, 152, 170
   see also stockings
soldiers 9, 43, 73, 76, 81, 125, 139–54
sound 172
Spain 9, 60, 139
Stallybrass, Peter 174
Steele, Valerie 76, 79
stockings 23, 99, 103, 125, 128
   see also socks
straight lasted footwear 14–15, 83, 135, 149, 156, 166, 171
Styles, John 75, 148
superstition 3
   see also concealed shoes
sustainability 178
Swann, June 14, 39, 81
Swaysland, Edward 49
sweat 42, 112–13, 133
Swift, Jonathan 55
Swing Riots 56

tanning 17, 42
Tory party 55, 60
Tosh, John 6, 69
trousers 86, 128, 142
Turner, David 102–3

Vickery, Amanda 76

Wahrman, Dror 68, 81
walking, 1, 26, 35, 43, 45–6, 59–60, 66, 73, 84, 114, 171–2
Walpole, Horace 97, 108, 113, 127
war 5, 103, 139–60
   American Independence 85, 146
   Crimean 146
   Napoleonic 74–5, 83, 139–40, 146, 149
   Peninsular 9, 75, 150–1
   South African 152
Waterloo, Battle of 69, 86, 140, 146, 148
wearing 161–81
   wearing in 133, 164
   wearing out 1, 131, 133, 164

Webb-Johnson, Cecil 139
Weedon Barracks 146
Weekes, Hampton 21, 41, 69
Wellington, Arthur Wellesley 1st Duke of 9, 69, 73, 86, 90, 139, 151
    Wellington boots *see* boots
Wheeler, William 145, 150
Whig party 55, 60, 103
wigs 28–9
Wilkes, John 46
Williams, George 65
Willich, A. F. M. 100, 113
Wollstonecraft, Mary 19
women, 1, 6, 9, 19, 23, 28–29, 43, 58, 79, 102, 179
    women's shoes 4, 26, 29–30, 47, 49, 73, 84, 133
wood *see* clogs
wool 15, 29, 43, 99, 128, 131, 135
Wraxall, Nathaniel 69